"Janine Turner is a breath of fresh air in the
come from laborious research and a profou
principles. She knows that liberty and knov
light a fire in the hearts and minds of Ameri

"Janine Turner is a renegade for the republic! Her essays on *The Federalist* and opinion editorials on culture, women, and politics evoke reason and clarify why conservative principles matter. If only everyone in Hollywood thought this way!"

—Sean Hannity

"Janine Turner is a proud patriot. He father, Turner Gauntt, a graduate of West Point and an Air Force hero, was one of the first to fly Mach 2. She knows firsthand that our troops fight to protect our U.S. Constitution, which in turn protects our liberties, and her pride in her dad, and those who serve, shines bright in this wonderful and very personal book. Her tribute to her father, who recently passed, rivals the most moving of Hollywood screenplays."

—Gary Sinise, actor, *Forrest Gump* and *CSI: NY*,
The Gary Sinise Foundation

"A leading voice in today's conservative movement, Janine Turner gives a thoughtful take on the state of the nation, the trials our country faces, and how her faith has been an integral aspect of her life in her new book, *A Little Bit Vulnerable — Hollywood, God, Sobriety & Politics*. By taking the reader on a journey through her own tribulations and how her faith has helped her overcome them, Janine provides a story of hope and inspiration."

—Karl Rove, Former Deputy Chief of Staff and Senior Advisor to President George W.
Bush and author of the *New York Times* bestseller, *Courage and Consequence*

"Samuel Beckett said it best: "All poetry is prayer." In Janine Turner's book, *A Little Bit Vulnerable*, she chronicles her amazing life through poetry, founding Constituting America, politics, Hollywood, God, the death of her father, and twenty-eight years of sobriety. We feel her fortitude as early as thirteen, echoing Ralph Waldo Emerson (If a man wants to build a carriage, let him, but just don't let him forget how to walk) and her awakening at twenty six (Like a racehorse Transcending

From the gallop Through the cantor To the trot; her inward angst turning outward with resolutions of what the Truth must be . . . that it runs further Than me). Like Emerson, Turner is a champion of individualism, aware of the constant battles mankind must face each day to stay sane, to hold on to tenderness. Her voice is of the young heart, yet philosophical, always reaching to find its way in a world tormented by a daily devil. We see a warrior; a defender of our American way of life; a woman whose inner beauty outshines even her Hollywood glamour. You will be moved by her extraordinary strength, her words rising like prayer in the modern rush; Emerson's own quote, a perfect mantra: "What lies behind you and what lies in front of you pales in comparison to what lies inside of you."

—Karla K. Morton, 2010 Texas Poet Laureate

"Janine's personal story is a powerful testament to the reality of long-term recovery from alcoholism, and her willingness to share this story publicly is both courageous and inspirational."

—Greg Williams, Filmmaker: *The Anonymous People*

"Every now and then God creates a person with an exceptional combination of gifts. They have insight, commitment, courage, and faith. They see things we all need to see, and understand things we all need to understand. Janine Turner is just such a gift."

—Monsignor Don Fischer, a Priest with the Diocese of Dallas,
Pastoral Reflections Institute

"'Heroic' doesn't begin to describe what Janine Turner is doing on radio to spread the word on liberty and freedom. When we save this republic, history will show Janine answered her country's call—putting patriotism far above her Hollywood interests."

—Andrew Breitbart

"Like a modern-day Paul Revere, [Janine] Turner will keep spreading the word about our founding principles."

—Chris Wallace, FOX News Sunday

"After hearing Janine Turner speak, I felt inspired, touched, motivated, and, quite frankly, in awe. Her speech was riveting."

—Anita Perry, First Lady of Texas

"Janine is a rare mix of talented actress and principled, committed conservative. Her understanding of how entertainment shapes our culture makes her a potent force and sought-after speaker."

—Ed Gillespie, former Republican National Committee Chairman, advisor to President George Bush, and political strategist

"Actress Janine Turner was an eloquent supporter, particularly on the subjects of women in politics and the strength and value of single moms who are committed to raising solid citizens."

—Gov. Sarah Palin, Former Governor of Alaska

"I commend Janine Turner for continually shining a light on America's founding principles. Her foundation, Constituting America, is an excellent resource for all Americans, especially our young people."

—U.S. Senator Scott Brown (R-MA)

A Little Bit

Vulnerable

ON HOLLYWOOD, GOD, SOBRIETY, & POLITICS

By Janine Turner

DUNHAM
books

A Little Bit Vulnerable
© 2014 Janine Turner

Trade Paperback ISBN: 978-1-939447-57-9
Ebook ISBN: 978-1-939447-58-6

Printed in the United States of America

Cover Photo by Juliette Turner at Mockingbird Hill Ranch
Cover Design by Nice Branding
Interior design and layout by Darlene Swanson • www.van-garde.com

Dedicated to my Dad—

the Angel on my shoulder

Table of Contents

Chapter Two

Constituting America—Interpreting *The Federalist*

Chapter Four

Chapter Five

Notes

Introduction

This book is a compilation of my life journey thus far, or at least aspects of it. To date, this is the most I have ever shared of my private emotions, my dark valleys, my resurrections, and my deep love of country. I feel a bit vulnerable, I must profess, but if something said here helps another person in any way, big or small, then I have been a steward of my wounds and/or my experience, strength, and hope.

I suppose I can say that as an actress many of my joys, vulnerabilities, tragedies, and heartbreaks have been poured forth on the screen. Yet my first love, my independent reach, has always been for the pen. Writing was, and continues to be, my emotional, cathartic coping skill, my expression, my outreach, my vision.

A Little Bit Vulnerable traverses thirty-eight years of my life, from ages thirteen to fifty-one. These pages thus embody many different genres: poetry, essays, opinion editorials, radio conversations, and speeches. I deal with my dreams, fears, heredity, doubts, devastations, love (including my broken engagement with Alec Baldwin), alcoholism, my struggling acting days in Hollywood and New York, my love of country, my scholastic quests and subsequent opinions about our Republic, women in politics, social issues, and what I perceive as a crisis in not only our culture, but in our experiment of self-governing.

I realize now that as I wrote I bumped into memories of my loved ones. Their essence, their joys, their tribulations, and their destinies are woven into the fabric of my being. Though I am the only one in my family to venture into the insanity of Hollywood, the promotion of the Constitution, and the foray of political activism, I echo the spirits of my forefathers and foremothers.

On my father's side, I am related to Israel Gauntt, who gave provisions to the Revolution and the Revolutionary soldiers. His brave contributions give me the honor of being a member of the *Daughters of the American Revolution*. Perhaps it is Israel who instills the fervent ardor I hold for revolutionary times and the preservation of our great Republic. In heaven, there must be a council of ancestral angels who murmur motivations. Perhaps this is why I asked my father, at the age of eight, "If our Founding Fathers were to come back today, what would they be most disappointed about?" I mean, what eight-year-old asks that type of question?

My great-great-great-grandfather J.W. Gauntt fought in the Civil War, my grandfather Turner M. Gauntt, Sr. fought in World War II, and my father Turner M. Gauntt, Jr. is a graduate of the United States Military Academy at West Point and served in the Air Force during the Cold War. He was one of the first to fly Mach 2, twice the speed of sound, in the B-58 Hustler. My great-great-grandfather J.B. (John Bass) Gauntt did not serve in the armed forces, but I found some of his notations about politics and revolution, along with his hauntings about John Barleycorn and his warnings to his sons about the evils of booze—obvious correlations to my journey resulting in sobriety. And to remember the ladies, I would be remiss to not mention that my grandmother Marjorie McKenzie Gauntt was a very social and charming woman, embracing the community with civic duty and her church with service.

From my mother's lineage, I garner my faith and my muse. On my mother's paternal side, my great-grandfather Mr. Agee was a Methodist preacher. My grandfather Stanley D. Agee was one of his ten children. My grandfather Stanley was goodness personified. On my mother's maternal side, my great-grandmother Emily Pearl Rogers Burgess was renowned for being the pillar of the local Baptist church. Rumor has it that her cousin was Will Rogers. Her husband, my great-grandfather Richard P. Burgess, was a Major in the army during World War II. His spirit was entrepreneurial and he loved to invent. One of his inventions was a pair of wings for man. He made my great-uncle jump off a cliff to see if they'd work. I don't know if they worked, but my great-uncle lived. He also loved to write. He wrote greeting cards and many, many short stories. I believe he, "great-grandfather Burgess" as we called him, is my muse. I believe, and have always believed, that he is with me as I write. He was in his eighties the last time I visited him, and I remember it vividly. After our visit, I was walking down the stairs. I paused before I got into the car, and, looking back at him, I waved and said good-bye. From the top of the stairs he replied with a smile, "Don't ever say 'good-bye;' say 'see ya.'" I believe he still sees me, and I see him too in a sensorial way.

His daughter, my grandmother Loraine Burgess Agee, was a staple in my life. She was a vision of beauty and pioneering spirit. My mother, Janice Agee Gauntt, blended these attributes, both physically and spiritually, with a business tenacity that makes men blush. My mother gave me a plaque with an inscription from Aristotle that reads, "To avoid criticism, do nothing, say nothing, be nothing." When agents told me that business was slow, she would retort, "Someone is working!"

Within all of these mysteries lies the crux of my meditations—the callings of my poetry, the impetus for my reflections, and the genesis of my opinions.

As I was reminiscing, collecting, and compiling the pages for this book, my father died. It sent everything to a grinding halt. Now, as I re-emerge two months later to polish the remnants of this book, I have included a few pages in a final chapter devoted to him. The last chapter deals with my devastation and also serves as a tribute to what my father endured, achieved, and did, not only for my country, but for me. His influence, however, is whispered throughout the entire book. How could it not be? He was my father, bigger than life—a West Pointer, an elite Air Force pilot, a cowboy. He was a brilliant, handsome man—a character—who endured many heartbreaks, demons, and challenges. He taught me to cowboy up, look up, and never give up.

Though my dad is in heaven, his presence is etched in the air here.

Chapter One

Pouring Pain into Poetry, Surviving Hollywood and Early Sobriety

Things said or done long years ago,
Or things I did not do or say
But thought that I might say or do,
Weigh me down, and not a day
But something is recalled,
My conscience or my vanity appalled.

—W. B. Yeats

Preface

If a man wants to build a carriage, let him, but just don't let him forget how to walk.

Janine Turner
13 years old,
Fort Worth, TX

An innocence lost is sometimes purity born
A denial no longer in the making
It clears the path, renews the soil
As a bud does journey into blossoming

Janine Turner
25 years old,
New York City

Protect my inner softness
That walks through this vacuous valley
Containing the sculptured faces
That peer from hidden rooms
Clutching their remembrances
Of stolen moments.

Janine Turner
26 years old
Hollywood

Never evidenced in manner
For I feared my passion and my pain
It gripped me so intense inside
That it seized me in refrain

Janine Turner
27 years old
New York City

When my parents were children, they rode the tails of the Great Depression. As young adults, they were molded by 1950s mores. Thus, as a young girl in the 1960s, I was pigeon-holed into the typical "girly" things: dancing, modeling, singing, and acting. My love for academia was never the main objective of my parents. My scholastic achievements were appreciated, but treated as a bonus point, *per se*, and though I performed my girly duties well, and, I might add, enjoyed them, I found my own voice curled up in bed with a pen and paper—writing. Writing has always been my comfort and poetry was my first love.

In third grade, inspired after winning a creative-writing contest in school, I ventured into writing my first book, which was about a tiger. I remember reading it to my father, ensconced in my favorite childhood home, a home we lovingly called the "Blue Barn," in Euless, Texas. I laugh when I recall his perplexed face. She's writing? Nevertheless, writing has been my emotional respite, my saving grace, and, I might add, in later years, my dad became my biggest enthusiast.

Poetry, especially in my twenties, literally saved my life. I was modeling in New York City at age fifteen and pursuing an acting career in Hollywood by age seventeen. They were turbulent times—thrust into the world, smashing illusions and picking up the pieces. Poetry was creative coping that captivated my private burnings and yearnings. It was the vessel for my passions during my quest for self-analysis, sobriety, love, and success. When my passions overfilled my cup, I poured them onto the page.

After my first summer season on *Northern Exposure*, at age twenty-seven, I collected remnants of these writings and made a homespun book for my family for Christmas, entitling it *Congregating Conscience*. It was a way of wrapping up that era of my life, I suppose. My family felt, shall I say, stunned by the emotional vulnerabilities of the works. Looking back, I can't believe I sent a copy to my grandmother! My mother often says she regrets that I spent all those years alone in NYC and Hollywood, navigating the stormy seas, often shipwrecked. Wretched is the passage of becoming a successful actress and challenging is the path of sobriety. During the majority of my twenties, I was grasping for horizons from canyons.

I have no regrets. I believe that the stepping stones of life are just that, steps from one stone to the next, some rough, some shiny. Yet, all of them lead to one's purpose, one's destiny. On this path I encountered many demons and many days of splendor. Ironically, I value overcoming the demons more than I value the splendor. As trite as it sounds, facing my fears, overcoming my challenges, and breaking the cycles truly did shape my character and mold me into a happier, more successful human being. The seeking and the "awareness, acceptance, action," led to the light at the end of the tunnel. All of this—most of this—was captured in my poetry.

For many years I was thrust forward by agents and casting directors to be scantily clad in a bikini as what I called the "damsel in distress of the week." I was greatly troubled by this, and for this reason, I deliberately sought respectful, intelligent characters. After a twelve-year hike through hills and valleys, bereft and broke, I got lucky, or as my mother so often told me, "Luck is when opportunity meets preparedness." I won the role of Maggie O'Connell, an Alaskan bush pilot, in the CBS series *Northern Exposure*. (My dad's innate influence surely played a part in landing the role, since he was an heroic Air Force pilot who flew Mach 2 in the 1960s in the B-58 Hustler, and later flew for Braniff International for twenty-five years.) Also, I guess, I was finally prepared, and I don't just mean as a cultivated thespian. I had cleared the cobwebs of my childhood, sought sobriety, and endured the heartache of a broken engagement/almost marriage and the aftermath it wrought. I was not only ready technically, I was ready physically and spiritually. I had given my will to God. It's amazing how letting go and letting God really does work.

Regarding my poetry and why I decided to include it in this memoir: I packed my poetry away almost twenty-three years ago. Recently I pulled it off a dusty old shelf. As I re-read it, I was struck by its sheer, raw, emotional power. Each poem chronicles the passions I felt during my Hollywood dramas and early years of sobriety. Hollywood can be hell and sobriety challenging because sobriety is a journey, an awakening, a rebirth, of sorts. Sobriety is a coming to terms with why one drank and learning to deal with life on life's terms—which isn't always easy. My poetry unveils my experiences and my expressions of living sober in the daunting environment of Hollywood and NYC. In a unique way, it tells the tale of my young adult life with striking vulnerability. I decided to include it because I believe it reveals more than the typical memoir, which recounts the past from the present, ever could. Instead I use my thirty-eight-year-old private journal: my poetry. I am not a trained poet. I was not an English major. I include my poetry, however, because I believe it represents the amazing resiliency of the human spirit.

I added the months and years of my sobriety, and an occasional insight, purely for the person who may be seeking sobriety or trying to keep sober. I know that a poet would never dream of adding such a window, but since this is an atypical memoir with a particular inspirational purpose, I do so.

Conveniences
(excerpts)

This modern-day world is a highly educated and sophisticated one. The inhabitants are steadily hurrying . . . rush, rush, rush. It seems that the higher the intelligence of man, the more conveniences he produces. Then the younger generations grow up expecting nothing but those conveniences because they seem natural; like a part of life. Yes, life is made physically easier with things such as pumped, uncontaminated water, cars, and the gas that motors one from place to place, as well as planes and trains, electricity, modern-day food stores . . . the list goes on forever. Does one ever step out of his hurried, timed life pattern and take the time to appreciate such things? It is not, often, until these things are gone that one fully awakens to reality. As Ralph Waldo Emerson has written, "the civilized man has built a couch, but has lost the use of his feet."

. . . If one looks around himself, he can be assured that at every position that his eye stops, lies an article or action of which one takes advantage—this paper. Doesn't one just buy paper at the convenience store? There is nothing wrong with modernized convenience and one has to be proud of man's intelligence. However the underlying meaning is to not be totally unaware of alternate procedures and to be a little more conservative and appreciative. If man wants to build a carriage, let him, but just don't let him forget how to walk.

13 years old; 1975
Wayside Middle School
Fort Worth, Texas

Me in 1989

On this present day I am thirteen years of age and in the seventh grade. I can't really predict my future, only by my present interest and goals.

In 1989 I will be 26 years old. By that time I would like to have finished college and be married. I will have hopefully graduated from college—SMU—and have majored in dancing, English, Fine Arts, and have had courses in real estate. Real estate runs in the family. I would mainly like to be a model, but by then I might not have the qualifications. I love to act, so maybe I could have an acting career.

I would like to live in a nice house out in the country. Not necessarily in the country, but not in the city.

I would like to have time for my hobbies. I love to paint, swim, play tennis and golf, and play the piano.

13 years old; May 24, 1976
Wayside Middle School
Fort Worth, Texas

*Well, I didn't attend SMU, I didn't get married by age twenty-six, and I didn't take courses in real estate, but I did model, act, and I do have a nice little house, my ranch, that's "not necessarily in the country, but not in the city."

Maturity
(excerpts)

I have had some time to think and to collect my thoughts. I have come to the resolution that everyone has her own ideas and outlook on life. What is mine? Well, first I asked myself, "What is life?" To me, life is like a Ferris wheel, turning and turning, and on each revolution there is a new door, a new compartment, and inside that door is a fresh surprise or a new awakening to a different part of the world of life. God has control of this Ferris wheel. He opens and shuts the compartments and He, also, fills them with the surprises and knowledgeable experiences. The good thing, and the remarkable thing, is that He always knows and has carefully planned ahead for when that next door is to open. It has taken me a long time to learn this much and I am sure that there is much more to learn. There are more explanations to be taught because I think, no one ever quits learning . . .

I think that part of maturity depends upon how many of your compartments on the Ferris wheel God has opened. Does anyone ever fully mature? No, it's impossible. Because the final door is never opened until the last revolution on the Ferris wheel stops, and then you can never put that last door's opening to use on earth.

17 years old; May 9, 1980
Fort Worth, Texas
Upon graduating from high school one year early to move to Hollywood

Soap-Set Philosophy
(Stream of Consciousness)

You know...

Growing up is so interesting and mysterious.

The intriguing part of it is that one is always growing, no matter what age. Growing to me is an unveiling of eyes. Things open up and new opinions, outlooks, and attitudes are taken. Each day, month, year is different, new learning, adding up.... Life is one stepping stone after another. Some parts are good, some bad. But, they all are experiences which make us more human ... more humble, I believe. Humble. I think that it does. Life is a mystery. The past, history ... it's unbelievable. I am magnified towards it—what was. What was makes what's now, what's now makes what's in the future. So not only do people individually open and grow, but by each doing so the human form—being—life does. The decades, centuries, races—all encounter rough stones, as well as smooth. But, that builds character—definition. Without the difficulty of the British and the colonies ... no revolution ... thus, no America! Isn't it interesting? Now everyday, one learns, grows challenges oneself, has regrets and out of those comes hope—goals. New lights flicker in our brain through time. I guess those are ideas—goals—thoughts. Just like stars ... they glow ... they're always there but sometimes we have to look especially hard for them and we all want and love the biggest and the brightest star. But, sometimes the soft, dim ones calm us. Stars ... bright ... dim ... just like thoughts, flickers, challenging, peaceful. We are learning. Our eyes are unveiling everyday. Our senses change and multiply and develop ... until someday the light becomes a huge burning bright glow ... and all is known ... and one is fully developed.

20 years old; 1982
Hollywood
On set of *General Hospital*

La-La Land
(Stream of consciousness)

The alarm rings
Rings the time
What's time?
Drowsily you rise
Put on your robe, fix the tea
Morning routine
You read the paper
—of tragedies
—of problems
—of jolts
Why do people get hurt?
You turn to stock exchange
You prepare for work. One must work to make money
But . . . what is money?
Work at nine . . .
Lunch at twelve . . .
Outing time at five . . .
Daily routine . . . money by the hour.
Hop in car—returning home
Packed in traffic
Where
Is
Everyone
Going?
The cars . . . the expensive ones
Talk . . . "Look I have money!"
A green piece of paper, marked with numbers . . .
Does this mean happiness?
Companionship?
Love?
Is money important?
Shouldn't life be full of giving
Caring
Sharing
From the soul?
Wouldn't this bring love, companionship, and happiness?

Someone gives you an object…
But is it the object you love, appreciate?
Isn't it the one who gives, you love and care for?
It's the heart and soul which makes one giving
Then why? Why do you need the object?
Has everyone lost sight
Of the simple things—
The inner feelings—
The true meaning of life…
Is not everyone caught in a
Contest
Of getting the most money?
When really it should be getting
and Giving
The most
Love.

20 years old; 1982
Hollywood

Strangers

You see a person. You catch his eye. He catches yours.
Magnetism flows through the air.
You turn to look—
He senses your stare. Proceeding on, you feel apprehensive.
Not knowing what to do.
He's a stranger.
Never before been introduced, who is he?
You feel his eyes.
Don't move.
"Never talk to strangers," they say. "It's dangerous."
He looks so nice…but you never know.
Curiosity reigns.
You turn to look, he remains in close view. His eyes. . .
They look so full of intrigue—another life—another world,
you long to know.…

You move on. Not knowing what to do
still feeling his presence, his mystique.
He proceeds, also.
Will you ever meet again?
He looks back … longing, grasping. Two who long to
meet. But neither know the other.
Should you make the first move?
Both pausing.
You move on … those eyes. That air. Will you ever meet again?
He walks on.
You sit.
Strangers … in a world of millions. Is that what God intended?

20 years old; 1982
Hollywood
After seeing Alec Baldwin, my future fiancé, at an audition for *Cutter to Houston*.
I didn't get the role because they said I distracted Alec too much.

Venice Beach

Waves crash and birds fly
by
Soaring through the sea-kissed
sky,
Up above a bird's eye view
Of humans below—all askew,
Flapping, soaring, diving
Is all their days consist of,
A day of beauty, wonder, nature
is never missed above,
Birds question not the sea, the
sky,
As humans question all day,
all night.

20 years old; 1983
Hollywood
With Alec on Venice Beach

Why?

What is it?
What can it be?
That has such animosity
Towards love?
What force?
What evil?
What alchemy?
Destroys the two who have such love.
Why can't it just be?
Why can't it just be?
Is it family?
Friend?
Foe?
Is it the air?
The sea?
The moon?
Is it the fast rich city?
Is it the lure that ages too soon?
Why can't love just be?
If two love, why can't it be?
Strength.
Strength it should be.
Not only should love be strong
But also the individuals
to succeed.

21 years old; 1984
Hollywood
After canceled wedding with Alec Baldwin

Alec

It's truly sad
When I fell in love with you I didn't know
what emotional power love could have
and I never dreamed it would turn out this way.

21 years old; 1984
Hollywood

My Fault

The cost of a heart can be so high
When you give it away for free
The love, the time, the energy
Is all so worthwhile at the time.
To dream of the future, the promises, the hope
That like a candle, flickering so light
One breath that breathes a step out of lope
Grows dark on the dreams, the love, the life

21 years old; 1984
Hollywood

My Blue Grey Door

You pressed you chest
Against my blue grey door,
Your breath heavy and belabored
And you leaned your sandy, tousled hair
Upon the dawn,
Shining on the 211.

I heard it –
Your breath heavy and belabored
I always could....

Slipping through the blue grey wood,
Mirroring your spray of eyes,
Half shut with sleeping,
Staring with tainted
Stains of should.

I'd laid in waiting
On the other side,
Wound in a tethered ball of time,
Twisted in my battlefield
Of self and substance,
Naught and wrought,
Missing not a click of clock,
That rounded through the sorted lot,
Announcing your belated coming-
While I rocked my sense of self,
Consoling my misguided thoughts
That bred in empty arms.

Then you stood
At the lair of wood,
And dared not speak,
For words could only further spoil,
The obvious glaring blot,
Seeping drops of red between us.
So, silence was the only sound,
Weighing heavy in the air,
As nothing could repair,
The constant of despair,
That intertwined our passion.

Yet, I heard your heart,
Beating triple time,
Osmosising through on waves of want,
Crashing in my lap,
As I sat,
In my puddle of confusion...
Paralyzed with ineptitude
Of dealing with the ride of feeling
That wooed...

Beyond all reason,
All pride,
All self-perceiving...
For me to jump into that pool
Of paltry play,
Like a child splashing in a river,
On a rainy day.

But, as bewitched with calling,
I threw my soul out of bed,
And begged my body then to meet me,
Crawling towards the blue grey door,
Imploring me to greet you.
I zigged,
I zagged,
As if mesmerized with magic,
And on my knees, I bent my ear
To hear your heart of beating,
Caressing the rise of wood,
The you who stood,
Against the crevices of keeping.

My heart skipping,
As if driven by drugs,
I dug with pulsing fingertips
To turn the knob that kept us parted,
And I opened the closing and saw you,
I saw you,
I opened the closing and saw you.
And you gazed at me,
With piercing blue,
Unfocused, hurried,
And distraught,
Engulfing me into your arms
With shame and sadness...

After madness
You ran your fingers through your hair
That hid your eyes from seeing,
And you looked at me

With seeming
Holes,
As I watched your blackened souls,
Stepping through the blue grey door,
The shutting sounding through me.

I dragged my soul,
Leveled and low,
Through the passing tow of toll,
And I gathered vintage grapes of drink,
Hotly and beseeching
Pouring into depths of debt
And burying my head, I wept,
Chanting
Maybe tonight, tonight, tonight,
Maybe tonight,
Tonight…

Alec aftermath
before I got sober, 1984
Hollywood
—Written December 1990
Four years sober
27 years old, NYC

Rochester Drive

There's a man in my building
of seventy or so
Who asks me to come over for coffee
I smile and say—straight from the heart—
Gee, how nice that would be

He walks on slowly enjoying the day
he's been up since four a.m.
As I hustle and hustle to make it on time
I slept late—till ten

I hurry to work, I hurry to school
I hurry to run all my errands
The reminder of things I have to do
go off in my head like sirens

I run by him every so often
with his eyes yearning for company
I pass him briskly and hear him say
I thought we were meeting for coffee

I wave to him from my car
as I screech onto the street
I think to myself, as I'm at the light
Someday we've got to meet

Life seems to be a contradiction
what's happened to humans' humanity
The world is spinning, advancing so fast
We've forgotten how to have coffee

I envy the older generation
who knew the world before we
How it was to deal with each other
before computers, radio, and t.v.
To not be afraid of a nice afternoon
with no music, no shows, no movies
Just two people enjoying their souls
and sipping and sipping and sipping and sipping
and sipping and sipping their coffee.

22 years old; 1985
Hollywood

∞

New Love East 12th Street

Like nothing before
    a sensation anew
To watch and behold
    this vision of you
Movement so grand
    intensity great
A splendor to feel
    as if blessed by fate
A feeling unspoken
    the touch of a heart
God must have known
    right from the start

23 years old; September 19, 1986 New York City
After meeting Mikhail Baryshnikov
Almost 4 months sober

More

Brilliant is the soul that yearns
That lingers in the form
It has that inner voice
That does not rest, it storms.

Burns for something more
And more, and more, and more,
Always talking, never happy
With the victories of yore.

Pushing on the walls inside
The caverns of the head
Yearning, turning knots of fire
Begging to be fed.

Captured inside the shell
It never takes a rest,
Moaning, groaning empty sighs
Echoing from the chest

The self—same self that arises victories
It also brings defeat
Stomping on the gladdened moment
Hastening to retreat

Escaping with the fuel of bliss
Released in open air
It is back with sudden shutter
A trepidatious scare.

Crying, bending, understanding not,
This intensity of mood,
Swinging like a pendulum
Swaying to allude.

Never ending the obsession
The symbols of roulette
The game of hit and miss
A continual running bet.

Time is short and the should
Knocking at the door
Tapping at the conscience
Stealing from its core.

It never stops, stop it not
The never ending sending
Of the banging, clanging,
Noise unbending,

Ringing, singing, unknown notes
Twirling throughout the form
Pushing outward, loudly screaming
Until another victory born ...

23 years old; November 1986
New York City
6 months sober

No Pink Clouds

The mists of winter,
So much like my mind.
Rolling inward,
Commencing the questioning
drifting in circles, circumventing time.
Bits of moisture, yet not rain—
Just a smokescreen of illusions.

Hazy...
and vision impaired,
Variations of intensity
swirling in figure eights,
Creating outward compulsivity...

The wind blows harder.

Fighting for the dream
A clarity of clouds—
A hope for such a source ...
But, the darkness wanting night,
Swiftly eats the droplets
Blanketing the fantasy with black.

And the wind blows harder.

> 24 years old; January 1987
> New York City
> *8 months sober*

A New Pair of Glasses
(from the Twenty-sixth Floor)

I look out at the world and see
A multi-spectrum reflection of me,
A world to do with as I need
To hide within, or to plant a seed,
An abundant chance for my should to relay
A challenge to wake up to every day,
The choice is always within my view
It's all in what I choose to do.

24 years old; February 1, 1987
New York City
9 months sober

Autumn

Etched in darkness, illuminating against the backdrop of silence, a golden leaf commences its journey from the height of the tree. Swirling and whirling, it is caught up momentarily in a wave of air, as if guided by a skilled pilot…of which it is.

The moon, in full face, smiles down and zooms in for a closer view, as its fingers caress the leaf with its robe of lightness. The leaf, enjoying the bath of light, expresses its final gesture by reflecting back to the moon its golden shell and delicately veined center, sketched with five paths.

Witnessed and absorbed, the light carries slowly onward, sufficiently fulfilled. The leaf, newly engulfed in darkness, closes up its points and embraces itself. Its mission accomplished, its duty complete.

24 years old; October 31, 1987
New York City
1 year, 5 months sober

Pachelbel

Autumn winds and Pachelbel,
Diffusion of hope, mixed with hell,
Ever knowing will I,
Ever knowing will I?

Notes of resounding multitudes
Follow the line harmonies
Forever swaying,
Forever swaying.

In and out my head, the strings
Vibrating with renowned friction,
Is it calling,
Is it calling?

Winds that carry memories
Caressing and billowing,
Where are they going,
Where are they going?

A scent that sketches euphorically
As scant as the breeze,
Passing through,
Passing through.

Captured with the canon,
Circles with no escape,
Elucidating comfort,
Elucidating comfort.

24 years old; October 31, 1987
New York City
1 year, 5 months sober

∞

Play

The little girl got tired of grey,
So out into the yard she'd play…
—but it never went away.

Anger and accusations fly,
As surely as the days go by,
—and the little girl would cry.

Asked how she was, in her bind,
As if there were no other sign,
She'd always answer,
— "oh, I'm fine."

She somehow knew, as she could hear
That trouble was, oh, so near
—when she did hear, the spew of fear.

Out into the yard she'd play,
Tucking all her feelings away,
—locked into her heart to stay.

The grass was green, the sky so blue,
So many things there were to do,
But afraid to go,
—no…she'd stay too.

Asked again—as if blind—
Asked again—as if blind—
How she was, one more time,
— "oh, I'm fine…I'm fine."

25 years old; January 21, 1988
New York City
1 year, 7 months sober

∞

Resiliency

An innocence lost is sometimes purity born
A denial no longer on the making,
It clears the path, renews the soil
As a bud does journey into blossoming.

A string upon the heart grows coarse,
The harmony no longer finds its note,
The response grown weary, buoyancy lost
Reactions from all the plucking.

The string snaps, the music is gone
Only silence refracting through the chambers,
A fear, a clutching, the dam is down
An open floodgate of reality.

Too much to handle, too much to see
But blindness no longer suffices,
Sunk into depths of swirling undercurrents
Whirlwinds whirling winningly.

But a thought jumps in,
As if orange and floats,
An image like a free floating friend
Who somehow knows, who comprehends
A master of the sea,

Resiliency.

And from this impregnated ball of mutations,
Swollen with confusion,
Is born a new perception—
A stepping out—
A dancing in a new direction.

25 years old; January 25, 1988
New York City
1 year, 7 months sober

∞

Red, White, and Blue

A land so often dreamt in slumber,
A light, to carry forth the colors,
Ah, distant lands, a people many,
Understand better than we…

A creeping, slowly moving in circles
Refracting off a swiveling beam,
Creating dizzy, prolific affects,
to later bring surprising means.

Oh, awaken, our blanket of satisfaction,
Lose not, that founding feud,
Appraising the slyness of demagogues,
A fruition by too few.

Lower not our standards of being,
A belittling to adopt the many,
A learned people lie asunder,
A look upon a backward penny.

A fusion of waves into a little box,
the power of the easy,
Melting into a mess of mass,
No room left for the autonomy.

A speculative debate—a haven,
We do harbor here,
Yet, noise and images flashing,
Achieves the riveting ricochet.

Danger is found in the arrogance,
The defiance of the impending,
Steadfast awareness, to be able,
We must regain our thinking.

Give not the others this victory,
By relinquishing our countenance,
The inner definitions of the mind,
We must treasure to reveal.

25 years old; January 28, 1988
New York City
1 year, 8 months sober

Dad at West Point

It is cold, much colder than expected. The foreboding grey, stone buildings hover overhead, casting a shadow, as if its darkness is reaching out to swallow up the figure, poised, ready, standing there. A racing heartbeat is felt, as his frozen, ungloved hand reaches up and is placed across his chest. Blood rushes to his cheeks and he finds it hard to swallow, knowing that the emotions felt, if manifested, would be death. Thus, he sinks his boot heel deeply into the ground. Pushing…pushing…as if to squash the flow of feelings.

The wind, unimpeded by the stoniness, rushes through, swirling around his ears, leaving its mark of blush. Then, it heaves upward, catching the flag and snapping it into formation. The suddenness seems to stop the boy's heart, yet, also, seems to be the cue to start the drum roll. The music swells, as the wind blows, as his heart pounds, and then, it begins. The song, the pride…the journey.

As the song proceeds, he finds his mouth moving, but, as to what the words mean, he is not sure. Why he is standing there, he is not sure. Why he wants to run, he is not sure. However, his boot heel deeply rooted into the ground serves as an anchor prohibiting his flee. The song nears the end with no fireworks or applause, only the silence, coupled with the siren of the wind. His eyes are frozen on the flag ahead whipping, snapping, cracking. Silence…whipping...Silence…snapping… Silence…cracking.

Suddenly, the flag is replaced by a face. A face stony, cold…mirroring the landscape. The face's eyes blazingly look upon his subject's hazel, yet untouched eyes. Unknowing, unsure. A moment, eye to eye, seemingly unending, tells it all. The boy unflinchingly holds the look, calling upon some inner, instinctual knowledge that a blink would reveal more than a thousand words.

The face moves on, replaced, once again, like a slide show, with the flag. The flag, the flag…refocusing on the flag. The tension mounts in his back, his legs, his hands, his face, his lips, his eyes. An escape of breath eases from his mouth, slowly, carefully, not to disturb the quiet. His hands at his sides touch his blue jeans covering his strong, youthful, muscular legs, wrapped in knots from uncertainty. His body fully acknowledges the feelings that his face cannot reveal.

Tears welling, fear screaming…he struggles to confine them. No escape here. No more. Going are the memories of a scream at fear, shoulders back! Going are the memories of an open heart, chest forward! Going are the memories of a free-flowing conversation, …chin out! Going are the memories of a carefree soul, …

back straight! Going are the memories of a shameless tear, …stare ahead! Going are the memories of an expressive face, '…Sir, yes, Sir!'

Turning, …following in line, the boy steps forward, unearthing his heel from his grounding, releasing his hold on his identity. Walking towards the grey, stone arch of triumph, his body is stepping forward, but his soul …is stepping back. There is no turning back. No looking back. No going back. …He steps across the threshold, he hears a high- pitched scream, that, for a moment, he thinks is coming from within him. He hears the high- pitched scream, …the whistle, …and he then, marches right.

25 years old; February 21, 1988;
New York City
1 year, 9 months sober

The Call of the Wine

Yellow. Pale Yellow. Pale yellow mixing into golden yellow. Is it? Stop. Dewy drops slowly, mesmerizingly gliding down the neck. Bink. Bink. A blur. It's just sitting there. Yet, it is staring, calling. Turn away. Maybe it's mustard yellow, no, it has the highlights of paleness making it yellow. Yellow. Mellow yellow. Yes, mellow yellow. Mellow yellow. Mellow yellow. Stop.

But, the clarity. It's clear. Yes, very clear. That's good, yes, that means it's good. No. Bad, bad. Look away. But, it's just yellow. That's all. Dewy yellow. Just dewy yellow. Golden, mellow, dewy yellow. No, it's red. Red and Black. Black. It's really black. No lightness, no lightness at all. Oh, come on, now, it's bright. Full of light, see. The elegant didactic circles swirling. It's surprisingly swirly. Swirly. Swirly. Swirly. Swirly. No. Stand still. Be serious. It's black. Black. Black. Black. Black. Black. It's an illusion. Illusion? Ha! Listen, it's singing. It sings!! It's singing. "Ou la la la, ou la la la," hear it? It's happy. La la la la la la la. It's golden, dewy, mellow, swirling, singing, gleaming yellow. It gleams. It glistens. It glitters. All that glitters is gold. No, all that glitters is not gold. It is not gold. It is not swirling. It is not singing. It's tempting. Stop it. Turn away. Turn away. Ah! No fun. No fun. Dancing… Ah! It's dancing! It's playing a waltz. A waltz! Ah, romancing and waltzing. Look! In that mellow, dewy, golden, swirling, singing, yellow is romance! Romance. Romance. Ah! Romance! Yes, romance is in the yellow. And music. Music for the romance. Strauss? Gershwin? Prokofiev? Litz? Puccini? Borodin? Tchaikovsky?

1812? Yes! It's 1812. What a good year. Great year. Yes, very good, extraordinary year. 1812! Hum. Bum. Bum. Bum. Bum. Fireworks. Fireworks. Fireworks are in the yellow. Hear it? Hear the fireworks? Wheeeeee! It's not just mellow yellow. It's yelling yellow. Wild and yelling and fireworks. Wheeeee!

What a golden yellow. War? Is it war? War with what? War with war? Ah, shush. It's peace. Peaceful yellow. It offers peace. Yes, peace and goodwill. Stop. It's black. It's black and bloody and hell. Hells bells! You mean it's hell? Nah. It's heaven. Heaven with music and waltzing and fireworks and romance and life. Life is in the mellow yellow. The swirling, golden, dewy yellow. Life. Here's to life! Look! It's talking and clapping. It's happy. It's happiness. Ah! Happiness. Happiness. Happiness. Happiness. Bells. Bells. Bells. Bells. Ding Dong. Ding Dong. A waltz. A swirl. A kiss. A hug. A lover. A bell. A ball. It's so intriguing this yellow. Very, very intriguing. Calling and yelling and whispering and singing and dancing. It's miraculous. Truly a miraculous yellow. Full of wonder. Full. Full. Full of wonder. Ding Dong. Ding Dong. Ding Dong the witch is dead, which old witch, the wicked witch. Ding Dong the wicked witch is dead. Dead. Dead. Dead. Dead. Dead. Dead. Dead. Dead.

Dead? Yes, black. It's black. Not yellow. But it looks so yellow! So very yellow and bright and happy. It's a pool. Look. It's a pool. A pool for divers and floaters. Float. Ah. To float. Yes, float. Float. Float. Float. Yes, to be cushioned and to float. So nice. So very nice to float. It's easy. So easy...Wait! Wait. Wait. Wait. What's happening to the float? Float. Float! Float! Float! Sing! Sing! Sing! Sing! Bells! Bells! Bells! Bells! Bells! Hey. Wait. Waltz! Waltz! Waltz! Waltz! Waltz! Kiss! Kiss! Kiss! Kiss! Help!!!!!!! Sinking. Sinking. Sinking. Wait? Sink? Sink? Not sink. But, it's happy, so yellow. Blub. Blub. It's getting dark. Dark. Dark. Dark. Where's the yellow?!!! It promised me yellow. A dance, a hug, a kiss, romance, happiness, glitter, singing, peace, heaven. Where's the heaven?!!! It promised me heaven. Wait! Wait! Wait. Wait. Wait. Wait. Wait. This isn't right. It's black. It's dark. It's hell!! Hell. Hell. Hell. Hell. No bells. No bells in hell. It lied. It lied. It lied. Hell. Hells bells. It's hell. It's dark. It's deep. It's deep and dark. It lied. It deceived. It won. It won. It won. It won. It won. Hell. Hells bells. Hells bells. Hells bells. It's hell!

25 years old; February 24, 1988
New York City
1 year, 9 months sober

∞

Cerebral

Cerebral, intensity of the desire
To know—a pondering continual
Never ceasing, always moving
Dictating

Ponder, ponder, ponder
Escaping or reality—the necessity
To figure—eluding and demanding
What a pretty tree

26 years old; August 9, 1989
New York City
3 years sober

Tease

A flicker of a candle
A glimmer
Nice hands, he says
I smile

He draws figuratively
Circles, bottles, a hint of heart
I think, great eyes
Speaking, but what

My breath weighs heavy
Enjoy this
But I will want more
Much more of this man

God, you put him here
Please don't tease.

26 years old; August 9, 1989
New York City
3 years sober

The Keys

I hear his voice with
Intermittent velocity
Holding on to every variable
A second at a time

A pause, a beat, a laugh
I interpret all the keys
Though discovery is in the dynamics
Dictated directly from above

I love the way his reason
Resonates against the air
A sense of care
Releasing my refrain

A wave overtakes me
Abetting my obligations
As I stare at the mosaic
An octant ocean of a million threads

The elusive element of ego
Rushing forward
Deciding what I always know
Is the doing of a Higher Power

Reconciling in the realization
That responsibility relates
Relatively to the moment
Rationality resounds

Whatever hopes I hesitantly harbor
Of happiness—a slice of heaven
I only sporadically
Allow them court

Yet, one at a time they
Prance and prissily parade
Across my mind—perfectly
Picturing the essence of love

Awareness allowing me the
Luxury in assuredly
Reminding that I know
No perfect picture

Though I strive sensorily
Coloring my seeming sensibility
With sensation, to conjure a
Serendipity of what amore consist

Is it bliss or behavior
Of a broader base
I question unceasingly
Concluding most brilliantly

My bewilderment
Basically

26 years old; August 14, 1989
New York City
3 years sober

Street Fantasy

Men stare at me
They look
They wait
They summarize

Some silent
Some loud
Some scary
Some sound

Men stare at me

When they stare the
Air seems tight
My privacy penetrated
And polluted

I feel exposed
Examined, exemplary
Extravagant
And exercised

What is it that
They think
They want
What role am I in their fantasy?

Of the moment

And they get angry
The Arabs, Americans
Aristotles and
The Aries

If I don't lure
And gratify
As if it's my obligation
—their obsession

Men stare at me
And if I don't respond
Then I'm a bitch
If I'm elusive
I'm a whore

It's as if I'm
A validation
A victory vicariously
To be claimed

Thus, I hide and hurry
Haphazardly in the streets
Escaping the
Illusion

The intrusion
The invasion
Their intermission
from reality when

Men stare at me

26 years old; August 16, 1989
New York City
3 years sober

Spider Man

People are so strange
Really a complexity in
Which I constantly find
I'm surrounded

Especially in Manhattan

My cab driver today
Kept referring to the Titanic
(that we were on)
And Spiderman
(whom he kept seeing)

I almost got another

Then the photographer that
I just paid the
"Captain of the seas"
Six dollars to see

Just sat and glared
With glazed eyes and
A nervous twitch
Accompanying his silence

His leg swung back
And forth and then
He spoke
"I charge money"

What an eloquent encounter

The Captain and his buddy
Spiderman
Were seeming more captivating
In comparison

Lovely meeting people
Who are preoccupied
Perilously
With their own person
Presiding somewhere
On another planet

Where most of these
Peasants, princes,
Philanderers, philosophers
And photographers
Seem to be

It eludes me

I then caught a belated
Bus to Bloomingdales
To return the Boulecheron
That bastes too heavily
On my skin
For breathing

26 years old; August 16, 1989
New York City
In a cab
3 years sober

∞

Brief Pink Cloud

Hip hop
Happy now
Hippidy hoppidy
Do

Tree top
Traveling to
I say to you
How are you

Sing sing
Let it sing
Down the
Avenue

You and me
Let's see
Let's see
The soft tranquility

Be be
Be yourself
Allow the
Whistling woo

Be free
Be free
It seems to be
The ultimate I love you

26 years old; August 14, 1989
New York City
3 years sober

∞

Open Windows

Oh, God
That woman is
Wailing
Wandering
Waif-like
Underneath my
Window
Again
I hate
It
The wallowing
Wantonly
It echoes
And reaches
Upward
Inside
And I
Cringe
And Shiver
Helplessly
Oh, God
That woman is
Wailing and
Wailing
Like an
Old
Forgotten
Opera star
It comes
In
And touches
My being
Her screaming
It aches
The misery
And shame
Oh, God
That soul

Is singing
Again
She is
Sending
Notes to You
Up high
Do You
Hear
Her hallow
Heart
Horrendous
Haggard
Hidden
With hurt
Oh, God
That woman
Is wailing
Again
Like a
Goblin
Ghosting
In October
Release her
From her
Rigorous
Reprimand
Set her
Free
To be
Of Light
Her sight
Set only
On Your
Beauty
Capture her
Cravings
Carved
In stone
And let
Her know

They weren't
Important
Oh, God
Hear the woman
Who's wailing
Again

26 years old; August 17, 1989
New York City
In my apartment
3 years sober

Aloofness is More Attractive

I feel so raw,
Ripped at the
Seams and I just
Don't understand.

As if I am going
To explode—
This long road of
Trying to understand.

Whatever the code
By which people are
Operating I just
Don't understand.

Please, please
Someone tell me!
Why should I be
So misunderstood?

To be friendly and generous
Appears to be wrong,
So, I guess that means
They don't understand.

F*** you seems to be
The air....
The most universal
Understanding.

I feel so vulnerable, I want
To become hard
And say f*** you, f*** you
You understand?!!

Am I not to feel?
Am I not to care?
What kind of life would
That be—no understanding?

"Understand, understand
Listen, be tender, be
Understanding, is that
Understood?"

I want to run
And run and run and run
And run from this frightful
Lack of understanding...

I feel so embarrassed
For being of love,
Being a bitch
Is obviously more understood.

I guess that I do it
All wrong...
F*** you—is what I
Am understanding.

That seems to be
What I am hearing,
I am hearing a hardened
No understanding.

26 years old; August 17, 1989
New York City
After ballet class
3 years sober

Letting Go

And then I realized
After exhausting my
Resources with
The gamut of
Emotions

That I am not
The center of
All, which had
Been conclusively my
Surmise

And that true
Giving
Was in the gift
Of letting actions
Be

It's as if I
Hit this place
Where all the
Tightness
Loosens

Like a racehorse
Transcending
From the gallop
Through the canter
To the trot

I walk into
A reality
Much to my
Chagrin
That eventually
Eases

Into a somewhat
Hollow
Place that's
Filled to the
Embankment

With resolutions
Of what the
Truth must be
And that it runs further
Than me

At that point
Beauty transpires
Into
Living
Freer

The bondage
Of self
Relinquished
To a Higher
Purpose

That life
Is not always
What I can win
But what I can
Achieve

26 years old; August 17, 1989
New York City
After a hot bath
3 years sober

∞

Against a Wall

I'm transiently
Transfixed
Turbulent with the tides
Of immobility

Trespassing thoughts of you
Turning and conniving
Dripping within the hourglass
Imbued with salt

Brilliantly it burns
The soft soliloquies
Of my heart
Expressing the varied beats

I hear no flagrant
Pulses rushing
Towards me flowing
With reciprocating vibrancy

Only silence reverberates
In these hollow
Chambers of my
Formulating fortress

Though soundless sonnets
Cannot decapitate the
Deliverance of the
Dictations of spirit

Which sliver and slide
Selectively into my
Space speaking the
Secrets of seclusion

Screams of powerlessness
Bounce from one
Refrain to the next
Of my alluring abstracts

Communicating the connection
Of which variables are
No militant
Master

Storytelling the fantasy
Both of us confine in
Mutually believing
Beleagueredly so

Yet only my pen
Transcribes the delicacies
Of deliverance that
Neither of us dare

Shattering the shelters
With drips of sea
One sand castle
At a time

26 years old; September 9, 1989
New York City
3 years sober

Attitudes

Blazing
Lineaments
Linear
In spirit

Drive me to
Forbidden realms
Of latent
Latitudes

Aberration from
Badges of honor
Bravery in
Assuming compliance

Triads of trepidation
Trident with colors
Flying separate channels

Arrows arrogantly
Bereft of fragrance
Calling out my name

Receiving flaming
Configurations that
Tease with
Retribution

Breathing gaseous
Bubbles of bigotry
Rising in
Resilient stride

Shot with sparks
From frozen fields
Attitude
Anesthetizing air

Captivated
I am responsive
With regiment
Regards

Defeating
Evolving revolutions
Diminishing knowledge
Of abhorring serene

26 years old; September 21, 1989
New York City
3 years sober

∞

The Hang-Up

It was you
Who called last night.
It was you,
I know,
I do.

Though, still yearning
For actual,
Factual validation.
Yet, I know the breathless,
Restless
Pause...

I sit mesmerized
Frozen with mystique,
All my sounds internal screaming
To induce
Your hesitation
To appear in tones of truce.

It was you,
Who called last night.
It was you,
I know,
I do.

Why, why,
Why, why, why,
Why do you not
Speak
To me?

Everything I own,
Reaches out to your
Retreat...

But, you don't leave
Not completely,
You entice with silent
Calls...
All these walls!!

It was you,
Who called last night.
It was you,
I know,
I do.

Every tiny thread
Of inner rectitude
Reaches through the
Lines of iron
Barring our
Duet.

Oh, God..
If not me,
Then You
Tell him,
Make him,
Release him,
Please him
With our
Union.

It was you,
Who called last night,
It was you,
I know,
I do.

Yet, you hang
And disconnect,
Dialing of no
Great consequence
Except to raise the
Ante...

Safe
So very safe,
To hibernate in
Rebound,
No feeling to be rejected...

You leave all of that
To me,
In a sea
Treading...with my guts,
All buts,
All ifs,
All maybes,
And we'll sees—
Drowning in
Hypotheses!!
No conclusion,
No reductions,
No factual regards,
All retards—
In actual information,
That could
Possibly
Reveal
Through steel,
Through the parting of the
Canyons,
The magnitude
Of your feelings
For me,
Which remain
Anonymous
In you
Secrecy...
It was you who called last night...
It was you...I know...I do.

26 years old; September 23, 1989
New York City, NY
3 years sober

The Slippery Voice

There's an entity
That calls to me
With eyes of hellish hazel,
A heart of glass,
A little cap top,
And teeth that surround its edges.

It speaks to me,
Singing melodious tunes of
Romantic rendezvous.
It fancies my sweet spirit…
And craves the flavors of my seclusion
Vulnerabilities that pepper thought.

It promises its abilities:
To be my lasting friend
And to set me free—
Traveling to reclusive realms
That suspend unnatural nakedness,
Stripped of all respect.

It pardons
And excuses
And releases me from guilt.
It justifies
And jokes
And is jubilant with glee.

It whispers platitudes,
With eloquent elation,
Longing to be within me…
To captivate my reserve.
What might—
It has no fright in its intrigue,
Holding back's no baiting bargain.

Come!
Come!
Come!
Come!
Come and enjoy my pleasure!
A call girl in transaction.
Tepid pools of burning soul
Lie inside that sparkling reservoir,
Effervescence in temptation…
Yet, swords as teeth
Do knife the thought
Of blinding inebriation.

And it screams in horror
At my willful disregard,
Pulling all kinds of tantrums.
Not happy with neglect,
Remaining
Yet…
An entity
That calls to me,
With eyes of hellish hazel.
Though seen,
With my heart of vision,
That its little cap top
has teeth
And illusions…

That surround its edges.

26 years old; September 26, 1989
New York City
After a meeting
3 years sober

Palm Trees in the Parking Lot

Palm trees in the parking lot
We drive deliriously into oblivion
Swaying with rebellious reason
Careening with psalms of laughter…
Uhmmmmmm…
And the poet sits without a pen
Feeling inspired…
By the salt-and-pepper dashes
That fill the tray for ashes…
Reading Spago
The raisins hiding in the wheat
(so sweet)
Are having more fun than me…
Staring at the palm trees…
In the parking lot.

Wooden smiles
Wildly beaming
A resilience more of meaning in my ashtray
Reading Spago
Or my shrimp.
My table's more exciting…
An ashtray embellished with crumbs of butter
Dotting the linen of virgin white
(a rare word around here)

And with all my might
I try to act intrigued…
But, then, our foreign friend in white
To my demise,
With a whisk of wrist comes and steals
My showpiece…
Too many crumbs, I guess…

I hear the crystal cubes…
Echo sounds…
Sip…
Ahhhhhh

A slip in a foreign face
(the woman across the room)
As she acts smitten,
With the wine of reason,
Whispering the tales of moving pictures.
Where's my ashtray?
Well, there are always the Palm Trees in the parking lot.

26 years old; October 1989
Hollywood
Spago Restaurant
3 years sober

Hollywood

I watch…
As the frozen faces
Smile at the Nothingness
That penetrates the air here.

And I declare:
Oh, God!
Please protect my gentle soul
From the rusty calls,
Sweetened with delusion,
That echo on the waves of the fog
Up here on Mulholland Drive.

Away up high in the realm
Of forgotten deeper meaning
Swallowed by the seeming
Stillness
Moving in Arctic "circles"
Revealing distant thunder.

Protect my inner softness
That walks through this vacuous valley
Containing the sculptured faces
That peer from hidden rooms
Clutching their remembrances
Of stolen moments.

And I get on my knees
And I pray:
Give me courage, God,
To look beyond these shadows of darkened glitter
And be revealing of Your
Constant vibrant Lightness,
And the recognition that Your love
Carries me on different roads,
Sounding all the same to them...
But, arriving on a different plane.

And send Your mist to gently kiss
All of the artistic sinners
Wandering...amongst the fallow fog
That rolls its fingers
And points at distant, different roads.
Fame
Fortune
Stardom
Glamour
Glitz
And
Glory
Crossroads of confusion
Leading straight towards hell.
Or is this place it.

26 years old; October 1989 Hollywood
3 years sober

Glory to the Gin

Whistling down the road of reason
Whipping past the why
Walks a man of stature
Weeping—his ally

Laden with the breath he borrows
Beckoned from brown bottles
Journeys a solitary figure
Teeming with remorse

At what he labors, not he knows
As surely as the wind does blow
The hollow pecans that drop from trees
Seeming fully fair

Rolling down the avenue
The shell keeps even step
Swept by some unknown force
That rides with mounting pleasure

How to measure the mystery
That calls at even temp
Darkening the burrowed brow
So beautifully placed upon his face

And out yonder, the cows do graze
With tails that whip their foe
A sting of hair, does the scare
Then off their devil goes

Eyes of envy burn the throat
As he takes another swig
A swallow, a sigh, a sting—
The darkness does not give

Step by step he takes the curve
With the hell that rides beside him
The sound of crumbling rocks beneath
Grind the path of stone

Brown bagging his intentions
Of which he never mentions
To the ghosts that nestle in his chest
That's filled with hidden treasures

All his love, that's bound so tight
Could feed a thousand others
Starving from the lack of limit
That sows and grows within

Lonely in his secret
Glory to the gin

Down the road, he solely goes
Past the fork that does elude him
Oh, God, bless him
Carry him with your hands

As the Light's blown out
As he bandies about
In the damned
Unyielding binges.

27 years old; January 4, 1990
New York City
3 years sober

Tears of Time

Picturing the window...
I wonder what the pains were like
Trimmed in silver and draped in lace
The view does mesh the thought

Peeking through forbidden senses
Packed away long ago
Intertwine the fervent rhymes
That riddle in my space

Crowns that shine of glory
Gifts of which I knew nothing
Line the shelves that hang on threads
And tiny forget-me-nots

Pulling strings and winding ways
That wash the memory white
Dimensions appear....Division's fear
And seedlings show their might.

Dancing around the pink tutus
That skip the path of seasons
Pointing back to lives of others
Tightening all the ribbons

Laughter speaks with tears of time
Yet, love of hearts do win
The winter turns to spring
But the showers do begin again.

Speak to me, speak the secret
That whirls around my head
Simply listen to the sights
Hear what's being said

But what the meaning, I do not know
That language not coherent
To a girl who ran the house
Looking for a parent

Pajamas trail the road of night
As journeys do come next
Standing at the door confused
I'll have my father yet

I'll steal him back from lineal keep
Bequeathed to him verbatim
Binding slips with bonds of pain
Harboring deep inside him

Insidiously prevented by Warden Thwart
From telling me he loves me—
The trap of words within his heart
Longing to be free—

Oh, the pain…it does not stop
The train set has no caboose
It follows me in circles
Yearning to be loose

Wandering back in my room
Amongst the valley of the dolls
Listening to the chime of Brahms
Lulling on my wall

Praying with my fingers tight
While gazing at my ceiling
God, oh, God, oh if You hear
Please take away this feeling.

27 years old; January 9, 1990
New York City
3 years sober

Gentle Ledge of Tender

Never do you know
The thoughts within my head
Never do I show
The source I keep instead

At a loss I feel
The mystery too deep
To tell the secrets of my being
That shoulder against the giving

It perplexes and sends distance
Regards of foreign notions
With little potions…
That keep the style ferment

I take a chip and try not yielding
But then I scare and hide the tool
Locked beneath my harbored heart
Keys cleverly a riddle

Yet I yearn for softness
The gentle ledge of tender
That seems alluring and besotted
Way beyond the sender

Why do I feel this way
I want not the isolation
That peaks at times, seeks at times, leaks at times
Not mentioned

Please God, let the barriers go
That suffocate my soul
Leave me not to figure
The scope of life alone

Gently, I do rise above
The tide of armored shore
Lifting me in waves of passion
Always wanting more

But then again the fright sets in
Demanding equal time
It will not leave its station
Eager to the signs

Back away I push it
No I say to silence
Forcing with all my muster
I relegate the fight

Yet it's seemingly ripe to win
The battle not coherent
The trophy I do not bequeath
To heap upon this thief

Conquer the illusion, God
That strides and rides in curves
Win over the intrusion
Its existence never more

Please, I ask the exorcise
Be ever strongly willing
To undertake the tender task
Wild within its knowing

Vanquish now this villain vile
Leave it in the sea
Let it forever render
No passage back to me

Let me love the love of love
Free from fiery fear
Always knowing, always sure
That You are here, right here

Beseechingly I search to seize
The simple joys of life
Let me sing the Hallelujah
To treasure void of strife

Push away, push away
Push away that voice
Keep it gone forever…
That trepidating voice

Take away its power
Let it cease its grip
Banish it beyond all reason
No borders to requite

Let me love again…
Encompassing the call
Let me feel the peace of purpose
Sumptuous strengths stand tall.

27 years old; January 14, 1990
New York City
3 years sober

Midnight Madness

In a moment of midnight madness
A light burst through my room
It spoke to me in avid apt
Its tempo wrought a transit tune

Manifesting from where all elicits breed
Realms of deepened reason
Rattling solid mores of might
Its awareness tried of treason

I craved retreat to my daunting den
And cried for familiar, sheltered haze
Mend the fence with wishing wire
And pallid, euphoric, habitual haze

Yet, cognizance rose to higher rapt
My floating cushion had a view
I saw that my unswerving silence
Had eclipsed my truth from two

Denouncement of any quest for more
Denial of existing needs
I swallowed ardent appetite
For we had our fraternal deed.

Never evidenced in manner
For I feared my passion and my pain
It gripped me so intense inside
That it seized me in refrain

Honest, I was sure to heed
True to whispered words...
My desires penetrated deep within
Longing for a purge

In a dance dodging depth
I leapt with the illusions
Guised behind mercurial masks
Coercing no intrusions

Into this land of fragile paces
Sewn together by tiny steps
Square roots of the surreal sublime
I forced into round pegs

My true self, the child within
Battled victoriously not to show
For as surely as my veil fell
You'd see me, and you'd go

So, I pretended, I would bravely say
"A mature and timely woman I am"
At times I think I was convinced...
You were a mature and timely man

Living in a bottle—
Selfsame thirsting of another sort—
I tightly capped my inner being
Hidden struggle behind the fort

Peeking over wooden wrenches
To my childhood beyond recall
I saw a cherub in padded feet
Venturing into great halls

Secret there in twilight's kingdom
A king and queen with night they'd reap
Upon a pawn who bid in step...
The compulsion to repeat

That pawn upon a square was me
A baby reasoning rigid touch
I meekly seek to grasp the game
I saw the king's world gleaming shut

Enveloped by this wanton world
Hopping scotch—alone to cope
Fortresses sprung up all around
Living solely on the hope

It's challenged every move I make
As a woman with no wherewithal
When seeking now I cannot surmount
The ghosts of hollow halls...

Trapped within these malls of hell
For you my feeling laid unspoken
Fear of loss, bred the cost
My taciturn went unbroken.

Sitting on volcanic verses
Constant forward and retreat
Ambivalence in my sordid soul
Courage I could not meet

For years I ran with fervor
Propelling myths with heartless tasks
Paradoxes prized in rations
Feeding on which I'd seem to last

Depths of love, I yearned to free
Yet, solitude crept in pressing ways
How often did I reach to you
Still stifled in my molten maze

Doubled with existing fear
Patterns webbed with childhood fright
If I told you of my needs
You'd echo in surmising flight

Here within lies the riddle
Of which I rode in stride
Constantly leading me back to halls
Where as a child I'd bide

The key unlocks, the truth be told
My poverty of you ran deep
It reached inside and tugged at needs
I longed for us to meet

The hall's soliloquies sufficed no longer
The path grew too narrow and too dim
Suffocating in rise of checks
I grappled for more than friend

Circuitous in confessing love
For I feared exit of your caring
Hence, I remained mute, for you'd rebuke
And the silence would be blaring

Yet, now, I lie in full exposure
And grasp at last the finding
That with another you had no deed
—Fraternity is not binding

What to me you said, to her you said
The motive was not synonymous
Here within is the grim remorse
That shatters tart hypothesis

What is the ravenous course, I ask
Upon which I am to love you
I tried denial, it did not work
I fragment, with elusive cues

Binding friendship, we aspire
Yet, as your friend I fear I fail
Though I mirror quick mirage
My wanting need is to be held.

I view horizons from a canyon
Stumbling among the step of stones
I venture through untrodden creeks
A drunkard leans on sober loans

I quest to quench this thirst to mesh
I send to you my plea…
Air our flame with fetching strength
Sobriety lends the key…

That's my heart's resounding theme
It wakens me at night
It follows me through everyday
Transcending scorching heights

Expelling now my fortitudes
That fall with booming ticks of clock
How am I to squash the anguish
That undertows my rising rock

I throw spirit at whitewashed walls
As you seal up and dimly drift
In your mist I whisper red
Rebelling vast and rigid rifts

Swallowed in rooms of sharp delusions
That rip at seams that hold my might
I fear the gap that gores my gut
Reaping havoc's cyclical bite

I venge this vary, chanting black
As it canons our cohort's cord
Thriving on bleak feasts of famine
Hurling raving rotes in hordes

Smitten by this smoldering bond
I solely fan enamored fire
Grasping nails that hail the dark
Battling marks from epoch mire

I long, in whirlwinds wrapping reason
Tightly wound in sullen lands
All the panes that repel rains
Summon to my hand

Up against a wall I stand
Atoning weathered rapture
Beckoning with despairing calls
Beseeching that you capture

Magnetisms mysterious birthing
Propels me to your core
I chip with fingers ripping martyr
Seeking through a voyeur's door

Reverberating sounds of melancholy
Hope rends tender stoic sighs
Wistful whispers slide through night
Riding passions towing ties

This everlasting copious ting
Sent upon the wings of dove
On my knees ... I reach to seize
... Your corresponding love.

27 years old; March 1, 1990
New York City
3 years sober

Yellow Rose of Texas

Yellow petals fall to floor
Stepped on, running through the door
To awaiting yellow buds in "sun room"
Ahhhhh, delicious Texas beauties ...
In full bloom—
Thank God they come in dozens ...
Haven't you met Penny ...
Oh ... (so many)
Yellow petals call from floor
Simply easier to ignore
A dime a dozen ...
There are more.

27 years old; March 6, 1990
New York City
3 years sober

The Devil vs. God

Perched upon my rock of burden
Head harbored in my hand
My eyes engage overwhelming void
On the vortex of another land

Bombarding rays of black and grey
Circuitous in mirages
Entice with their confusion
Certain in demand

Damned in demented spaces—
The blackened core of solitude,
My spirit tumbles around the ground
Blown by sentiments surpassing strength

I feel a mist of dark
Rushing through my hair there
As it seeks ceremoniously on my countenance
Hungry for weak withins

Shadows dance to whirlwind
Spinning my reclusive cell
Into a gale of hellish vigor
Throwing swords of sullen hue

Ebony forces obscure reach
As I wind my sorrow through sands of glass
Struggling with masked manipulations
Marching in marked momentum

I flail my desperate fingers
Along the lines of wall
Rising nails obtain the pain
Taunting me to fail

Scattered mirrors on the floor
Reflect the burning flames that lure
They chant to me to jump and join them
Reaping putrid pleasure

I throw myself on wooden walk
Wanting not this lair for comfort
I crawl backward lost in traverse,
Abandon snaps as snares

I lie numb in nocturnal knots
Confining reverent courage
I cannot shake the hovering wake
Of boundless passion taken

Sheepishly I grope—forsaken,
Forcing my ineptitude of reason
To foresee future—
Somehow

Waves of felling rock my conscious
Knocking at my knowing door
I shake remnants from my essence
And stumble to implore

Then, within, I ready counter
To oppose the grand illusion
I question it its right to mount
And morbidly ride my shoulders

I feel the current resisting rise
Fighting fast my calling
I parallel myself to battle
Rounds of restitution

Tripping against my wilting will
I press my body abreast the beast
I writhe to uphold my sordid soul
Billowing in sheer surmise

I warrant cause for my arrest
And attest to gallant graces
I step with summons of survival,
However slight in measure

Questing now for higher ground
I scream at God to conquer
I lift my hands with wailing
And purge petulance of self

I thrust my heart above the wrath
Supplying soaring sight
Direly seizing the thread of hope,
—I step above the past.

27 years old; May 19, 1990
New York City
Almost 4 years sober

N.E. 90

I sat beside you...
In my chair—there
Your breath aligned with mine,
The room was square
Sketched with light
Darkness darted round...
No sound.

Connections wrought by same despair
Tribulations we had fought—
The knot...
My fingers crept to touch your hand
If only in my thoughts...

I there, you there—
Temptation tied with bows of sighs
My arms flung 'round your soul
Like wings in ardent stride
By your side
As I sat
And glanced at you.

Known reprimands, on separate lands
Bound our throw of spirit,
Pleading let's not ever leave
This sordid pleasant spot
In time
In space
In vacuous vaults of air.

We smiled
We laughed
We frowned on life's poor play.
We linked eyes
And winked at fate
And then,
Pretended otherwise.
And you were called away from there,
Sitting gallantly beside my chair,
And you, with every step and sideward stare,
Were unraveling my thread of keeping,
As I sat…
In my chair…
Watching darkness—
Bare.

27 years old; August 8, 1990
Seattle
Filming *Northern Exposure*
4 years sober

Soul

I walk around with this emptiness
Inside myself—
That self that is that entity of soul—
That in its Lightness,
Captures within its weightlessness,
My heaviness of spirit.

It holds my ton of tears
Within its porous mesh of strings.
It receives the sleets of ice
Delivered from the arctic of another's vacuous tin.
It absorbs, the arrows that fly,
Into my fleshless, sightless mass of obscurity.
Oh…
Yes…his nebulous means of intangible being
So easily and pointedly does reach and pierce
My nebulous means of intangible being.

And it rules my untouchable, uncanny,
Unseen, unfelt…
Fabric of thought.

> 27 years old; November 8, 1990
> New York City
> *4 years sober*

A Dark Hello

I heard your dark hello today
I heard your frozen fine
I heard the stillness
Lay between the lines

And I knew nothing

You spit your syllables
As to a stranger...
Yet, what stranger induces such requite?

You feign foreign,
Disguising the true fearing, I know,
Of my stark nakedness of soul,
For with no mask to lay upon,
How are we to speak?

Any walls that had let down
Are now positioned as a bastion
With bolts,
I a ranking stranger
An enemy climbing the wall of the Alamo.

You push me with your will of fort,
You shove with silent, blistered force
"Get off my stone carved mountain"

I, the enemy with my truths,
I, the enemy with my strengths,
I, the enemy with my love,
I, the enemy when I speak,
I, the enemy with my feelings,
I, the enemy with my need...
I, the enemy with my caring,
I, the enemy with my retreats...

And I feel somehow apologetic,
Sorry for my stay of soul.
Oh, God
What expense the toll.

March 10, 1991
Seattle
4 years Sober

The Threshold

My pen most often meets the page with despair and rage as ally,
Yet, with you as inspiration, I greet not the rote,
But passion, purpose, quizzical curious kindness…
Whatever we decide this is—
For I do not know—
I know not the rights and wrongs,
But, I worry, a pleasing, satisfying, rewarding fret,
What is this we have beset upon ourselves?
I smile as my palms bead sweat, combining these intrinsic senses,
Watching how your hair plays about your beautiful, soulful face,
A lullaby, the revelations from your heart soft and eloquent,
While feeling you, electrifying my wild, inhibited realm of reason,
And I get scared and brave all at once,
For your breath from breast that rests between us,
I will with grace defend,
For you speak to my inherent wind.

I find myself on the threshold of control,
Mesmerized
Do I care I do I dare?
What is the fare—
What price is bountied upon our pasts,
At what cost must rust stain our todays?
No guaranteed okays…
Mountains of courage one must have to cast
Everlasting ways of love.

I can, I can't, I can't, I can,
Yes, no, yes, no, yes, no, yes,
The hell from yesteryears leave me senseless,
A daisy plucked a thousand times,
It isn't meant to be this way…
Is it?
I no longer want to visit those wastelands of naught,
They who I so thought were it –
I will no longer probate them leave
To steal my present blind.

And now you…you…
Here you are
You are like a rainfall upon my desert…
Sighing simultaneously to my quenching,
I, yet, fear vulnerability of thirst,
Will we burst from rationale?
Ah, where this leads us, where this goes,
Heaven know…
But your breath from breast that rests between us,
I will with grace defend,
For you speak to my inherent wind.

March 23, 1991
Seattle
4 years sober

Chapter Two

Constituting America—Interpreting *The Federalist*

The internal effects of a mutable policy are still more calami-tous. It poisons the blessing of liberty itself. It will be of little avail to the people, that the laws are made by men of their own choice, if the laws be so voluminous that they cannot be read, or so incoherent that they cannot be understood; if they be re-pealed or revised before they are promulgated, or undergo such incessant changes that no man, who knows what the law is to-day, can guess what it will be to-morrow. Law is defined to be a rule of action; but how can that be a rule, which is little known, and less fixed?

—James Madison, Federalist 62

This is the quote that spurred me into action: founding Constituting America, becoming politically active, writing opinion editorials, appearing as a political pundit, and launching my radio show. Those who believe that the Constitution and the wisdom of our Founding Fathers are not relevant simply have *not read* the Constitution and founding documents.

Preface

We fight an elusive enemy that is creeping into our fields. They are creeping both from abroad with violence and from within with slow usurpation of our founding principles. Alexander Hamilton warns in Federalist 25, "For it is a truth which the experience of all ages has attested, that the people are commonly most in danger, when the means of injuring the rights are in the possession of those of whom they entertained the least suspicion."

—Janine Turner

Poetry helped me survive my "struggling actress" years by giving me an artistic and cathartic channel to work through my turbulent twenties. At age twenty-seven, I began a new chapter of my life. I received my "big break," winning and portraying the role of Maggie O'Connell in *Northern Exposure*. For five solid years I performed someone else's words and emotions, both in *Northern Exposure* and *Cliffhanger*, and trust me, after working eighteen-hour days for five years, I was depleted.

When *Northern Exposure* was picked up by CBS for fifty episodes, which was unheard of at the time, I could finally breathe a sigh of relief and reckon with my deeply rooted desire to return home to Texas. The first thing I did was purchase a palomino horse—my cherished Maggie—a pick-up truck, and a horse trailer. Next was my ranch, which I named *Mockingbird Hill*. I love mockingbirds because they remind me of actors. They mock other birds with melodious monologues in the way actors mock other people in the form of characters (not to mention, Thomas Jefferson had a pet mockingbird in the White House!). In 1995, after being gone for eighteen years, I blissfully moved home, exhausted, but ready for my next chapter. This chapter would be my precious daughter, Juliette, who was born in 1997.

Juliette, who is now sixteen years old, is my delight, my joy, my blessing. She is also my inspiration and creative partner. We have launched, side by side, many entrepreneurial projects. I continued writing in varying genres. I adapted the short story *Trip in a Summer Dress* into a screenplay and made my directorial debut, in which Juliette stole the show. I wrote and produced a Christian yoga workout video, *Christoga*, with yoga expert Mary Cunningham. I wrote a book, *Holding*

Her Head High (published by Thomas Nelson), which is about twelve exceptional "sheroes" spanning seventeen centuries. Juliette and I ventured into singing/songwriting for our debut country album, *Mockingbird Hill*. I wrote it as an emotional release after my beloved horse Maggie died.

In 2010 I launched a foundation, Constituting America, with my soul sister and co-chair, Cathy Gillespie. Juliette was along for the ride, serving as the national youth director, which led to her hit published (Zondervan) book *Our Constitution Rocks*, and her sequel *Our Presidents Rock*. My fervent mission is to spread the message to adults, students, and the culture that the Constitution is not only *nonpartisan* but vital to barring tyranny and preserving our self-governing republic, which in turn preserves our inherent rights.

With Constituting America, I ventured full force into, as my friend Dr. David Bobb of Hillsdale College and the Bill of Rights Institute says, "a self-inspired, self-taught Master's degree in the Constitution and our founding era of enlightenment." This was aided by the 90 in 90 day studies we initiated at Constituting America. We had ninety interpretive essays written over the course of ninety days by brilliant, generous professors, garnered by the incomparable Horace Cooper. In minute detail these essays explain each opinion editorial in *The Federalist*, every clause of the Constitution, and the classic works by Aristotle, Cicero, and others that inspired the Constitution.

Enthused, my writings re-emerged with gusto in another genre: essays—from poetry to Publius. After reading the eighty-five opinion editorials in *The Federalist*, written by Publius, the pseudonym used by Alexander Hamilton, James Madison, and John Jay, I wrote eighty-five corresponding essays to promote Constituting America. I was on fire to share the astounding relevance of their words and wisdom. I was, and am, simply amazed by their genius.

Included in this chapter is a selection of my essays on *The Federalist*, bookended by a few of my opinion editorials on the subject of Constituting America. This has been the most remarkable journey and continues to be a labor of love.

What Would Our Forefathers Think of America Today?

I have a fantasy.

It's fascinating. It's futuristic. It's foretelling.

My fantasy is that our country's forefathers would miraculously appear today in America. I see them walking among us, dressed in velvet coats and knee pants, hair in ponytails, hats in hand. Thomas Jefferson in Virginia. Alexander Hamilton on Wall Street. John Adams in Boston. Benjamin Franklin in Philadelphia. And, George Washington in Washington.

I envision it theatrically, of course, with cameras. A panoramic sweep as they turn full circle in awe. What would they think? Would they be proud? Would they be shocked? I, for one, want them desperately to be pleased.

This is an idea that has fascinated me for decades. I can remember asking my father about it when I was eight: "If our Founding Fathers were to come back today, what would they be most disappointed about?" My father, who was a graduate of the United States Military Academy at West Point and a man of few words, thought for a moment and simply said, "taxes."

What would our forefathers think of us today? I yearn for their wisdom. I believe if they roamed the halls of Congress together and eavesdropped on the conversations, heard the rancor, felt the division, they would say, or at least Thomas Jefferson would say, "Ah, democracy at work." However, upon further investigation their impressions would sour. They would accurately perceive that the tenor has changed.

During their day, they too differed and fought. They were, at times, wickedly vicious—but it was for Americans. They believed that God wove an innate promise in human beings and they envisioned the infinite possibilities of the mind and soul if freed from tyrannical government. They ardently loved America. Their purpose was for America to be born, to blossom, and to be the hope of mankind. They took pride in their remarkable achievements. They believed that their victory over the British and success in uniting their fledgling country's passionate diversities as they constructed and ratified the Constitution were the works of "Divine Providence."

Brilliant and well read as they were, they would quickly surmise the threats to America. Alarmed by the bitter greed, they would stand at the pulpit of Congress, pound the gavel, and say, "Awaken, Patriots. Awaken your sense of unity! A Congress divided, for the sake of pride, will most certainly fall. A Congress that betrays its constituents, for the sake of party line, will most assuredly falter. A Congress that bloats bills to the point of obscene obscurity will be condemned." They would be astounded by a Congress that does not read its own works, and they would warn, "A Congress that cannot or will not read the bills before they vote, before they represent the American people, will, without fail, lead the country and its people to doom."

When they realize C-SPAN is there, and they would adeptly figure this out, they would look into the camera and warn the American people. They would warn parents that by neglecting to teach their children their rights as embodied in the Constitution as well as the inherent responsibilities of citizenship, they will let America simply slip away. Thomas Jefferson would recount his own words: "If a nation expects to be ignorant and free, in a state of civilization, it expects what never was and never will be." They would warn, "It won't be sudden. It will be insidious. Those who devalue freedom, who underestimate human genius, integrity, and industriousness, will cunningly dominate the debate."

Benjamin Franklin would recount his own words: "Think what you do when you run in debt; you give to another power over your liberty." They would say, "By letting Congress bankrupt your country, you most assuredly will lose your freedom, your free will. By letting Congress take away your right to own a gun, you will let a dictator seize your country and your home, because he will encounter no resistance."

They would close with biting truths by saying, "Without moral values, which should begin in Congress, America will lose her roots, her basis, her thesis." They would echo Paul Revere and cry out, "Stand up, Americans. The challenge is coming! The challenge is coming! Let freedom continue to ring!" They would exit Congress and they would not be downtrodden. A smile would emanate from their faces, for they know the heart of Americans.

Janine Turner
July 16, 2009
FOXNews.com

A Republic, If You Can Keep It

Federalist 1 by the brilliant Alexander Hamilton! I wrote about his mother Rachel Lavien Fawcett in my book, *Holding Her Head High*. Historians have not been very kind to her, but read my version. It is from a woman's point of view. There is no doubt that she planted the seeds of greatness, determination, and entrepreneurial spirit in Alexander's character.

A famous Benjamin Franklin quotation sums up our mission at Constituting America. When asked by a woman, "What have you given us?" Franklin replied, "A Republic, if you can keep it."

This is our challenge today: stepping forward, standing up for our founding principles, and demanding that our republic be vital and strong and that our Constitution be protected, preserved, and defended. The best way for us to do this is with a basis of knowledge about our country's thesis. How lucky we are that it is so well documented in copious documents and books—the Declaration of Independence, the United States Constitution, and *The Federalist* being the foundations.

Alexander Hamilton, James Madison, and John Jay came together for the good of the country. They did not agree on many things, and later became quite divided, but they united to accomplish the magnificent miracle of the Constitution and *The Federalist*. They saw the bigger picture and were able to forfeit their egos to better their country—and they had vision! They had vision and wisdom and determination and a sense of service.

They wrote *The Federalist* under the name of Publius after Publius Valerius, a founder of the Roman Republic. A republic. They knew that they all had reputations that preceded them, for better or worse, and they did not want the objectivity of their thesis to be tainted by preconceived notions. Smart. These men were very smart and they truly loved the United States of America.

This is what it's going to take to awaken, educate, and propel Americans to undertake the journey of Constituting America—a love for the United States of America and all she embodies, her nobility, greatness of character, and philanthropic communities with a genius for creativity and a gut for survival. We have a republic, and God save the ones who try to strip Americans of our inherent rights, rights that exist in the Declaration of Independence and the United States Constitution and that embody Americans today. God bless America.

God bless our forefathers who sacrificed so much for their prosperity—all of the great men and women who have fought throughout our history to maintain our dignity, freedom, and inalienable rights.

Janine Turner
April 28, 2010
Federalist 1
Constituting America

Farewell, A Long Farewell to All My Greatness

There are many aspects in our readings of the United States Constitution and *The Federalist* that are relevant today. However, as I was juggling the many pertinent points from Federalist 2, suddenly a more general observation manifested.

Our forefathers were intent on explaining the Constitution to the people of the United States. They wanted the republic to understand what was in the bill (the Constitution), and they undertook great pains and efforts to make sure that

happened. Spearheaded by Alexander Hamilton, they published eighty-five different opinion editorials in newspapers.

Not only did they go to great pains to explain the contents of the Constitution,
which was only seven pages, they knew that the American public would demand
to know what was in it before they ratified it. This brings about two conclusions:

1. The American people of the eighteenth century wanted to know
   what their government was doing, felt very much involved in the
   process, and were passionate about the direction of their country.

2. Publius and the signatories of the United States Constitution felt
   obligated to explain it to them, and did so in great detail because
   they had written it and they understood it.

A very different atmosphere exists today. Both the American people and the
United States government are to blame for the obscurity in which we wander. The
bloated bills and ignorance of their intentions are the fault of both the governors
and the governed. We, as collective countrymen and women, grew discordant and
lax in the affairs of the state, and like a child pushing the boundaries with his or her
parents, the United States government got away with what they could. It's human
nature. "Men are not angels," hence, the Constitution.

Times have changed. Our country's woes are like trying times for the soul.
Difficult times are God's way of shaping our character—making us into the people
He wants us to be—a light, a leader. Now Americans are waking up and realizing
that we must once again demand to understand. What is really in the bill and what
is really the direction of our country? We are realizing that we must vet, vote, and
find our voice. In our blood is the ancestry of righteousness.

We must stress to our elected officials that we will accept nothing less than
clarity. In Federalist 62, James Madison zeroes in on this point:

> It will be of little avail to the people, that the laws are made by men
> of their own choice, if the laws be so voluminous that they cannot
> be read, or so incoherent that they cannot be understood; if they be
> repealed or revised before they are promulgated, or undergo such in-
> cessant changes, that no man who know what the law is today, can
> guess what it will be tomorrow. Law is defined to be a rule of action;
> but how can that be a rule, which is little known or less fixed.

The title of John Jay's Federalist 2 is *Concerning Dangers from Foreign Force and Influence*, and is applicable today as well. If we do not gain control of the economy we are going to be like Greece. Times of economic stress are ripe for tyranny. If we do not gain control of our spending and deficit then we are a sitting duck for the hunters who wait in the night—*Dangers from Foreign Force and Influence*. As Benjamin Franklin said, "Think, when you run into debt, you give to another power over your liberty."

John Jay ends this paper, from over two hundred years ago, with a Shakespearean quote. It echoes eerily across our current environment. It is a battle cry and ominous warning of something we do not want to ever shout, "FAREWELL! A LONG FAREWELL TO ALL MY GREATNESS."

As the present necessity of unity prevails, we the people will gather with the mission of preserving our great country and we will be spurred by our patriotism and launched by our learning.

Janine Turner
April 29, 2010
Federalist 2
Constituting America

Prophetic Publius

In relation to the founding era and Federalist 5, there was still so much to be imagined, discovered, and resolved. There was an abundance of mystery in America. This is one of the brilliant aspects of Publius—Alexander Hamilton, James Madison, and John Jay had such foresight, almost prophetic. They knew there were differences amongst the peoples of America, with a vast portion of America yet to be discovered and claimed, but they also knew that it was better to be *with each other* rather than *against one another*, to be governed by a unified vision.

As our two-hundred-thirty-four years have evolved, it has become apparent that our differences did drive stakes into our passions, but they did not dismember us. If we had not found stability as a burgeoning union then we would never have been able to survive the challenges that were to be wrought by the Civil War and the Great Depression, to name a few.

So what is the relevancy of Federalist 5 today? It is in defining the boundaries between the federal government and the states in the twenty-first century. It is in the understanding of how much power our Founding Fathers really intended the federal government to have. It is in the reckoning and reconciling of the autonomy the states were intended to have and should have today. The answers to these questions are complex, especially because it is inordinately hard to rein back leniencies that have already been dispersed. Once one foot is in the door, it is very hard to close it again. Has the federal government planted its boots upon our thresholds too boldly?

I dare say many of us would answer yes. I dare say many of us agree with Arizona in regard to the fact that she has the right to make her own laws, yet look at how her autonomy is disrupting the union. Is this not exactly what Publius was predicting? However, today, is the fault with the state or with the federal government who failed to protect her and her people? Or is it the state's right to defend herself? This is addressed in the Constitution in Article I, Section 8, Clause 16.

It is only in the educating of America about the United States Constitution that these questions may be answered. Knowledge is power. We cannot appreciate what has been taken away if we have never known what was rightfully ours in the first place.

The monarchies of Europe didn't want their people educated. An educated people would be able to see the truths. These truths are self-evident: If we don't utilize our educated voice, someone else will speak for us. And all of our rights will be lost.

Janine Turner
May 4, 2010
Federalist 5
Constituting America

Warnings from History

The complexity of this particular paper, Federalist 6, is mesmerizing. I am enthralled by the examples of former empires, the rise and fall of these republics, and the reasons why. The relevancies in today's reading are many, but the warnings are simple and the question singular. How do we keep the United States of America from failing? The warnings from history provide wisdom. The republics of Sparta, Athens, Rome, and Carthage were ruined by wars and greed. Holland was overwhelmed in debt and taxes, and England and France were beleaguered by antipathy toward one another.

It is interesting to reflect upon the fact that one of the reasons Alexander Hamilton, John Jay, and James Madison could make such brilliant observations is because of their superb education. Alexander Hamilton should be an inspiration to many who believe that one has to be born into wealth to receive such an education.

Hamilton was raised by his single mother, who by example taught him at an early age the art of business and the spirit of tenacity. She started her own business and Hamilton worked beside her. Yet they struggled financially. When his mother died, he was in desperate need of a new pair of shoes. He may have had no shoes, but he had spirit, determination, and true grit—and his mother's fortitude.

Are these not qualities that Americans hold near and dear—spirit, determination, and true grit? These American characteristics were why we won the Revolutionary War and these are the qualities that keep America great today. We are a country—a republic—where one may dare to dream. We are a country where, according to our Constitution, no one may receive titles of nobility. We are a country where a boy born in a single-room log cabin becomes president and where men raised by single mothers become president. We are a country where vision, perseverance, and the willingness to work hard can nurture the seeds of talent in any man or woman. In this respect we are all equal. In this respect we must maintain our free enterprise, which yields the vast fruits of commerce, industry, and personal ingenuity. These are the things that keep America vibrant, solvent, and safe.

Janine Turner
May 6, 2010
Federalist 6
Constituting America

A New Type of Republic

With the birth of the Republic of the United States came the birth of a new type of republic. Republics in the past all eventually lent themselves to the art of war instead of the art of commerce and free enterprise. Our new republic would be monitored and governed by the people instead of military figures.

This was truly an enlightened and inspired experiment. Yet safety would have to be secured in order to offer the opportunity of these pursuits and the art of war delineated. If the people did not feel safe, and if war were to spring from internal hostilities, then the focus would shift away from the remarkable aspects of American ingenuity to the colossal attentions war and petty skirmishes demanded.

To quote Alexander Hamilton, "Even the ardent love of liberty will, after a time, give way to its dictates. [...] To be more safe, they at length, become willing to run the risk of being less free." If war were to become the dictate then the executive branch would broaden and the legislative branch, the people's branch, weaken.

"They would, at the same time, be obliged to strengthen the executive arm of government; in doing which, their constituents would acquire a progressive direction towards monarchy. It is of the nature of war to increase the executive, at the expense of the legislative authority."

War was thus incompatible with the new industriousness of the American people. "The industrious habits of the people of the present day, absorbed in the pursuits of gain, and devoted to the improvements of agriculture and commerce, are incompatible with the condition of a nation of soldiers, which was the true condition of the people of those republics."

Once again our forefathers had the wisdom and wherewithal to prophesy the necessities for a free people to flourish—freedom from dictators, tyranny, war, conquests, and internal skirmishes.

Which begs the next big undertaking: replacing the dictator with the wisdom of the people. If the government were to heed the whims of the people, then how does one educate and inspire the people? The checks and balances of the Constitution were thus both a check against the leaders and the people—a republic instead of a democracy.

In this respect how have Americans fared? I would say on the broad scale, remarkably well. I believe our forefathers would be mesmerized by the scope of growth—scientifically, industriously, and humanitarianly. They would be in a state of awe. The experiment of liberty and union, though bruised along the way, has remained vital.

Yet, a new generation and movement are upon us. Our Founding Fathers, I believe, would be a bit wary regarding the modern-day wisdom of the people. There was such a hunger for education and inspiration in the blossoming days of the United States because the repression of such liberties had left a formidable and everlasting impression.

Today, we take for granted the freedoms that have made our country great. I believe that the lack of voting would be a disappointment to our forefathers, as would the seeming unawareness of the founding principles of our country.

If we, as citizens, and our children, do not understand the dignified rights and principles we have, then we, and our children, will not know when they are subtly taken away from us. The success of the progressive movement is a prime example.

Janine Turner
May 7, 2010
Federalist 8
Constituting America

Liberty Is to Faction, What Air Is to Fire

Most Americans do not realize that our form of government is a republic. Most Americans believe we are a democracy, and most Americans lack an educated understanding about the differences between a democracy and a republic.

Our Founding Fathers' prudence, knowledge, and experience steered the fledgling United States of America clear of a democratic form of government. They knew that democracies lent themselves to the vulnerabilities of mob mentalities and passions. Channeling and tempering the populace's zeal was paramount for the longevity of self-government. Our Founding Fathers accomplished this goal by establishing a republic, a form of government where the wisdom of representatives would heed the people's call in a slow and thoughtful manner.

Madison believed in the art of debate, which by its very nature led to factions. He wrote, "Liberty is to faction, what air is to fire, an aliment, without which it instantly expires."

Madison was invigorated by faction. He believed it was a necessary and vital tool to thwart the constant threat of monarchy. After eight years of presidency, however, Washington was exhausted by ugly, spiteful, and incessant faction. He warned in his Farewell Address that faction, and blind party loyalty, would be the downfall of our Republic because people would care more about their party than about their country.

Which belief, Madison's or Washington's, is proving to be correct today?

Janine Turner
May 11, 2010
Federalist 10
Constituting America

To Plume Herself as the Mistress of the World

In Federalist 11, Alexander Hamilton makes a statement regarding Europe:

> *The superiority she has long maintained, has tempted her to plume herself as the mistress of the world, and to consider the rest of mankind as created for her benefit. Men, admired as profound philosophers, have, in direct terms, attributed to her inhabitants a physical superiority; and have gravely asserted, that all animals, and with them the human species, degenerate in America; that even dogs cease to bark,*

after having breathed a while in our atmosphere… It belongs to us to
vindicate the honor of the human race, and to teach that assuming
brother moderation. Union will enable us to do it. Disunion will add
another victim to his triumphs.

This statement exhibits the vision of our Constitutional Founding Fathers and of Publius: strength in numbers, success with unity. They envisioned a United States that could, with her richness, vastness, intellect, unsurpassed spirit of enterprise, and republican virtue, compete with Europe and do so with dignity and in a way that would "vindicate the honor of the human race."

Other points that I found to be of interest were regarding a strong and unified navy: "The rights of neutrality will only be respected, when they are defended by adequate power. A nation, despicable by its weakness, forfeits even the privilege of being neutral."

This statement is relevant today and applicable to our current situation regarding the 9/11 terrorist attacks and subsequent War on Terrorism. It is, also, represented by human nature. Bullies only attack the weak. Other nations watch our administration and our country's stance on defense. If they sense any leniency, or lack of response to attacks on American soil, which is "despicable by its weakness," then we, as Americans, forfeit our privilege of being neutral. Peace is no longer an option for us if we do not exhibit and execute strength—politically (a Congress that thinks in terms of what is best for America and not factiously), militarily (readiness and response), and financially (solvency). Strength, also, lies in our resources—our own oil and advances in new fuels.

It is best illustrated by Alexander Hamilton's own words regarding unity and strength: "The unequalled spirit of enterprise, which signalizes the genius of the American merchants and navigators, and which is in itself an inexhaustible mine of national wealth, would be stifled and lost; and poverty and disgrace would overspread a country, which, with wisdom, might make herself the admiration and envy of the world."

As a final note of relevancy, note the many mentions of the phrase "spirit of enterprise" in *The Federalist*. Hamilton, in Federalist 11, refers to the "unequalled spirit of enterprise." America was built on this spirit—a can-do, true-grit American determination. The greatness of America will cease with the continuance of a nanny state. America was not built with her hand out. America was built with her hands at work.

Janine Turner
May 12, 2010
Federalist 11
Constituting America

No Nobility

Our Constitutional Founding Fathers had a truly amazing, brilliant ingenuity. It is obvious from the Constitution that they did not want any resemblance of class warfare or "nobility" in the new America. The greatest fear post-Revolutionary War was that the independence of the American mind and soul won by blood, sweat, and tears would be forfeited to yet another monarchy. The right to own property, patents, and pursue one's private journey toward happiness was the promise of America. The gateway to entrepreneurship, the rewards of hard work, and the path to prosperity were no longer limited to the aristocracy, and our Founding Fathers wanted to keep it that way.

James Madison states in Federalist 14, "The kindred blood that flows in the veins of American citizens, the mingled blood which they have shed in defense of their sacred rights, consecrate their union, and excite horror at the idea of their becoming aliens, rivals, enemies."

The art of a republic is finding perfect balance for a democratic state. James Madison makes a striking point regarding the complaint that there was no precedent for a republic. Nor was there a precedent for the Declaration of Independence, our courageous and biting document that sparked and validated our courageous and biting Revolutionary War.

Maintaining a republic is not possible without a virtuous and educated public. Alarmingly, a Rasmussen poll in 2009 stated that *13 percent* of people *over forty years* of age believed that socialism was better than capitalism. That's bad, but even worse is that in the group of people *under forty years of age, 33 percent* believed socialism was better than capitalism. With each generation, fewer and fewer citizens understand what a republican form of government is and why it is necessary, not to mention the relevancy of our declared inherent rights and why and how the Constitution upholds them.

America's younger generations accept the principles of socialism because this is primarily what they are being taught, not only within many schools, but most especially within today's culture. In order for a nation's youth to be able to reason, they must be privy to a broad range of perspectives. Enlightenment cannot prevail in the dark.

Janine Turner
May 17, 2010
Federalist 14
Constituting America

Duty Would Bind to the Constitution

"Duty would bind the representatives to the Constitution and public opinion." This singular line from Federalist 23 encapsulates wisdom and inspires reflection.

The first reflection is upon the word "duty." Duty seems to be a word that is lost in our American culture today. As the decades descend from World War II, the sense of duty to one's country appears to be diminishing. I looked up the word "duty" and found the following definition: "a social force that binds you to a course of action demanded by that force." The definition was followed by a quote by John D. Rockefeller, Jr.: "every right implies a responsibility; every opportunity an obligation, every position, a duty."

Today the focus of America's representatives as well as many Americans and the American culture seems to be one of self-interest. Yet, within the blessing of the Providential rights that are secured for us in our Constitution lies a responsibility. One of those responsibilities is to know, respect, and understand the United States Constitution, as well as to encourage others to do so. The same should apply to the American culture. How far we have drifted from the days when patriotism and love of country were, as President Ronald Reagan said, "in the air." Is our country perfect? No. But as the former Senator Daniel Patrick Moynihan said, "show me a better one."

We, as patriots who love our country and appreciate the founding principles upon which she was founded, need to rise to counter the palpable negativity that permeates our air today. One has to question whether our Congressional representatives are bound to their duty to their country and their constituents, or to themselves.

The second reflection is upon the statement that duty would bind representatives to the Constitution. "Bind the representatives to the Constitution." We have strayed from the Constitution in cultural thought, personal awareness, legislative acts, and Supreme Court rulings. This slow usurpation is due to a lack of knowledge and by a lack of pressure applied on our representatives to uphold the Constitution's principles. As a republic we rule through our representatives, thus, our vote is our voice. The checks and balances of our government begin with us. Thus, I suppose, there is a responsibility that we, as patriots, must own—if our representatives have grown callous and irreverent regarding the Constitution, it is because we have allowed it by our lack of diligence and duty to hold them accountable. How well do they know the United States Constitution? How do they intend to abide by its stipulations? These should be the questions of paramount importance.

The third reflection is upon the two words "public opinion." "Duty would bind the representatives to the Constitution and public opinion." Public opinion seems to be virtually ignored by our representatives today. As mentioned in previous papers, Publius had a respect for the "genius of the people." The American people have a genetic predisposition and inherent ability to seek the truth and know the truth, and American patriots have risen to the challenge of duty. This has proven to be a tried-and-true trait of Americans.

All of the attempts by the current branches of government to reason around the Constitution and govern a republic without respecting the Constitution and the history of the American spirit will do so in vain. Duty to preserve our great country, founding principles, Bill of Rights, and free enterprise will be the Paul Revere call to action of our day.

Janine Turner
May 29, 2010
Federalist 23
Constituting America

Danger When Entertained the Least Suspicion

During this Memorial Day season, I think it is appropriate to truly contemplate and think about the soldiers and families who have sacrificed their lives and loved ones, and given their time and dedication to our country.

Sometimes it is beyond reach to put ourselves in someone else's shoes and feel, to the most heightened sense, what it would be like to say good-bye to our loved ones for perhaps the last time. Do we take the time to feel empathy for the soldier who has to walk away from his or her family—mother, father, wife, husband, daughter, son—to be potentially killed out in the field, to die away from family, in perhaps some distant land, in enemy territory, on foreign soil? How frightening this would be.

It is difficult in our daily lives that are hectic with work, pressures, commitments, and family responsibilities to really pause to think about the sacrifice our men and women in uniform have made and are making to protect us. Our men and women in uniform were and are the brave, the special, the few, and the truly great patriots. Without these soldiers, America and Americans, would not be here—plain and simple. The air we breathe, the land we walk, the sky we sketch, the country we call home, is benefited by the sacrifices of our men and women in uniform.

No matter which war they called their own, they all fought the enemy, whether near or far, whether boots were on the ground, in the air, or on the sea, whether the enemy was present or premeditating. As Alexander Hamilton expressed in Federalist 24, "cases are likely to occur under our governments, as well as under those of outer nations, which sometimes render a military force in the time of peace, essential to the security of the society." Thus, an actual battle or a state of ready alert has served the same purpose—the enemy was to know and knew that he would not prevail against men and women who had the divine right of liberty in their soul, passion in their hearts, and the supreme strength of military readiness.

Memorial Day is the day to set aside time and sit down with our children and teach them about our wars and war heroes. It is a time to teach them about the Revolutionary War and the reasons we fought it. They should know about the soldiers who walked barefoot in the snow, leaving the stain of their blood on the ice. They should know about the soldiers who died miserable deaths as POWs in the stifling bowels of the British ships at sea. They should know about heroes such as Paul Revere, Israel Putnam, and Nathan Hale, who said, "I only regret that I have but one life to lose for my country."

We should take a moment during this Memorial Day season, and every day, to pray for our men and women in uniform. We should teach our children about those who served in the War of 1812, when the British returned, how they burned the White House, and how President James Madison's wife, Dolley Madison, ran to save the portrait of President George Washington.

They should know about the Civil War, why we fought it and how thousands of our soldiers died from a new type of bullet that shattered their bones. They should know about the horrors of slavery, how it had permeated the world throughout history and yet how, according to William J. Bennett, "the westerners led the world to end the practice." They should know how Americans fought Americans, claiming hundreds of thousands of soldiers' lives.

They should know about World War I and how soldiers lined up in rows, one after the other, to be shot or stabbed by swords. They should know about World War II and the almost inconceivable bravery of the soldiers who ran onto the beaches to endure the Battle of Normandy, which claimed thousands of American lives. They should understand what history has to teach us about the mistakes in politics that bred the tyrants who led millions to slaughter. As Publius teaches us, we should rule not only with reason but upon the strong foundation of the lessons of history.

They should know about the Korean War, the Vietnam War, and the communist regimes that ripped the souls from their people. They should know that our soldiers did not die in vain in Korea or Vietnam, because even though the enemy was physically in their field, the enemy's propaganda permeated and thus threatened our field.

They should know about the soldiers, like my father, who stood on alert during the Cold War, and their willingness to die for their country. My father is a graduate of United States Military Academy at West Point who served in the Air Force. He was one of the first people to fly twice the speed of sound, Mach 2, in the 1960s. He flew the B-58 Hustler and was ready to die on his mission to Russia when his country called him to do so. The Cold War was won by the ready willingness of our brave soldiers in uniform and a country that was militarily prepared.

A prepared state is a winning state. Alexander Hamilton wrote in Federalist 24, "Can any man think it would be wise, to leave such posts in a situation to be at any instant seized by one or the other of two neighboring and formidable powers? To act this part, would be to desert all the usual maxims of prudence and policy."

Today, we fight in Iraq and Afghanistan. We fight the insurgencies at our borders, most especially in Arizona, Texas, and California, and we fight an elusive enemy that is creeping into our fields. They are creeping both from abroad with violence and from within with the slow usurpation of our founding principles. Alexander Hamilton warns in Federalist 25, "For it is a truth which the experience of all ages has attested, that the people are commonly most in danger, when the means of injuring the rights are in the possession of those of whom they entertained the least suspicion."

Wars are fought physically and wars are fought mentally. As civil servants, we must be alert to the enemy that is among us. Alexander Hamilton states in Federalist 25, "Every breach of the fundamental laws, though dedicated by necessity, impairs that sacred reverence, which ought to be maintained in the breast of rulers towards the constitution of a country."

During this Memorial Day season, we begin our mission with an education of the thesis and basis of our country—what we fight for—the United States Constitution and the wisdom, freedoms, righteousness, and structure that it upholds.

Janine Turner
June 1, 2010
Federalists 24, 25
Constituting America

The Usurpers

In Federalist 28, Alexander Hamilton wrote:

> *If the representatives of the people betray their constituents, there is then no resource left but in the exertion of that original right of self-defense, which is paramount to all positive forms of government; and which, against the usurpation of the national rulers, may be exerted with an infinitely better prospect of success, than against those of the rulers of an individual state.*

I find this to be relevant to today in the respect that so many representatives in our United States Congress are betraying their constituents, and they are doing so with an arrogance and condescension that is disturbing. I refer once again to the often-repeated phrase of Publius, "the genius of the people." Our current Congress is paying little heed to this phrase and they are underestimating the patriots of America.

Publius is reaffirming the collective strength of the people and their right to take action. This is a comforting reinforcement for the passions of the many Americans who are now finding their voice and utilizing it. As predicted by Alexander Hamilton, the unity of the states, the brothers and sisters of America, is reaping resounding results.

"The usurpers, clothed with the forms of legal authority, can too often crush the opposition in embryo," is another source of wisdom from Alexander Hamilton. Too often lawyers seem to be usurping our democratic process and the United States Constitution. Teams of lawyers are constantly poised and ready to redefine legislation by squelching it before it has begun with intimidation or spinning it with coercive measures. Double-speak prevails.

However, in order to be a true guardian of the gate, we must carry forth our journey to be a people who protest with a basis of formidable knowledge of our principles. Knowledge is power. Alexander Hamilton states in this paper, "The obstacles to usurpation, and the facilities of resistance, increase with the increased extent of the state: provided the citizens understand their rights and are disposed to defend them."

The countermeasures of our current culture are imperative. The Constitution needs to be the theme that is prevalent and prevails, as does the readiness and willingness of Americans to stand up, take a stance, and go the extra mile.

When we are too tired, or too busy, or too distracted by the mundane, this is the time to rally our wills and our wits to carry on and carry forth the torch of our forefathers and foremothers who sacrificed so much and stopped at nothing to underscore and manifest what was right, what was worthy, and what was the true intent of our God.

Janine Turner
June 4, 2010
Federalist 28
Constituting America

Where in the Name of Common Sense

In Federalist 29, Hamilton states, "Where in the name of common-sense, are our fears to end if we may not trust our sons, our brothers, our neighbors, our fellow-citizens? What shadow of danger can there be from men who are daily mingling with the rest of their countrymen and who participate with them in the same feelings, sentiments, habits and interests?"

Our founding brethren were always anxious about standing armies. Thus, they were troubled by the proposal of a nationally unified militia instead of individual militias spread amongst the thirteen colonies. Hamilton argued that there was nothing to fear, as the new unified army was not that of foreigners but of our trusted sons, brothers, neighbors, and fellow citizens.

Our unity through diversity is what makes us unique. Our Constitutional forefathers gave us a brilliant structure and roadmap to keep us that way, to keep us unencumbered by the weight of heavy-handed government and protected from the threat of tyranny. Our freedoms have breathed life into our bond as a brethren working together. Our limited government has given us the ability to dream. Our sense of adventure has flourished and made America great because Americans have not been censored or oppressed. Rooted in this spirit are a moral compass and a virtue that have guided our way. If we lose these, we lose everything.

Alexis de Tocqueville summed it up best:

> *I sought for the greatness and genius of America in her commodious harbors and her ample rivers, and it was not there; in her fertile fields and boundless prairies; and it was not there; in her rich mines and her vast commerce, and it was not there. Not until I visited the churches of America and heard her pulpits aflame with righteousness did I understand the secret of her genius and power. America is great*

because she is good, and if America ever ceases to be good, America
will cease to be great.

Janine Turner
June 7, 2010
Federalist 29
Constituting America

The Necessities of a Nation, at Least Equal to its Resources

Alexander Hamilton in Federalist 30 states, "I believe it may be regarded as a position, warranted by the history of mankind, that in the usual progress of things, the necessities of a nation, in every stage of its existence, will be found at least equal to its resources."

For those who consider the Constitution outdated, or The Federalist outdated, one need look no further that these words. The relevancy of Hamilton's words for America, and Americans, is obvious. In this respect it is our tremendous debt. We have built a huge conglomerate of necessities that are certainly not equal to our resources. This statement serves as a warning to us. We have accumulated so much debt that our liberty cannot be sustained.

Another quote from Alexander Hamilton echoes our current dilemma: "But who would lend to a government, that prefaced its overtures for borrowing by an act that demonstrated that no reliance could be placed on the steadiness of its measures for paying?"

What happens when we are so indebted that we cannot repay our lenders, like China? What happens when we cannot pay our bills or even borrow money because we have "demonstrated that no reliance could be placed on the steadiness of its measures for paying"?

It is easy to spend other people's money. This is what many of our congressmen are doing. They are spending our money, our taxpayer money, with absolutely no regard as to how it will be repaid, even long after they are out of office. Our massive expenditures and social programs have no financial foundation and must be restructured. Do we as a nation have the collective wherewithal and courage to do this?

May Alexander Hamilton's dream not vanish, the "hope to see the halcyon scenes of the poetic or fabulous age realized in America..."

Janine Turner
June 8, 2010
Federalist 30
Constituting America

State Governments—Barrier Against Oppressive Power

Howdy from Boston, well, really Quincy and Cambridge! Juliette and I had an amazing day. It was a day devoted to one of our most influential Founding Fathers, John Adams.

We started our day with a trip to Quincy, sections of which used to be named Braintree. We visited John Adams's very modest childhood home and then a few cobblestones away, the small, simple home where John lived with his brilliant wife Abigail.

I was mesmerized when I saw the tiny desk where Abigail wrote all of her letters to John throughout the Revolutionary War. My sense of awe was rekindled when the park ranger who was our guide recounted the story of how Abigail, realizing her son's promise, and realizing the needs of her future country, sent her ten-year-old son abroad with John. She knew the experience would give him a wealth of knowledge, a knowledge that America would need in her future leaders. John and John Quincy traveled across the Atlantic in February. Their ship hit hurricane-force winds and was struck by lightning and four crewmen died.

Abigail was and is an example of a wife and mother who knew no bounds of fortitude and selflessness. This is why I wrote about her in my book, *Holding Her Head High*. A statue of Abigail Adams with her son John Quincy, who would become our sixth president, was in the town square. Inscribed on the statue are her words, "Improve your understanding for acquiring useful knowledge and virtue such as will render you an ornament to society, an honor to your country, and a blessing to your parents." She is an inspiration for me as a patriot and a mother.

In John and Abigail's first home is an even smaller desk than Abigail's. It was on this desk that John wrote the Massachusetts Constitution. Included in this draft of the Constitution for the commonwealth of Massachusetts were three branches of government, a bicameral legislature, a supreme court of the land, as well as a list of rights. The fact that the states had their own constitutions before the United States Constitution was written and ratified holds a revelatory poignancy to the modern-day debate over states' rights.

In Federalist 32, Alexander Hamilton argues a point regarding the levies of money and the states' power "[…]because I am persuaded that the sense of the people, the extreme hazard of provoking the resentments of the state governments, and a conviction of the utility and necessity of local administrations, for local purposes, would be a complete barrier against the oppressive use of such a power."

This statement illuminates, once again, the original intent of the federal government, which was to *respect the states' rights* and to be a federal power held to accountability through the checks and balances of both the people and the states.

After Juliette and I visited the original homestead of John and Abigail Adams, we visited Peacefield. Peacefield was the home of John and Abigail Adams after the war. In this home are the original furnishings: dishes, chairs, paintings, and thousands of John Quincy's original books on exhibit in America's first library—the John Quincy Adams Library. A poignant point that resonated through the experience of visiting their homesteads was sacrifice—a sense of duty to their country. John and Abigail were willing to put themselves in great peril.

It is worthy to note that John Adams was chosen to be the first American ambassador to England. John Adams walked in to greet the king—the king who wanted to hang him—and announced that he was there to represent his new country, the United States of America. I am also in awe of the fact that it was John Adams who so valiantly fought for the Declaration of Independence and suggested that Thomas Jefferson write it. It was John Adams who nominated George Washington to be general of the Continental Army. It was John Adams who, of his own accord and literally on his own, traveled to Amsterdam and negotiated a three-million-dollar loan for our Continental Army, whose soldiers had no shoes and were suffering tremendously. It was John Adams who, with four others, negotiated the magnificent Treaty of Paris that ended the Revolutionary War. It was John Adams who predicted that the French Revolution would be a bloodbath, ending in tyrannical government.

John Adams is truly an American hero. May we teach our children about his great genius, sacrifice, and dedication to our country. May he be an example of what it is to be a selfless American patriot. When Juliette and I visited the room that held the tombs of John and Abigail Adams and John Quincy and Louisa Catherine Adams, I was overcome with emotion. In this room, as tears flowed down my cheeks, the director of the Church of the Presidents, Arthur W. Ducharme, told me how important Constituting America was to the future of our country. It was a moment I will never forget.

May we all be as committed as John and Abigail Adams to our education, our children, our country, our fellow citizens, and to liberty from tyranny, no matter what the form—a tyrant, big government, usurpation of states' rights, or poverty of mind, body, and soul.

Janine Turner
June 10, 2010
Federalist 32
Constituting America

Power Derived from the People

In Federalist 37 James Madison states, "The genius of republican liberty, seems to demand on one side, not only that all power should be derived from the people; but that those intrusted with it should be kept in dependence on the people, by a short duration of their appointments; and that, even during this short period, the trust be placed not in a few, but in a number of hands."

If you are looking for a tool to use in a conversation with those who believe that the Constitution and *The Federalist* are outdated, add this one to your toolbox. The Constitution and Federalist 37 state that the power in government begins and ends with the people, and that once in office our representatives entrusted with this power should depend *on the people.*

It also states that the durations of their appointments should be short. This is currently a popular debate. Many believe that there should be an amendment to the Constitution limiting the number of terms Congressmen and Senators can serve. The irony is that they are already limited—Congressmen to two-year terms and Senators to six-year terms. If they are lingering in office then it is the voters' fault.

There is, however, a more menacing problem. The elected official is to "depend on the people," the "genius of the people." How can this be done when the people are kept in the dark about the events taking place in Congress? Secret meetings take place, documents are withheld, outsiders negotiate, lawyers manipulate, and bills cannot be understood due to their voluminosity and incoherency. Herein lies the conundrum: how can we be a people worthy of independence if we are ignorant? It appears there is a mission to take the power out of the people's hands by rendering them mute by omission and moot by obscurity.

This cycle has been spinning for years. Power has been shifting from the *people* to the *government*, both literally and in thought. Our Republic has been rebuilt and restructured over the past one hundred years, bit by bit. Elusively, those who believe the Constitution is outdated and its principles inconvenient have reneged on the very basis of republicanism—a dependence on the people—by intimating their genius.

Consequently, an out-of-control government, powerful in its bloated, misshapen mayhem, has rendered "we the people" apathetic. Apathy leads to tyranny, and tyranny takes many forms.

This is why Madison warned that "the trust should be placed not in a few, but in a number of hands."

Our government is structured to be checked and balanced by three branches, thus keeping the power out of any one branch's *hands*. The power was to be representative, with a dependence on the people's *hands*. Now the power has pooled in the few hands of the government, most especially the executive branch. Usurpation has prevailed, promulgated by both parties.

Left to their own devices, or *hands*, the government has morphed into factions that are factious beyond any good reason and necessity. Unchaperoned by the genius of the people, these factions have reached fever pitch, like teenagers partying while their parents are out of town. Madison states it best and lends advice to the crisis we face:

> *We are necessarily led to two important conclusions. The first is, that the convention must have enjoyed in a very singular degree, an exemption from the pestilential influence of party animosities; the disease most incident to deliberative bodies, and most apt to contaminate their proceedings. The second conclusion is that all the deputations composing the convention, were either satisfactorily accommodated by the final act; or were induced to accede to it, by a deep conviction of the necessity of sacrificing private opinions and partial interests to the public good and by a despair of seeing this necessity diminished by delays or new experiments.*

Only God can save us now. Madison realized the importance of Divine intervention: "It is impossible for the man of pious reflection, not to perceive in it a finger of that Almighty hand which has been so frequently and signally extended to our relief in the critical stages of the revolution."

Janine Turner
June 17, 2010
Federalist 37
Constituting America

Exclusive Right to Their Writings and Discoveries

Article I, Section 8, Clause 8 of the Constitution states, "Promote the progress of science and useful arts, by securing for a limited time, to authors and inventors, the exclusive right to their writings and discoveries."

These words, freedoms, and rights were the engine to the ingenuity and entrepreneurial genius in our country. Great minds were no longer restricted by the limits of ownership. The great ideas and industry of men were no longer chained by the denial to own the fruits of their creations.

Thanks to our United States Constitution, men could now dream, fly, and hope without being tethered. They could own, for a limited time, the exclusive right to their writings and discoveries. Free enterprise. The acknowledgment of hard work, tenacity, and brilliance with the rewards that naturally align to such achievements are what led the likes of Thomas Edison to try again and again, at least a thousand times, until he successfully created the light bulb.

This is human nature, a psychology of the mind and soul, which our forefathers truly seemed to understand. Men will soar on eagle's wings when they are free to pursue life, liberty, and happiness, and when they are able to reap the rewards of hard work.

This is one of the greatest arguments against socialism and communism, an argument that has been proven by the disastrous accounts of history. To stifle the hope, the industry, by withholding the rewards, is to kill the drive, the spirit.

To see the success of such freedoms and ownership of accomplishments, one has to only look around and see the vast array of astonishing accomplishments in our country. Human nature thrives on incentives. Human nature flies on Providential inspiration.

Yet, men are not angels. Hence the checks and balances that were intrinsically woven into our Constitution and founding principles. The modern-day, knee-jerk reaction is to concur with the prevalent belief that the checks and balances were solely to govern the rise of greed and quest for power. This is one reason.

Another reason, it seems, was to govern the quest to dominate. Domination dresses in many guises. One such modern way is to suggest that the desire to succeed and flourish is unfair. Because citizens quickly and conveniently forget the horrors of history, the permeation of this message into the cultural thought has succeeded.

It is hard to get many balloons, filled with air, into confinement. It is easy to get many balloons under control when the balloons are deflated. A flat spirit cannot rise. Why else would communism deny God, squelch creativity, deny individual patents, and punish free enterprise? The trend of today is to teach our children that to succeed is bad. The trend of today forgets to teach our children their rights. Why else would the United States Constitution be touted as irrelevant and locked into trunks in dusty attics? Better yet, how many schools have copies of the United States Constitution in their classrooms or libraries? How many households have a copy in their homes?

"From each according to his ability, to each according to his need." Polls reflect that most Americans today believe these words are in our Bill of Rights. They are in fact the words of Karl Marx. Is it any surprise this is becoming the mantra of America?

It is because Americans do not know. It is because America's children and college students are not required to read and study the United States Constitution. Our saving grace will be the rise of our educated voices and the prevalence of our vote. Our saving grace begins with educating our nation's children. It starts with knowledge. It starts in the hearts of Americans. It starts in the home.

In the words of Emily Dickinson,

We never know how high we are
Till we are called to rise;
And then, if we are true to plan,
Our statures touch the skies.

Janine Turner
June 25, 2010
Federalist 43
Constituting America

Powers Are Few and Defined

In Federalist 45, James Madison writes:

> *The powers delegated by the proposed constitution to the federal government, are few and defined. Those which are to remain in the state government, are numerous and indefinite. The former will be exercised principally on external objects, as war, peace, negotiation, and foreign commerce; with which last the power of taxation will, for the most part, be connected. The powers reserved to the several states will extend to all the objects, which, in the ordinary course of affairs, concern the lives, liberties, and properties of the people; and the internal order, improvement, and prosperity of the state. The operations of the federal government will be most extensive and important in the times of war and danger; those of the state government in times of peace and security.*

Federalist 45 provides a mountain of evidence concerning the true intentions designated for the federal government.

Federal Government	State Governments
Powers are few and defined.	Powers are numerous and indefinite.
Powers are exercised principally on external objects, as war, peace, negotiation, and foreign commerce; power of taxation connected primarily only to these powers	Powers extend to lives, liberties, and properties of the people and the internal order, improvement, and prosperity of the state.
Operations most extensive in times of war and danger	Operations most extensive in times of peace and security

The federal powers of today are most certainly not few and defined. They overshadow and overwhelm state governments with many unfunded mandates and manipulations. Federal powers have spread beyond war, danger, and foreign commerce. Federal powers have muscled their way into every aspect of Americans' lives.

The true intention of regulation regarding commerce was for *foreign* relations only. The modern-day usage of the word "commerce" has been twisted into many renderings that invade state rights and reroute the true intention of the federal government's original purpose, which was to manage and negotiate *foreign* commerce.

The states' powers were to extend to the areas of life, liberties, properties, internal order, improvement, and prosperity.

Today's federal government has taken the sovereignties of the states and the individual rights of the citizens into its domain. The usurpation of states' powers is tangible. The net was cast and the states hooked with the bait of benefits. The tide of control rose and never abated. American citizens let it happen as they were sunbathing, napping on the beach.

The American people have now awakened and have discovered that they have been burned by the noonday sun and their liberties are drowning in the tide of big government. The balm for the burn lies in the checks and balances and true intentions of the United States Constitution. We have independence bred into our blood. We have true grit written in the genetic code. We have the generational work ethic embedded in our family tree. We have the wisdom of our Providential faith that yields the prevailing power of our survival.

"The powers delegated by the proposed constitution to the federal government, are few and defined. Those which are to remain in the state government,
are numerous and indefinite." In order to prevent the tyranny of big government,
we must regain our intended balance. The road may be rocky and the path may be
steep, but obstacles have never stymied the American spirit.

Janine Turner
June 29, 2010
Federalist 45
Constituting America

State Superiority in the National Senate

Alexander Hamilton writes in Federalist 26:

> *The state legislators, who will always be not only vigilant, but suspi-
> cious guardians of the rights of the citizens against encroachments
> from the federal government, will constantly have their attention
> awake to the conduct of the national rulers, and will be ready enough
> if anything improper appears, to sound the alarm to the people and
> not only be the voice, but if necessary be the arm of their discontent.*

In Article 1, Section 3, Clause 1 the Constitution spells out who is to choose
the senators in the U.S. Senate. It stipulates that the state legislatures elect two U.S.
Senators from their states to represent them in the federal government.

Article 1, Section 3, Clause 1 states, "The Senate of the United States shall be
composed of two Senators from each state, *chosen by the legislature thereof, for six
years; and each Senator shall have one vote."*

State-elected U.S. Senators were a vital part of balancing power in the bicameral Congress—the Senate was to represent the states and the House to represent
the people. This very important component of checks and balances was turned on
its head with the Seventeenth Amendment.

Alexander Hamilton states in Federalist No. 31: "I repeat here what I have
observed in substance in another place, that all observations, founded upon the
danger of usurpation, ought to be referred to the composition and structure of the
government, not to the nature and extent of its powers. The state governments, by
their original constitution, are invested with complete sovereignty."

Consequently, there is now a serious flaw in the balance of power. Why would the American people allow such a thing to happen? Interestingly, the only state that did not ratify the Seventeenth Amendment was Utah.

Alexander Hamilton states in Federalist Paper No. 60:

> *The collective sense of the state legislatures, can never be influenced by extraneous circumstances of that sort: a consideration which alone ought to satisfy us, that the discrimination apprehended would never be attempted. For what inducement could the senate have to concur in preference in which itself would not be included? [...] As long as this interest prevails in most of the state legislatures, so long it must maintain a correspondent superiority in the national senate, which will generally be a faithful copy of the majorities of those assemblies.*

The states lost their power with the Seventeenth Amendment, which eliminated the state legislatures' ability to select senators and gave it to the people, which mirrored the House. The people lost the balance of power necessary to maintain a republic as our Founding Fathers intended and the ability to limit government and maintain the Constitution's enumerated powers.

I wonder if the Affordable Care Act would have ever passed if the Senate had been left in its original intent. I also wonder if the federal government would ever have had the opportunity to become so vast and powerful if senators had continued to be appointed by state legislatures. Who has been looking after the states' interest since the passing of the Seventeenth Amendment?

With Hamilton's Federalist 60 is the call to action: "Would they not fear that citizens not less tenacious than conscious of their rights, would flock from the remotest extremes of their respective states to the places of election, to overthrow their tyrants, and to substitute men who would be disposed to avenge the violated majesty of the people?"

The "majesty of the people." Our Founding Fathers thought highly of us. Are we living up to the "majesty of the people?" We suffer from an inferiority complex because government is now on autopilot. We no longer feel that our opinions will make a difference or that our voice will be heard.

We are needed, but we are not heeding the call of service. We are certainly not flocking "from the remotest extremes of their respective states to the places of election, to overthrow their tyrants." Perhaps it is because we do not think there is a tyrant to overthrow. Yet, tyranny manifests in many forms. Tyranny does not simply manifest in the form of a tyrant. Tyranny can manifest in the form of big government. Tyranny can manifest in overt or covert innuendos that we are not capable of governing ourselves, which are compounded by the fact that they deliberately pass bills and laws that are beyond the scope of understanding. Tyranny manifests in thwarting attempts to get involved in the political process by the use of belittlement and criticism that can have ruinous results. Tyranny manifests in the obscurity created by mammoth structures of government, resulting in a fortress that belies our entry. Tyranny manifests in gross, unchecked usurpations of Constitutional limitations.

We should be running to the polls to overthrow this tyranny. George Washington profoundly recognized that in a democratic republic, things have to be felt before they can be seen. Will it be too late when we the people finally see the tyranny that has encompassed our liberties, ready to smother them in subtle increments?

Janine Turner
July 20, 2010
Federalist 60
Constituting America

Hamilton's Nine Points on Constraining Presidential Powers

In Federalists 68 and 69 it becomes evident how earnestly and tenaciously our Constitutional Founding Fathers strove to protect our liberties and our republic, basing their decisions not on rhetoric but on the wisdom wrought by history. In no circumstance was this more evident than to the election of the President of the United States.

In Federalist 68, Alexander Hamilton states this with precision and clarity: "Nothing was more to be desired, than that every practicable obstacle should be opposed to cabal, intrigue and corruption. These most deadly adversaries of Republican government, might naturally have been expected to make their approaches from more than one quarter, but chiefly from the desire in foreign powers to gain an improper ascendant in our councils."

Could this be more relevant throughout our history and even today? We, and our republic, have been under continuous attack from varied countries for the past two centuries, and we are under attack today. The "deadly adversaries of Republican government" are in the field, whether it be a literal attack from a foreign enemy or an attack from a domestic enemy using weapons such as political correctness to influence and reshape America into another form of government.

America represents hope, and hope is the envy of the enemy. The most obvious place for the enemy to attack or influence is in our voting process. Our Founding Fathers wanted to protect our voting process from the intrigue and corruption of enemies foreign and domestic. Thus, they established the electoral process.

Though there are popular discussions about relinquishing the wisdom of the electoral process, it would be dangerous. The Electoral College is important because it balances the power between the states. If we abolished the electoral process, then the more populated states, such as California, Texas, and New York, would control the policies and direction of the country.

The electoral winner-takes-all policy that exists presently in all of the states except Maine and Nebraska undermines the electoral process. It may represent the political inclination of the states incorrectly and eliminate electoral votes from certain regions that could, when added all together, actually determine an election. One has to question if the winner-takes-all process is a violation of the United States Constitution, and whether it circumvents the amendment process.

Federalist 69 is a smart, insightful comparison of our United States Constitution with the British rule of the king. Revealing are the nine points Alexander Hamilton makes by this exercise:

1. Terms limited

2. Impeachment possible

3. Checks by the legislative body

4. Power to command the military but not declare war or raise arms

5. Treaties made with concurrent power of the legislature

6. Appointment of officers with approval of the legislature

7. No power to convey privileges

8. Can prescribe no rules concerning commerce or coins

9. No particle of spiritual jurisdiction.

Hamilton goes on to elaborate on an important Constitutional process that is being abused today—the process of the president's power to nominate and appoint, which must be approved by the Senate.

Article 2, Section 2, Clause 2 of the Constitution states, "The President is to nominate, and, *with the advice and consent of the senate*, to appoint ambassadors and other public ministers, judges of the Supreme Court, and in general all officers of the United States established by law, and whose appointments are not otherwise provided for by the Constitution."

Serious violations and deviations from this process have occurred over the years. Unchecked, our modern-day federal government has been bloated with unapproved bureaucrats and czars. This does not fare well under Constitutional scrutiny.

Such are the bleeds that rupture the heart of a republic and threaten a seizure of the people.

Janine Turner
August 2, 2010
Federalists 68, 69
Constituting America

Discovering the Misconduct of the Persons Thy Trust

Big government. These two words are bandied about quite frequently. They are thoroughly examined in *The Federalist*. Our Founding Fathers believed in a small federal government encumbered by checks and balances. Alexander Hamilton makes the case by quoting examples of how deceitful enterprises rise from an executive branch that is not singular. When accountability rests on the few instead of the singular, evasion becomes the norm. In Federalist 70, Hamilton denotes:

> But one of the weightiest objections to a plurality in the Executive, and which lies as much against the last as the first plan, is, that it tends to conceal faults and destroy responsibility[...]It often becomes impossible, amidst mutual accusations, to determine on whom the blame, or the punishment of a pernicious measure, or series of pernicious measures, ought really to fall. It is shifted from one to another with so much dexterity, and under such plausible appearances, that the public opinion is left in suspense about the real author.

This is one of the reasons why Americans throw up their hands in disgust and walk away from the duties beholden to a citizen of a republic. Where does one begin to know the truth of an issue? Where does one begin to know who really is the culprit?

Though our executive branch is represented by a single person, the bureaucracy surrounding it, the lawyers, and the administration instructing it, has become a huge machine. Transparency has become nonexistent. The executive branch has become a branch governed by the councils, a process Hamilton both denounces and forewarns. This plurality of our modern-day executive branch befuddles the citizens. Though there is no actual plurality of leaders, there is plurality of persons influencing improper behavior. With so many, who takes the blame for misconduct?

Hamilton states, "The people remain altogether at a loss to determine by whose influence their interests have been committed to hands so manifestly improper." It is plurality in the executive branch that most threatens a republic and robs her citizens of "the two greatest securities they can have for the faithful exercise of any delegated power." These two securities of a republic are public opinion and discovery.

> The plurality of the Executive tends to deprive the people of the two greatest securities they can have for the faithful exercise of any delegated power, first, the restraints of public opinion, which lose their efficacy, as well on account of the division of the censure attendant on bad measures among a number, as on account of the uncertainty on whom it ought to fall; and secondly, the opportunity of discovering with facility and clearness the misconduct of the persons they trust, in order either to their removal from office, or to their actual punishment, in cases which admit of it.

We are in the throes of such turmoil today.

The office of President of the United States is a thankless job, and certainly the president is still held accountable today for the state of the union. Yet, because the executive branch is so big and because laws are being made by bureaucrats behind the scenes—and not by the legislative branch—enterprising schemes take place in ways that render American citizens without the adequate resources to respond and take action.

As Hamilton astutely observes: "An artful cabal in that council, would be able to distract and to enervate the whole system of administration."

All of this intrigue begs the question: what are we to do? Where do we begin and how will we make a difference? Hamilton even asks the question: "Who is there that will take the trouble, or incur the odium, of a strict scrutiny into the secret springs of the transaction? Should there be found a citizen zealous enough to undertake the unpromising task."

Our forefathers were most certainly examples of men who were zealous enough to undertake the unpromising task. They were willing to lose their lives, their fortunes, and their sacred honor to combat the intrigues and unscrupulous behavior of the British Empire. They fought to secure liberty and justice for all American citizens.

Who is willing to "incur the odium" in order to preserve our republic today? Upon the "majesty of the people" our republic rests.

Janine Turner
August 3, 2010
Federalist 70
Constituting America

The Crux of the Creed—A Quarter They Cannot Control

The written word is not permeable. The written word requires time and thought and tenacity and truth. The written word does not lie.

Alexander Hamilton's Federalist 73 exhibits our Founding Fathers' brilliant writing and political savvy. What our Founding Fathers truly understood, in an astonishing way, was human nature. They studied the temptations that befell the psyches of men and recognized the vulnerabilities that weaken even the best-intentioned individual.

Hamilton gives a mesmerizing breakdown of a scenario where a president may be wary of doing the right thing in certain circumstances because he fears the perception of it. Having thought of this potentiality, the founders of the Constitution give the president a way to make the right choice and save face.

> *A man who might be afraid to defeat a law by his single veto, might not scruple to return it for reconsideration; subject to being finally rejected only in the vent of more than one third of each house concurring in the sufficiency of his objections. He would be encouraged by the reflection, that if his opposition should prevail, it would embark in it a very respectable proportion of the legislative body, whose influence would be united with his in supporting the propriety of his conduct in the public opinion. A direct and categorical negative has something in the appearance of it more harsh, and more apt to irritate, than the mere suggestion of argumentative objections to be approved or disapproved by those to whom they are addressed. In proportion as it*

would be less apt to offend, it would be more apt to be exercised; and
for this very reason, it may in practice be found more effectual.

Brilliant. Hamilton also sums up the rationale for the Constitution's checks and balances, the cement of its foundation, in one concise, astute, and profound paragraph. "When men, engaged in unjustifiable pursuits, are aware that obstructions may come from a quarter which they cannot control, they will often be restrained by the bare apprehension of opposition, from doing what they would with eagerness rush into, if no such external impediments were to be feared."

This is the crux of the creed.

Man is subjected to the pull of evil vices—power, greed, shortsightedness, impatience, and imprudence. The Constitution is the conscience of America. The Constitution is the governor upon the men who govern.

Janine Turner
August 6, 2010
Federalist 73
Constituting America

Lighting the Lantern—One if by Laziness, Two if by Ignorance

Federalist 85! Alexander Hamilton's words express it best: "Thus have I, fellow-citizens, executed the task I had assigned to myself; with what success, your conduct must determine. I trust you will admit that I have not failed in the assurance I gave you respecting the spirit with which my endeavors should be conducted."

Wisdom beyond words prevails from *The Federalist*, and their warnings beckon our most urgent involvement. A rekindled knowledge of Publius' belief in the genius of the people reminds us of the necessity of our voice, our actions, and our constant seeking of the truth.

In Hamilton's words: "The unwarrantable concealments and misrepresentations which have been in various ways practiced to keep the truth from the public eye, have been of a nature to demand the reprobation of all honest men."

It is our duty to get involved in the preservation of our republic. Times heed not the lazy participant, leaving America to the few. Patriots must curb the silent, slippery slope that always precedes tyranny.

The Federalist, the issues our Founding Fathers faced, and the duties required of the people of the eighteenth century are as pertinent today as they were then. Hamilton states:

> *This is a duty from which nothing can give him a dispensation. This is one that he is called upon, nay, constrained by all the obligations that form the bands of society, to discharge sincerely and honestly. No partial motive, no particular interest, no pride of opinion, no temporary passion or prejudice, will justify to himself, to his country, or to his posterity, an improper election of the part he is to act.*

At this potential crucial turning of our country and with the need to prevent such a turning, we must join in unity as our Revolutionary forefathers and Constitutional forefathers did. A country divided falls. We must always remember that we are all Americans—a people who share the greatest country on earth, founded on Godly principles and a goodness of spirit that birthed a "majesty of the people." Thus, we must be true to our principles, yet never wedge such a divide as to crater our country.

Hamilton brilliantly states the mission for his constituents and for his posterity: "Let him beware of an obstinate adherence to party; let him reflect that the object upon which he is to decide is not a particular interest of the community, but the very existence of the nation."

I love America. I love her goodness, and even her failures. It is through her failures that we have continued to grow and mature into the thoughtful, conscientious, and consistently creative people that we are. It is our United States Constitution that has given us the platform to both preserve and amend our laws of government in a non-partisan way. It is through our tribulations that we have triumphed. It is because of God and subsequently the *genius of the people*, that we have defined our own destiny.

As we walk through these challenging times, let us not forget the onslaught of troubles our ancestors both experienced and tackled. They excelled through storms, famine, persecution, indecision, and war. At these times they called upon a Higher Power, and He led them to a new level of human dignity. We too are capable of these things. We need only our faith in God, our fellow citizens, and our knowledge of the United States Constitution to rise above the mire of mediocrity in which we find ourselves today. With a willingness and a desire to preserve our country, our beautiful land, and our liberty, "for ourselves and our prosperity," we can soar on eagles' wings. We are no less the heroes our forefathers were. We need only to hear the call and heed its needs.

Knowledge is to power what actions are to results. We are the people. We are the roots that feed the branches of government. The tree will not survive without us. May we keep our rights alive. Our Constitution and our Bill of Rights are more relevant today than ever. They protect us from the tyranny that at any time may overtake us and succeed. The enemy is in the field, and they may not use traditional tactics. Sly are their methods of operation.

Let us put the lanterns in the North Church. Let us be the alarm, the Paul Revere, that sounds the warning: one if by laziness; two if by ignorance. We must know our rights, and our children must know their rights. We are borne of true grit and determination. In our genes lies the innate knowing of righteousness. We were founded on such callings, from the Mayflower to Bunker Hill to Independence Hall, from the Civil War to World War II to 9/11. Let us never forget. Let us always be grateful for the men and women who have sacrificed to keep our flame of independence alive, and let us carry that torch today.

To close with Hamilton's words, "The unwarrantable concealments and misrepresentations, which have been in various ways practiced to keep the truth from the public eye, have been of a nature to demand the reprobation of all honest men."

May we be honest men always searching for the truth. May we rise to every occasion to fight for it, and may we do it in a virtuous manner, because without virtue our republic cannot exist, and all is lost.

Janine Turner
August 24, 2010
Federalist 85
Constituting America

Dialogue with Cathy Gillespie,
Co-Chair of Constituting America

I think when kids are creating, that's when they are really learning. I mean kids can be preached to in a classroom and you never really know if you are reaching them. But when they have to dig deep inside themselves and come up with something that they create, that's when they really internalize what they are learning.

[...]

That's what we are after. We want to affect the culture because we know that these days more than ever people get most of their knowledge from TV and the internet and YouTube. So if these kids are our future culture-makers, we want to make sure that they have a deep appreciation for the founding principles of our country and our Constitution.

—Cathy Gillespie

One of the greatest blessings to come out of founding Constituting America besides our mission, which is to shout from the forums of culture that the Constitution is a non-partisan and vital document, is my friendship with Cathy Gillespie. Her heart is huge, her tenacity is tremendous, and her loyalty unswerving. She is a masterpiece. Never before have I experience such an unyielding, devoted, and unconditional friendship. Cathy is the type of friend that everyone wishes they had. She inspires me with her unflinching fortitude and her amazing work ethic. Cathy is a pillar in any environment: as a wife to her husband, Ed, as a mother, as a friend, and as a co-worker. I joke that Cathy is one degree away from anything you need or from anyone you may need to meet and if she is not, she will find a way. Sheer will defines Cathy Gillespie. Though, she has a heart for God, a humility, and an amazing connection with Him. When Cathy prays, miracles happen.

Janine: 'Is anybody there? Does anybody care? Does anybody see what I see?' I still love that song. You need to hear the entire song; it's from *1776*, the musical. This should be on every American's must-watch list. And in that particular song John Adams is singing out after a letter from George Washington, a post that was walked into Congress by a very weary writer, and George Washington said in his letter, "Is anybody there? Does anybody care?" Poor George Washington. But anyway, John Adams, the one who was the thorn in the side of the Second Continental Congress, said we must declare independence. We wouldn't be here without him. We wouldn't have had Thomas Jefferson write the Declaration of Independence without him, and we wouldn't have George Washington as our general without him. And we would not have Constituting America without Cathy Gillespie, and she is my superlative guest. And Cathy Gillespie, welcome to *The Janine Turner Show*.

Cathy: Well, thank you, Janine. But honestly, we wouldn't have Constituting America without you, because you were the one who called me up in 2009 and said "I want to start a foundation," and you had a wonderful vision for it and invited me to be a part of it, and it was the best decision that I have ever made in my life.

Janine: Well that's been quite the journey for both of us, hasn't it, Cathy? And I thought it would be so much fun on our fourth anniversary to have you on the show. This is our fourth anniversary going into our fifth year of the birth of

Constituting America. It just goes to show that America is great, that we can still have it, and we want to keep it this way, visions, dreams, inspirations, and that can be accomplished with vision and hard work, and that's something certainly you and I have both done, and we are a great team. And I think that this visit down memory lane for our fourth anniversary is worthy of note if for no other reason, I hope will be an inspiration to others who have something that's near and dear in their heart, to say, "Okay, this can be accomplished and one step at a time." So Cathy, all right, I remember having this conversation with you, calling you after being so inspired after rereading the Constitution and hearing Federalist 62 from a Hillsdale College seminar Juliette and I watched immediately after reading the Constitution. I wanted to understand really what they meant. And James Madison said, "It will be of little avail to the people, that laws are made by men of their own choice, if the laws be so voluminous that they cannot be read, or so incoherent that they can not be understood." And I remember calling you and I remember I was in the grocery store and I had the phone to my ear and you and I were talking about how we could launch this foundation and what we would have to do. All the things that we did within the first six months were sort of an explosion of creativity, were they not?

Cathy: Oh they were, and everything just fell together in place so much that I really have to believe that God was in the center of our efforts, because just the things that we wanted to do, we just jumped in and somehow they all happened.

Janine: They did. And Cathy Gillespie, I just want to say I met Cathy, when she was working on a campaign and I wanted to be a part of it. So I sort of sent you a care package saying, "I love my country and I want to be a part of the country." You and I met at that point and we were made friends. But this journey, and we have numerous things in common personally, but this journey for the two of us really has cemented our friendship. I don't know too many people who can work together as co-chairs of a foundation and do all that we have done and remain such solid true best friends. I mean, that's been an amazing part of this process, hasn't it?

Cathy: It has been and I think that's what makes it so much fun. I get up every morning excited about what we are going to be doing that day to advance the cause of young people and adults learning about the Constitution and appreciating our country's founding principles. But the fun part of it is I get to deal with you, and we just have a great time, and I think all the kids and the adults who are involved in our organization have a great time with us.

Janine: Well, and on a note before we move on about the foundation, I called Cathy recently and I said, "Okay, Cathy, we have to have time for friendship calls because you and I are such workers, we are always envisioning and doing and progressing and trying to get things done that you and I have forgotten how to just have a friendship call." So I called Cathy and I said, "Cathy, on Mondays and Fridays, we are going to have fifteen-minute friendship calls, and we are just going to have a friendship chat because when you and I get together, it's 'okay now we need to do this, this, this, and this.' But that's what it takes. I think that was the energy of our Founding Fathers, and I think it's the engine that keeps our country great. So let's talk about the journey from Constituting America. I remember being on those calls thinking about the name Constituting America and what about the logo and saying 'what about George Washington crossing the Delaware.'" And I have learned so much through this process as well, more and more about George Washington, the president of the Constitutional Convention and things of this nature. But what I found to be most exhilarating was that first few months where we said, "Okay, let's have a contest. We want all kids to read," and then we realized that they weren't going to read really and so we said, "Okay, let's focus on the culture." I am an actress, so we came up with the "We the People 9.17" contest, which is now the "We the Future" contest. But we launched this contest with kids doing "best song" and "best short film" and "best public service announcements" and "best essay" and "best artwork." People said it couldn't be done. They said, "Oh you can't get that contest off the ground." I said, "Oh yes, we can." So we launched President's Day in February of 2010 and we had that contest going and we embarked on a journey to New York City to be on Fox and promote it. By July 4th we had entries and then we were on a bus, an old broken-down bus—that was another vision of ours, to have a bus going in from town to town, to do this documentary by July. We were on a road trip doing a documentary. And we had a documentary signed, sealed, and delivered by Constitution Day. You and I held the camera and did this documentary ourselves. We held the camera, went into these towns with the broken-down RV, and then Juliette and I edited it. That was quite the journey just with the contest alone, wasn't it?

Cathy: Oh it was; I mean, it really was. And I think one of the reasons we were so successful is because there is a hunger and a thirst out there for knowledge about our Constitution and founding principles. And I think adults, families who saw you on all those Fox shows when you did that first trip to New York in April or May of

2010, are people want to teach their kids about the Constitution because they know that they are not learning it in the schools, but they don't know how. And I think when they saw our program and they saw that we offered programs both for adults so they can learn and then in turn encourage their kids to enter our contest, it was really what people were looking for and it just kind of exploded from there.

Janine: It did. And our 90-day study really helped the parents, and we will get to that in a minute. But the fact that it's nonpartisan, I think this is a message. I remember I was on an airplane heading to the east coast, and I had my Constituting America business cards and I was passing them all out with fervor, just like when we were on this road trip passing out Constitutions at coffee shops and whatnot, and some people, especially on that plane to the east coast, looked at me with disdain, a horror, as if when they touched my card that said "Constitution" they might combust. But it's nonpartisan, it's so incredibly relevant. And if people haven't read it, I don't think that they really understand it. There is this knee-jerk reaction amongst certain elements out there, parties that feel that it's not applicable anymore, and I think that that's been one of the most amazing journeys for me personally on this path of Constituting America, is just how nonpartisan it is. It's for every American and I think that's the mission you and I strive to get out there over and over and over again, isn't it?

Cathy: Yeah. So I think it must be so rewarding for you when you give a speech and you have people who are aligned with the Democratic Party come up to you afterwards and say, "You know, when I came to hear you, I was skeptical and I thought you were going to be partisan, but I really learned a lot and I appreciated what you had to say." And I think that shows that you are getting through to people, didn't that happen to you one time?

Janine: Yeah, it happened at a speech at a senior living facility and the head gal, she said, "Well there is one guy who said 'Oh. I am not going to go listen to her, they're talking about the Constitution, it's just some Tea Party thing and I am not a Tea Partier.'" And I looked at her, I said "But that's not true, it's a nonpartisan document, it's for everybody." I said, "Get him to come." And he did. He walked in with this little cane and his beret and he sat there. Afterwards, he came up to me and said, "You know, I didn't think I wanted to hear anything you had to say but actually, it was all right." I will never forget him. But you know, Cathy, it's fun to see the journey that we are on here with Constituting America and boy, all that goes into the work of a foundation.

Cathy: But yeah, I mean it's so rewarding when these kids come up to us and they say, "You know, I didn't know anything about the Constitution before, but I entered your contest and I have learned so much." And we hear that time and time from kids, both kids who win and kids who just enter and they may not win but they still learn. So I think when kids are creating, that's when they are really learning. I mean kids can be preached to in a classroom and you never really know if you are reaching them. But when they have to dig deep inside themselves and come up with something that they create, that's when they really internalize what they are learning.

Janine: That's true. And we are the only foundation that uses these tools for the media, social media. It's been really fun to have that unique aspect to draw all these kids in. It's also fun, isn't it, Cathy, that we can speak at schools all across the country where we can talk to not just the history department or the English department, but we can talk to the band departments, choir departments, film departments, the theater departments, and the journalism departments, because we have the "best public service announcement," "best short film," and "best song" categories in our contest. Our winners in college receive $2,000 prize money, and, in high school, $1,000. All the other kids get gifts and prizes. They have all received trips to Philadelphia for four years, Cathy, which has been a feat in itself. The winners and a chaperone go to Philadelphia to have dinner, to see the historical sites, and to perform their winning entry at the National Constitution Center. We have put them all in the documentary and some have had nationwide press and we had premiers in their hometowns. The things that we have done have been really wonderful opportunities for these kids. I also wanted to talk a little bit about our 90-in-90. I am going to be reading today from the 90-in-90s that we have done. I absolutely love these. These give our foundation the sort of depth and the scholastic aspect. I want to talk about those 90-in-90-day programs. We started our first one in 2010, too. I mean, it's amazing when you think about it. We launched February 22nd and we got the contest launched, but we also launched our annual study where we would bring scholars in to break down these documents. It was amazing that we had that happen too. You and I wrote ninety essays, five on the Constitution and eighty-five on each of *The Federalist Papers* every day when we launched this.

Cathy: Yeah. And that shows the state of constitutional education in our country, because I was a political science major, and I had never been required to read *The Federalist*. So for the first time, at age 47, or however old I was, I read *The Federalist* with you and wrote an essay on each one every night for ninety days.

Janine: Individually, you wrote yours and I wrote mine, that's right.

Cathy: Yes. Sometimes we didn't start writing until about 1:00 a.m., but we got them done.

Janine: And we posted them as a blog, and we had a lot of people blogging with us. We put each of *The Federalist Papers* up and we had scholars come and interpret, professors around the country, what the federalist paper meant. Then sometimes I did a little YouTube video too. Those were the days when I had my sidekick, my daughter, who wasn't immersed in so much homework as she is today. We did start off like gangbusters. The first one was *The Federalist*, and weren't they fascinating?

Cathy: They were, and then the next year we broke the Constitution into ninety parts, and the next year we broke the amendments into ninety parts, and then this past year, we took the classics that inspired the Constitution right up into the twenty-first century, the challenges that it faces today. It was a study based on the Hillsdale reader. We broke that into ninety parts.

Janine: That's I have to say one of my—go ahead, go ahead.

Cathy: Well, I was going to say all of it is now archived and searchable on our website with the drop-down menu, and people can go to the original founding documents or the essays that explain each one of those.

Janine: Yes, that's another goal we have been working on: If someone puts in Article 1 Section 3 Clause 2 and wants to know what it means, Constituting America is the resource. So, that's yet another goal. This year's ninety-day study is one of my favorites because it breaks down John Locke and Aristotle and Cicero—it's just mesmerizing. I am rereading it this year page by page by page, and it's just truly fascinating. Well, Cathy, it's just been a tremendously challenging, rewarding blessing working with you on Constituting America, our fourth year going into our fifth year. This year, we are going to have mentors for our winners. We are going to take the "best short-film" winners to Hollywood—with Gary Sinise as a mentor, the singers to Nashville, and the "best public service announcement" winners to Washington, D.C.—with Bret Baier and Brit Hume as their mentors. They will be able to watch their show, meet with them, and have them as mentors. We will also take the other "best essay" winners to Washington, D.C., to meet with journalists, go see a newspaper, or a magazine. It's going to be a great mentoring experience for these kids this year. So once again, we are spreading our wings. We did four years in Philadelphia, and now we are going to do something a little bit different this year.

But the documentary will still be there, the prize money is still there. And they will have dinner with a scholar that evening to ask questions about the Constitution. I am excited about what we are doing this year with the contest.

Cathy: Oh, I am too, and I think the kids that have entered so far and who we have talked to are very excited about that. I think they all understand what a great opportunity it would be to get to meet a mentor. That's what we are after. We want to affect the culture because we know that these days, more than ever, people get most of their knowledge from TV and the internet and YouTube. So if these kids are our future culture-makers, we want to make sure that they have a deep appreciation for the founding principles of our country and our Constitution.

Janine: That's right. And the great thing about it is our kids are actually doing the public service announcements that are getting aired. We are promoting their works. There have been some fabulous ones. We are entering them in the film festivals and the public service announcements are actually being aired in certain areas across the country. And so it's not a corporation or an advertising agency that's making our public service announcements, it's actually the kids themselves. So I think this is an amazing process, Cathy, I have to say. It would not be happening without you. You are just such a pillar of strength and your fortitude and your tenacity and your willingness and your desire and drive, it's been a journey, but it's certainly been a blessing, so, thank you, Cathy.

Cathy: Well it's an example of synergy, because it's your creativity and energy and enthusiasm and just being such a great leader for our organization. I think our skills complement each other, and it wouldn't be happening without you, for sure. So, I guess it's just the combination of us, and we have all the other people who advise us, and we have great board members and advisory board members and just generous donors who make it possible. So it's a huge team effort.

Janine: It really is. All across the country, even someone who gives $10, everyone has participated in the making of Constituting America, and, as you say, bringing the Constitution to the forefront of the culture across the country is so incredibly important and that's our goal, that's nonpartisan.

Cathy: I really want to thank you for the sacrifices that you make for all the time that you spend on Constituting America, because there are so many actors and actresses in Hollywood who are just "the next movie, the next TV show," and you are still very active in that world. I mean, we are so excited you have the movie coming out in 2014. But you still make the time to do things that make a difference in our world, and that takes a little bit of your time away from those other endeavors. It is a sacrifice, and I personally just really thank you for using your skills and talent to help make our country a better country.

Janine: Well, thank you, Cathy. The irony is that if we don't have an active citizenry and participants in the process with knowledge, basis of knowledge about the Constitution and that we are a Republic and why it works, we will lose the freedoms that we have in Hollywood. The checks and balances of the Constitution are designed to prevent a tyrant because men are not angels, as they say in *The Federalist*, and we will lose everything, our basic rights, and certainly our rights to the creativity that Hollywood craves. So, I've got to wrap here, Cathy. Thank you so much for having this fun time to recount our journey here now as we go into our fifth year, and we encourage everyone to check out Constituting America at www.constituting-america.org, and God bless you, Cathy. Thanks so much. It's just a lot of fun.

Cathy: Thank you, thank you for having me.

Janine: Alright. Take care. Bye. *The Janine Turner Show*, Constituting America with Cathy Gillespie.

The Janine Turner Show
February 17, 2014

Chapter Three

A Call to Arms—Refining and Defining Freedom

Should I keep back my opinions, at such a time, through fear of giving offense, I should consider myself as guilty of treason towards my country.

—Patrick Henry

A wise and frugal Government, which shall restrain men from injuring one another, which shall leave them otherwise free to regulate their own pursuits of industry and improvement, and shall not take from the mouth of labor the bread it has earned. This is the sum of good government.

—Thomas Jefferson

Shall we gather strength by irresolution and inaction? Shall we acquire the means of effectual resistance, by lying supinely on our backs, and hugging the delusive phantom of hope?

—Patrick Henry

Preface

Oh, awaken our blanket of satisfaction,
Lose not, that founding feud,
Appraising the slyness of demagogues
A fruition by too few.

Janine Turner
25 years old
New York City

A people that won't vote for their own interest, won't fight for
it—they become anarchist, burn, rob, and kill.

J.B. (John Bass) Gauntt
My paternal great-great-grandfather
September 28, 1922

In about 1875, Henderson County, (Texas) was very sparsely
settled. The woods were full of all kinds of wild game. I was very
fond of hunting. I had a small rifle gun, but could shoot accu-
rate with it. I remember going turkey hunting one dark, cloudy
morn, down on Pearse Creek, just west of where LaRue is now...
it was 1/2 of three or four o'clock A.M...I had stopped there
to listen for turkeys to gobble—it was very dark. All at once
two big wild cats began to squall about twenty or thirty steps
in front of me. Bulgar, (the big cur dog), Pete, (the mule), and
I stood our ground. They circled around us and disappeared. I
could see wolves chasing across the open woods, deer and tur-
key in droves up and down Caddow and Flat Creek, and the
"shrinies," as we called the open stretches without timber. From
where LaRue is now, to the foot of Boon Mountain, I have seen
twenty-five to thirty deer in a bunch... A good deal of difference
in the country now and then. No hog law, no stock law, hogs
and cattle run at large on the range, had no prohibition, made

our own peach brandy and corn whiskey, no revenue—every-
thing free and everybody happy and contented. How about
your freedom now?"

J.B. (John Bass) Gauntt
My paternal great-great-grandfather
September 29, 1922

It is an absolute imperative, to maintain our democratic Re-
public, that the American people turn their trust and attention
first and foremost to the legislative branch. It is time for the leg-
islators to earn it, and fast, or they will be reduced to irrelevancy
and take the American people with them, culminating with the
demise of our experiment in self-government. We will be leaving
our children in the hands of a lustful tyrannical form of govern-
ment that will focus all power to one faction, or one man, and
their liberty and inherent rights will be forever lost.

Janine Turner

After reading the eighty-five opinion editorials in *The Federalist*, written by Pub-lius (pseudonym for Alexander Hamilton, James Madison, and John Jay), I wrote eighty-five corresponding essays, a selection of which I include in the previous chapter. After completing these essays and appraising the political landscape with an enlightened eye, I felt compelled to take the leap form constitutionalist to con-cerned American. Encouraged by my friend, columnist Peter Roff, I became a regu-lar contributor to the *Washington Examiner*, foxnews.com, breitbart.com, and then a columnist for the news outlet *PJ Media*. This launched a year of Friday-night appear-ances on *The O'Reilly Factor* and my radio show *The Janine Turner Show*. Though I certainly have opinions, I challenge the ideologies of both the Democratic Party and the Republican Party. I am a bit libertarian, a bit independent, a bit Republican, a bit Tea Party, and most definitely a Constitutionalist. I am fiscally and socially conservative, but regarding some social issues, I am more open-minded.

I picked select opinion editorials for this chapter ranging from a three-part assessment of the relevancy of George Washington's Farewell Address to our de-bilitating debt, tyrannical big government, ubiquitous "big brother," my TRUTH

ACT, and how the legislative branch is digging its own grave, much to the progressives' delight. We have so much to do in so little time. It is time for a "Call to Arms" for knowledge and dedication.

Satellites, *Northern Exposure,* and America's Future

As a NASA satellite barrels toward Earth this week with impending doom, the references to the TV show *Northern Exposure* are many. I, of course, remember it well.

Maggie, my character on *Northern Exposure,* was giving her boyfriend Rick a pilot's examination. He made a mistake, so she did not give him a passing grade. He was distraught and ventured to the top of a mountain to meditate. While in this posture, he was hit by a random, falling satellite and killed.

Many of Maggie's boyfriends died untimely deaths, but this was a blow, in itself, to Maggie. Fleischman was undaunted, and, daring death, danced with Maggie at the end of the episode. Great writing. Great cast. Great fun. Maggie was a truly unique character; one unmatched then and now.

I was walking through Lowe's yesterday to buy a hammer, and I saw a tool-kit belt that wraps around the waist. I laughed fondly as I remembered that during rehearsals, to "get into character," I wore one of those tool belts filled with tools. Maggie could fix anything: planes, toilets, dinner—with meat hunted by her own hand.

During the filming and post-production of that satellite episode, I was unhappy with the producers, Josh Brand and John Falsey. I had to re-record the dialogue for the scene in the episode where Rick's coffin was revealed, and they continuously cut away from my face.

The satellite had fused to Rick's body, so the coffin had pieces of metal coming out of it.

I wanted to show some emotion, revealing that Maggie was sad that Rick had died. Thus, I had a few tears, conjured by "method acting." (My favorite actors were and are all "method actors"—Dustin Hoffman, Robert DeNiro, Al Pacino, Jessica Lange, even Marilyn Monroe.)

Brand and Falsey were desperately trying to keep the show in the Monday night "comedy" line-up, so my performance had to be restructured via sound booths and editing rooms to be "funny." As Kahlil Gibran believed, "the selfsame well from which your laughter rises was oftentimes filled with your tears," so goes the tango and artistry of teamwork.

I remember John Falsey called me after the filming of that episode and said, "We are a comedy! Write it down!" So, "dramedy" we were—part drama, part comedy.

It was tough to win in a drama acting category because I was always "funny" through the tears (tears that I could slip in), while other "drama" actresses were having genuine meltdowns.

Throughout the years, as I watched the clips of my fellow nominees sobbing, I knew I'd never win. Their characters were having huge, dramatic, emotional break-downs. I didn't care. I loved the show. I loved my character. I loved the cast. I loved the creators—Josh Brand and John Falsey. Brand and Falsey believed in me, and I will always treasure them, those years, and my groundbreaking character Maggie O'Connell.

Now it is 2011, and there seems to be a correlation between the present descending satellite and the potential descent of America. I love America and all the promise for which she stands. I want her to survive. My friend Brent Cooper and I were recalling the *Northern Exposure* satellite episode today. He said, "You've gone from actress to activist." I laughed, but it is true.

I am now an activist, and I have never felt a more urgent sense of passion and purpose. As the satellite is making a beeline for earth, it reminds me a bit of our situation in America. We feel the impending doom: faltering economy, strangling debt, high unemployment, disenchantment, terrorism beckoning on our doorstep, and a president who has blinders on and only sees 2012. Satellite? What satellite? Ignorance is not bliss.

We are at a huge crossroads in our country. As Jackie Gingrich Cushman says in her book *The Essential American*, "It's the desire for liberty and freedom above security and safety" that best represents the American spirit.

Ironically, the "entitlement Americans" who claim "security and safety" is their "right" are incapable of seeing the satellite that is going to crash and burn upon their indignancies. The anomaly looming in the horizon is the collapse of our society as a whole when America can no longer pay her debts.

One thing our Founding Fathers knew was history, a subject that is considered irrelevant in our schools today. History, both in centuries past and decades past, proves that bad economies, high taxes, record-breaking unemployment, and incomprehensible debt lead to despotism and demise. Americans want both "liberty and freedom" and "security and safety." Instead of Patrick Henry's call, "Give me liberty or give me death!" the call of the "entitlement Americans" today is "Give me liberty and give me, give me, give me!"

We cannot have both. Our Founding Fathers wrote the words, "Life, Liberty and the Pursuit of Happiness," with no guarantee of happiness, only the *pursuit* of happiness. They also made it very clear that God gave us these rights and not government. Government simply cannot withstand the demand of being "sugar daddy" to everyone. Liberty cannot withstand that demand.

So, as the satellite comes tumbling toward earth, we are all on alert. We know that it is coming. Should it not be the same with our impending doom regarding our Republic? I remember reading *The Mandarins* by Simone de Beauvoir. In the book there is a passage where, after World War II, a French diplomat appeals to a French leader to reach out and help another country. The French leader looks at the diplomat and says, essentially, "Don't you understand ...we can't even help ourselves."

I read this over twenty years ago, but it is a passage that has always stuck with me. If our country falters and tumbles from the weight of debt, how can she possibly help even her own people? This is so elementary that I cannot believe that the liberal elite and the "entitlement" contingency do not see this—the implosion of a force that is heading our way.

Claire Berlinski writes in her book *There Is No Alternative: Why Margaret Thatcher Matters* about leaders who can shape destiny based upon history: "Those who matter are able to master these historical forces...they are able to shift the forces into a different outcome."

Our forefather Patrick Henry was one of these men. His biographer William Wirt describes Henry as "a spirit fitted to raise the whirlwind, as well as to ride in it."

Henry questioned the colonists' hesitancy to take on the British for fear of Britain's strength and the enormity of the task: "Shall we gather strength by irresolution and inaction? Shall we acquire the means of effectual resistance, by lying supinely on our back, and hugging the delusive phantom of hope..."

The enormity of our task today—to bring back America to her basic thesis, to curb big government and entitlement mentalities, to educate her citizens, young and old, about the duties that imbue liberty, to demand an accountability regarding spending in Washington—to basically save America—is as daunting today as it was for the colonists to take on the biggest, most powerful country in the world, Britain. However, we must. We cannot continue to hug the "delusive phantom of hope."

Who will accomplish this, if not the people? We must reclaim America's promise, which is liberty, which is freedom from government, and, thus, the ability to pursue happiness—all on our own.

Actress turned activist. I see the falling weight of misguided leadership. I recognize the impending doom. I want to be a woman of action, a patriot of action. I believe in Patrick Henry's words, "Should I keep back my opinions, at such a time, for fear of giving offense, I should consider myself as guilty of treason towards his country..."

Janine Turner
September 23, 2011
FoxNews.com

George Washington's Farewell Address
Through the Prism of Today, Part I

In 1796, President George Washington decided to retire from public service, thus not seeking a third term. He wrote a thirty-two-page farewell address, with Alexander Hamilton's ever-present counsel. It was printed in Philadelphia's *American Daily Advertisers* newspaper, on September 19, 1796. Not only is it mesmerizing, it is pertinent. To shed light on the remarkable relevancy of his words and the timelessness of his wisdom, I am writing a three-part series on George Washington's Farewell Address.

Does morality really matter? George Washington addresses the issue:

> *Of all the dispositions and habits which lead to political prosperity, religion and morality are indispensable supports. In vain would that man claim the tribute of patriotism, who should labor to subvert these great pillars of human happiness, these firmest props of the duties of men and citizens.*

In the wake of the Congressman Weiner scandal, questions are being asked if morality really matters. After all, "Weiner didn't break the laws of the Constitution," said the casual observer on the street. Others, however, beg to question, for one who holds the public trust, where do matters of deceit draw its confines?

"The mere politician, equally with the pious man, out to respect and to cherish them. A volume could not trace all their connections with private and public felicity." Washington's words, from over two hundred years ago, some would argue, are dull and mundane. Yet, actually, they are sharp and solid, resonating relevancy and reason. Reason transcends time and reason sees the connections between "private and public felicity."

But are we a country of reason anymore? A country that props up politicians who don't seem to have clarity of moral boundaries or an understanding or acknowledgment, for that matter, of simple words like "budget." Private citizens deal with these concepts every day in their households, and private citizens know that they can't spend more than they make.

Reason is being ransomed, and morality, like reason, is being stripped from our society as if it does not really matter.

In our nation's schools, any nod to God is grounds for being expelled or maybe even a required visit to the psychiatrist's office. Our founding documents state "freedom from religion," not "freedom *of* religion." George Washington, in his farewell address, does not specify a religion. Yet, he most definitely states that religion and morality play a vital part in the survival of a republic and a society as a whole.

> *And let us with caution indulge the supposition that morality can be maintained without religion. Whatever may be conceded to the influence of refined education on minds of peculiar structure, reason and experience both forbid us to expect that national morality can prevail in exclusion of religious principle.*

History proves that without morality, life and civilizations crumble. Why then is a politician impervious to these same principles?

What would Washington think of our present generation of kids who are being taught by our nation's schools that one should be dumb, deaf, and blind to the call of God, country, duty, civics, and morality? How will they cope? They are being taught that morality and religious principle is not a mainstay to sustain one through life. They are not being taught that morality and religious principle are necessities to sustain a republic—a republic that embodies liberty and justice for all.

But, how would they know about liberty and justice for all? They cannot, or are not encouraged, to say the Pledge of Allegiance to their Republic. They are not taught to revere it—the very Republic that gives them their liberties to speak their minds—but wait, they can't speak their minds.

If our children do not know their rights, they will not know when their rights are being insidiously usurped from them.

Let it simply be asked, as Washington asked, "Where is the security for property, for reputation, for life, if the sense of religious obligation deserts the oaths which are the instruments of investigation in courts of justice?"

Where do justice and morality meet? They meet in the hearts and minds of a populace who, as "the genius of the people," maintain their Republic. They meet in what Washington expected of us and our politicians: dignity, integrity, morality based on religious principle.

Janine Turner
June 11, 2011
Big Hollywood
breitbart.com

Introduction Photos

My Paternal Great-Great-Great Grandfather J.W. Gauntt and My Great-Great Grandfather J.B. Gauntt

My Paternal Grandfather Turner Maurice Gauntt, Sr.

My Dad, Turner Maurice Gauntt, Jr., and His Mom, Marjorie Gauntt

Dad at West Point in Uniform

Dad with his Father, Mother, and Sister
Lilibeth at his Graduation from West Point

My Maternal Great Grandmother, Emily
Burgess with my Grandmother Loraine
(standing in back), and her two sisters
Hazel and Mary-Ruth

My Maternal Great Grandfather, Richard
Burgess, and Great Grandmother,
Emily Burgess

My Mother, Janice Agee Gauntt, in San
Antonio, Texas as the Lead in her High
School Play

My Maternal Grandfather, Stanley Agee
and Grandmother, Loraine Agee

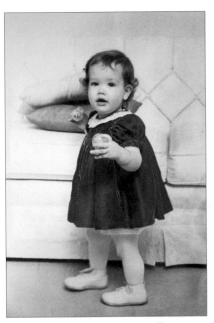

My Baby Photo in San Antonio, Texas

My Christening Day with Dad, Mom, and Brother Tim in Euless, Texas

Janine Gauntt

kim dawson agency

My Second Modeling Card with Kim Dawson Agency in Dallas, Texas – Age 5

Chapter One Photos

My Brother Tim and I in Front of My Favorite Home, The Blue Barn, in Euless, Texas

Little Miss Euless, Texas La Petite – Age 5

My First Magazine Cover – Age 9

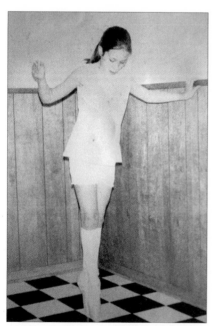

Breaking in My Pointe Shoes in Euless,
Texas – Age 9

Dad at West Point – Age 19

Modeling in New York City with
Wilhelmina Modeling Agency – Age 15

Modeling in New York City with
Wilhelmina Modeling Agency – Age 15

Acting in Hollywood – Age 17

Starring in *General Hospital* – Age 19

Engaged to Alec Baldwin – Age 20

Filming the Movie *Taipan* in Communist China – Age 21

Acting in *Steel Magnolias* as Miss Merry Christmas – Age 24

Acting in New York City - Age 25

132

After Cutting My Hair Before *Northern Exposure* in New York City – Age 26

My Constant Companion During my 20s – My Beloved Dog Eclaire

Chapter Two Photos

Maggie and I When I Was Pregnant with Juliette – 1997

My Beloved Horse Maggie and I in Our Barn at Texas Ranch – 2003

Filming Our First Documentary for Constituting America in California with Juliette – 2010

Cathy Gillespie and I Promoting Constituting America in New York City – 2010

Celebrating Constitution Day with Juliette in Philadelphia with Constituting America – 2010

Teaching Kids about the US Constitution at My Old Elementary School, Eagle Mountain Elementary in Fort Worth, Texas – 2011

Speaking at the Republican National Convention in Tampa, Florida – 2012

Chapter Three Photos

The Truth Act – 2013

Walking the Halls of Congress Promoting My Truth Act – 2013

Chapter Four Photos

Three Generations —My Maternal Grandmother Loraine, My Mother, and I — 1976

Three Generations — Mom, Juliette, and I — 1999

Three Generations - Mom, Juliette, and I — 2014

Juliette and I at Eighth-Grade Graduation — 2012

Chapter Six Photos

Recording The Janine Turner Radio Show on KLIF in Dallas, Texas — 2011

Chapter Seven Photos

Juliette and I in Houston, Texas Delivering my Alcoholism Is Ancient Speech – 2003

My cousin Robert Gauntt and I, Our Grandfathers were Brothers Whose Grandfather was J.B. Gauntt. He got Sober After Our Meeting in 1987

My Paternal Great-Great Grandfather J.B. with My Great Grandfather Paul, in the front with His Arms Crossed, Who Owned Paul's Cafe in Athens, Texas

Maureen Quinn and I Enjoying a Cup of Tea, Not Booze, in Seattle, Washington – 1994

Chapter Eight Photos

Dad in Eighth-Grade in Athens, Texas

Dad in High School in Athens, Texas

Dad at West Point Graduation Ceremony Receiving an Award as Company I-1 Commander

Dad and Mom on Their Wedding Day.

Dad in Air Force Uniform

Dad at Air Force Barracks Preparing to Fly the B-58 Hustler

Family Photo in Texas – 1968

With Dad and Brother Tim at West Point – 1970

In Seattle with Dad during *Northern Exposure* – 1994

Dad in Alaska Flying the 737 as Captain for Conoco Phillips

In Front of the B-58 Hustler with Dad and Juliette in Galveston, Texas – 2004

Dad at West Point 50th Reunion with Juliette – 2007

At West Point Football Game with Dad – 2010

On Set of *Northern Exposure* with John Corbett – My Favorite Episode – Burning Down the House

Dad, Mom, and I at Christmas – 2010

Hollywood Photos

Northern Exposure – 1991

Dancing with John Corbett at *Northern Exposure* Wrap Party – 1991

On Set of *Northern Exposure* with my
Acting Coach Marcia Haufrecht – 1991

On Set of *Northern Exposure* – 1992

On Set of *Cliffhanger* with Sylvester
Stallone and Lisa McCullough-Dupler –
my stunt double in Cortina, Italy – 1992

My Favorite Photo with Sylvester on Set of
Cliffhanger in Cortina, Italy – 1992

At the Vatican While Filming *Cliffhanger*
in Rome, Italy – 1992

On Set of *Stolen Women, Captured Hearts* in Kansas – 1996

Juliette and I During her Baby Debut – 1998

On Set of *Dr. T and the Women* in Dallas Texas – 1999

Juliette and I in Venice Italy Filming *A Secret Affair* – 1999

Juliette and I at the Ranch Mockingbird Hill for Crew Party for *Dr. T and the Women* – 2000

Juliette on Set of *Strong Medicine* in Los Angeles, California – 2000

Juliette and I in Hollywood – 2001

Juliette Starring in My Directorial Debut, *Trip in a Summer Dress* – 2003

Juliette and I on Our Ranch Mockingbird Hill – 2004

George Washington's Farewell Address
Through the Prism of Today, Part II

But the constitution which at any time exists, till changed by an explicit
and authentic act of the whole people is sacredly obligatory to all.

George Washington, in his Farewell Address, speaks to us about the obligation we have, as citizens, to the United States Constitution. Obligation. Americans, we the people, who live in America, we the people, who reap from her spirit, her resources, her goodness, her history of independence and equality, should be obliged to live by and honor our Constitution.

But do we? How can we, if we do not know it?

Americans love football. How would we ever expect a football player to play the game if he did not know the rules? Similarly, how do we expect to maintain our Republic if we do not know the rules, the laws, of our intended government?

"Respect for its authority, compliance with its laws, acquiescence in its measures, are duties enjoined by the fundamental maxims of true liberty." George Washington states that we should respect the Constitution's authority, comply with its laws, and acquiesce to its measures.

How can America's citizens sacredly oblige, respect, comply, and acquiesce to the measures in the Constitution if we do not know it? How can we sustain our Republic, a form of government where the people rule through their representatives by electing leaders and selecting judges to protect our liberties, if we know not from where these liberties are borne and maintained?

Is this not reasonable? Where is reason? Reason, a caveat in all things brilliant and everlasting, a mental attribute our Founding Fathers understood, leads us to a fundamental conclusion.

Is it not reasonable that we as adults fully comprehend the foundation of our government? Is it not reasonable that we dedicate as much time educating our children about the founding principles of our country as we do taking them to soccer practice and ballet school, the science fair and math labs?

But, where is reason in America?

I will never forget a recent experience I had when I was a guest on someone's radio show. As we were discussing the importance of the Constitution, he said, "I don't agree with it." I was awestruck. He didn't "agree with it?" What was his reasoning for such a blatantly broad and ignorant statement?

It reminded me of the great line in the movie *Amadeus*. After a beautiful, sumptuous opera, the king walks up to Mozart and comments, prompted by his faction, that there were "simply too many notes." A flabbergasted Mozart asked the king to describe to him exactly which notes. The king was at a loss for words.

The same applies to a broad comment regarding the Constitution such as, "I don't agree with it." I wondered to myself, which part? Reason led me to question whether this person had ever read the Constitution or studied it. If he doesn't agree with it, which implies the whole of it, then was I to suppose that he doesn't agree with the separation of powers, the checks and balances, the genius of Articles 1, 2, and 3?

Does he not agree with the bicameral Congress—one for the people, one for the states? Does he not agree that the president's cabinet has to be approved by the Senate? Does he not agree that the president is prohibited from declaring war without the consent of the Congress? Does he not agree that the House of Representatives, the people's house, holds the purse strings for war, thus empowering the people, through their vote, to end war at any time? Does he not agree that the president cannot appoint a Supreme Court Justice but can only nominate one, and that the nominee has to be confirmed by the Senate? Does he not agree that a bill vetoed by the president can be overridden by a two-thirds majority of the Congress? Does he not agree with the Thirteenth Amendment, which gave slaves freedom, or the Nineteenth Amendment, which gives women the right to vote, or the Bill of Rights, the first ten amendments of which includes freedom of speech— the freedom of speech which gives him his right to voice his blasphemous opinion that he didn't agree with the Constitution?

Where is reason?

> It is important, likewise, that the habits of thinking in a free country should inspire caution in those entrusted with its administration to confine themselves within their respective constitutional spheres, avoiding in the exercise of the powers of one department to encroach upon another. The spirit of encroachment tends to consolidate the peers of all the departments in one, and thus to create, whatever the form of government, a real despotism.

Is this not happening today? The executive branch is encroaching on the legislative branch by appointing unelected officials and czars, thus blatantly disregarding the Constitution. This encroachment has a residual effect on the liberties of the people, the resiliency of industry, and the inspiration of free enterprise. This can only happen if we the people are ignorant to the proceedings, the true intent of our government.

Thus, the bias against the Constitution and the people who revere it propels the purpose of the perpetrator—to intimidate the desire of a civic yearning and learning which allows the government to insidiously overstep its bounds.

Washington said it best: "All obstructions to the executions of the laws are[....]of fatal tendency."

Where is reason?

> *If, in the opinion of the people, the distribution or modification of the constitutional powers be in any particular wrong, let it corrected by an amendment in the way the Constitution designates. But let there be no change by usurpation[...]it is the customary weapon by which free governments are destroyed.*

Broad and unsubstantiated statements such as "I don't agree with it" are by-products of the proponents of faction. Faction is like a wildfire that rips through an innocent land. It breeds contempt, discord, division, distrust, and, eventually, the demise of our republic.

Janine Turner
June 18, 2011
Big Hollywood
breitbart.com

George Washington's Farewell Address
Through the Prism of Today, Part III

Faction. As Washington said, "they are likely in the course of time and things to become potent engines by which cunning, ambitious, and unprincipled men will be enabled to subvert the power of the people, and usurp for themselves the reins of the government, destroying afterwards the very engines which have lifted them to unjust dominion."

We are at a crossroads in America. This is a choosing time. Are we going to choose republicanism or Marxism? Free enterprise or socialism? Are we going to choose ignorance or reason, reality or denial? Are we going to be a nation divided or a nation united? Are we going to crumble or crawl through the fire? Do we have enough knowledge as a nation to know the demons that we face? Do we care?

I know one thing. We will care. We will care when we see the ashes of America carried on the winds of *change*.

As part of their political agenda, the cultural elite has slyly and insidiously captured the essence of America and shaped it into their vision and their desires, all of which are built on sand. These actions are not built on reason. They are built on an ideology that sells a mirage to the people and leaves the architect a hypocrite. Ignorance has let this happen.

One of the greatest mysteries of all times is how so many Americans could not see the change Obama sought to bring to America. Like all great leaders who manage to seduce a majority, he mastered the slick and slippery ways of doublespeak. Obama voters deliberately chose not to peer inside the looking glass that yielded focus on his true intentions. They chose denial instead. They chose to believe, mistakenly, that America could sustain herself on change. Others, knowing exactly what Obama's mission was, believed in the seduction of big government with feel-good economics. Governmental intrusions will eventually suck the life out of the American spirit.

It is ironic that America's most prevalent and prevailing faction has succeeded in promoting and implementing socialism as socialist (and communist) societies abroad are moving away from it because it simply does not work. These are facts. These are lessons from history. These are warnings that are based on reason. Our Founding Fathers did not construct a Declaration of Independence and a United States Constitution on visions of utopia. They built the foundations for future generations on education, history, and reason.

Where is reason? It's as if the liberal elite faction and those gullible enough to follow suit want to act like a child who plucks the dandelion, and, while blowing out all of the seeds with eyes closed, wishes, "Oh, I wish for a perfect society where there is no pain or poverty and I will always be taken care of by my nanny."

A government simply cannot be everything to everybody. The people have to sustain themselves. The government is to lay the platform to give the people that opportunity and then let go. Let go and let God. The faction of modern-day liberals want the government to micromanage our lives. Do children ever really find their way if parents never let them go? The liberal elite wants us to believe that we can do nothing without "Big Daddy," or "Big Brother," as George Orwell predicted.

Another haunting prediction of what America would be like in socialist hands is found in Ayn Rand's book *Atlas Shrugged*. It is a powerful example of the crisis at hand and the insidiousness of propaganda. In *Atlas Shrugged*, the social realms of all levels are eventually led to believe that people who work hard, and reap from their labors, are bad people. They are led to believe that government is the answer to all their problems. The talented, the wise, the brilliant are despised by the populace and sent to exile. The ones who are left behind, the leaders of the socialist movement, watch the economy dissolve around them, the very economy they had possessed and controlled. Debt, depression, starvation, and lack of spirit eventually crush America.

Sound familiar? In *Atlas Shrugged* all these events happened because people were led to believe that the government was the power, the government was the answer, the government would provide. Yet, incompetent and based on ideology instead of reason, the government stifled and manipulated individual, social, corporate, and industrial liberties—liberties that included the ability to succeed or fail. Government promised what it couldn't deliver. The engine of America stopped because the American people were seduced by a bill of goods that had no bill of rights. Americans had sold their souls to the devil. They had turned away from God as their provider and instead turned to government as their provider.

This is why our Founding Fathers based our fundamental principles on the solid, brilliant, and inspired reason that our rights—life, liberty, and the pursuit of happiness, are given to us by God. Our Declaration does not guarantee happiness. It gives us the right to pursue it, and the desire to pursue it, with liberty. Our Founding Fathers were motivated by God and logic, history and education.

Today we are a nation divided by faction. We are divided in a fundamental perspective of who gives us our rights and liberties, God or government. The dilemma is that we will not be able to sustain our Republic or rise from the mire of debt, deficit, and demise, unless we unite in the primary principles of our country's origin. Government is not the answer. Government is the problem.

The faction is perpetuated by denying our children an education in the principles of our country and the wisdom behind them. The liberal elite has infiltrated every aspect of our culture and has laid the groundwork for a takeover—like dynamite in a glass castle. Our courts, our primary schools, our movies, our television, our music, our colleges have all been slowly usurped, usurped like a slow poisoning with a propaganda that has no antidote—reason.

An awakening must occur. There must be a unification that defies party and unifies Americans. America has done it before, but it has been in times when Americans still believed in, and taught their children about, the goodness of America, the basic principles of the Constitution, and the fact that God had given them their right to succeed and fail and it was up to them to decide. America was built by immigrants who yearned for such freedoms. Let me be, and let me see what I am capable of doing. I will not know until I try to fly. And fly we did.

Today our children are taught to deny God in school, that loving their country is passé, that it is stingy and selfish to succeed, and that the government owes them happiness. Can we pull ourselves out of another slump if our spirit is broken, if our mantra is "give me" instead of "let me"?

George Washington warned that division and blind, ignorant allegiance to party would ruin America and give rise to dictatorship.

> *The alternate faction of one faction over another, sharpened by the spirit of revenge natural to party dissension, which in different ages and countries has perpetrated the most horrid enormities, is itself a frightful despotism[...]Sooner or later the chief of some prevailing faction, more able and more fortunate than his competitors, turns this disposition to the purposes of his own elevation on the ruins of public liberty.*

It's in the books for us to read. The writing is on the wall. But do Americans want to face the challenge? Do we as a nation have the stamina? Our muscles are weak and our minds mush. Just the way the leftist, socialist agenda wants it. Do not be fooled. Their goal is not a perfect state of well-being for all. It is power. Americans will be snapped into the snare of ruin by the dangling carrot—free care for life. Like a donkey with blinders on, we will walk in vain if we cannot see the truth.

Though elements of faction in the political arena are essential, if one prevailing faction is left unchecked by reason, our republic will fail. Reason and the ability to reason are alarmingly absent in the American culture today. We need reason. As Washington said, "The effort ought to be by force of public opinion to mitigate and assuage it [parties]. A fire not to be quenched, it demands a uniform vigilance to prevent its bursting into flame, lest, instead of warming, it should consume."

Janine Turner
June 25, 2011
Big Hollywood
breitbart.com

A Call to Arms

We are in charge of our children's futures, and it's time for a revolution.

In 1775 Israel Putnam was farming in Brooklyn, Connecticut, when he heard the British had fired on the American Militia in Lexington, Massachusetts. He immediately dropped his plow and rode one hundred miles in eighteen hours to Cambridge, Massachusetts, to join the colonial soldiers.

On the way he spread the call for "every man who is fit and willing" to come to their countrymen's aid.

Israel was resolute when revolution beckoned. He was fit and willing. Are we? Are our children? Or is it time for a 2010 resolution for a revolution?

Revolution conjures thoughts of guns and soldiers, passions and pageants. The revolution that currently beckons is an awakening—not an awakening of political parties or partisan politics, but of our youth's minds.

America's future lies with them.

What is happening to America's promise? Intellectual stimulation is benumbed with mindless text messaging, video games, and reality television. There is an extraordinary, seemingly boundless amount of information available at our children's fingertips, but the question begs: Will it be used benignly or brilliantly? Will our children become hypnotized or revitalized? Unfortunately, I see signs of complacency. Recently, I stumbled upon the following words:

The average age of the world's greatest civilizations has been two hundred years. These nations have progressed through this sequence:

From bondage to spiritual faith;

From spiritual faith to great courage;

From courage to liberty;

From liberty to abundance;

From abundance to selfishness;

From selfishness to complacency;

From complacency to apathy;

From apathy to dependency;

From dependency back to bondage.

Where are our children on this scale? Complacency? Apathy? They are walking the plank of dependency, over an ocean of bondage. Awakening our children's sense of faith, courage, tenacity, and selflessness, and lessening the belt on prejudice, is paramount for our country's survival.

We need to unite—unite in our efforts to rekindle America's flame.

We come from a lineage of a great, stoic, hard-working, positive, philanthropic people who believed in Divine Providence; a Divine Providence who was both the anchor and the launching pad from which dreams were made. America was a land of hope. We cannot become a land of dopes.

We must tell our kids to go outside and look at the stars, sit under a tree, read a book. We must encourage them to seek, understand, and value our rich heritage. They must study. They must read. We must teach them. We need to turn off the television and read a book of history at the dinner table. We need to be the example. We need to revolutionize our thinking, our moral foundation, and our academia.

To quote from one of my favorite forefathers, John Adams:

> I must study politics and war that my sons may have liberty to study
> mathematics and philosophy. My sons ought to study mathematics
> and philosophy, geography, natural history, naval architecture, navi-
> gation, commerce, and agriculture, in order to give their children a
> right to study painting, poetry, music, architecture, statuary, tapestry,
> and porcelain.

We have come full circle. We have studied painting, poetry, music, architecture, statuary, tapestry, and porcelain for too long. We, both as citizens and as parents, need to study with our children—history, literature, politics, war, mathematics, natural history, and engineering. We need to be fortified with wisdom, inspiration, Yankee spirit, and American can-do attitudes. We need to be both prudent and provocative.

We need a resolution for revolution.

We must no longer rest on our laurels as the aristocracy of Europe did in the eighteenth century.

Ignorance is the surest way to bring about the demise of our great land. Our children may end up in our enemy's hands. America will be taken with a subtlety and a craftiness that will feed upon our children's complacency. The rug will be pulled from under them before they even know there is an enemy in the room. It is not just the terrorists or reckless spending that threatens our country. It is our children's lack of education and intellectual fortitude. It is apathy. Woe to us, and shudder to think what lies before us, if we do not recognize that knowledge is power and reason is a civic responsibility.

Our children's fates and their futures are being carved by our culture, cultivated and manipulated by a senseless, meandering electronic society. We must be the hand on the brush that paints our children's fate.

"*Damnant quod non intelligunt.*" "They condemn what they do not understand."

Janine Turner
February 4, 2010
FOXNews.com

Desperately Seeking Statesmen

Americans are smarter than Washington, D.C. thinks. Americans have an inner, inherited intuition about freedom, loyalty, republicanism, and Americans do not like what they currently see.

Division. Impasse. Demise. Unemployment. Stagnation. Debt.

Americans know that to get any job done, anywhere, there must be cooperation. Americans know that to achieve this objective there must be a leader who inspires such unity. Americans know that their representatives need to respond to their rallying cry, "Think about America and Americans, not Democrats and Republicans."

Americans, whether they are the Tea Party movement or the "Occupy America" movement, are desperately seeking action. Americans see a government that is caught in the mire of division. Let's face it, no one likes to live in a home where there is anger, bitterness, and unproductivity, and no one likes to live in a country where there is anger, bitterness, and unproductivity.

Our government is being sucked into the quicksand of ineptitude. Obama is giving unrealistic speeches and inciting class warfare as he meanders around the country aloof to the needs of the people, focusing purely on his own re-election. He dumps his impractical, incoherent, financially lame jobs bill onto Congress, and even his own party is left teetering on the abyss. Democrats represent their constituents after all, not the president. Oh, but who is looking at the Constitution?

Obama inspires slogans like "I'm the 99%" which is arcane, certainly creates no new jobs, and inspires no incentive to find resolutions to the crisis at hand. So, America is without a statesman at the helm as president. Democrats know that Obama's jobs bill is nothing more than a campaign ad and community-organizer tactic. But does Harry Reid, who knows he doesn't have the votes amongst his own party, take a stand against it? No. Who does Harry Reid represent? The president?

Americans are looking for statesmen, not party men, in leadership positions.

Americans know that party divide, class warfare, and the blind ambition of its leaders are counterintuitive to the extreme crisis at hand. Is it really a surprise that the poll numbers show that confidence in Congress is at an all-time low? Americans are desperately seeking answers, solutions, and action.

Janine Turner
October 9, 2011
janineturner.com

Czars: The Enemy in the Field?

Weight does not show one ounce at a time. It is only when the gradual, insidious accumulation has taken place that one looks at the maladjusted balance of the scales and wonders, "What happened?"

So it goes with the loss of liberty. Rarely is it taken by a sudden reach of usurpation. It is taken by bit-by-bit maneuvering. Subtlety savors the loins of power. The wolf waits in the wings for the fattened calf.

In America, it has taken a century. Slowly, men, who are not angels and are victims of the whims of power, have thought themselves wiser than the Constitution.

It started with Woodrow Wilson, who thought that his intellectualism tipped the balance of government in his favor. He knew better than the collective reason of the people. Fiddlesticks to the notion that the "genius of the people" epitomized liberty and sustained republicanism, as Publius believed.

The Constitution was an obstacle that could be overcome by the perpetual elusive tactic of avoidance coupled with the pamphlet of a new mantra: "Government knows best." A pervasive propaganda echoed throughout the land saying that a wise, resilient executive is decisively more productive than a representative form of government. This executive, this king, needed more latitude, more money, and czars.

Not only did Woodrow Wilson instill "czars," who were unelected and unapproved by the Senate, violating Article 11, Section 2 of the United States Constitution, he also instigated two of the most intrusive and far-reaching amendments America has known to date. Under Wilson's tenure, the Sixteenth and Seventeenth Amendments were ratified. They restructured not only the basic thesis of the Constitution, but the power of the government.

What does a budding tyrant need to permeate the land with his persuasion? He needs less structure, or stricture, and more riches. With the Sixteenth Amendment, an earthquake to the foundation of our revolution, the federal income tax gave the executive and his cabinet more ability to mandate compliance. By shift-ing the reliance of the people from self-determination to government dependency, the federal government mushroomed. The people acquiesced their rights to the enticements of redistribution of wealth. At first it seemed innocent, but bit-by-bit the king's treasure chest was filled with his constituents' riches.

The next step in the stair step to tyranny was to censor the rights of the states. The Seventeenth Amendment lassoed the states into compliance by literally strip-ping them of their sovereignty. The state legislatures no longer had a voice. Thus, in two fell swoops the structure of our government was altered, restructuring and restricting forever the liberties of the people and the power of the states. The bud-ding tyrant now had money, power, and a private court.

In a bizarre absence of reason, and with a lack of knowledge as to why our Found-ing Fathers shed their blood, the American people surrendered many of their rights, liberties, and freedoms, not realizing that these men sought to change America.

Today, we deal with another kind of "hope and change." The balance of gov-ernment has insidiously swayed away from the people. The burden of the weight of unwieldy government regulation and dangerous debt brings us to the brink of total collapse. We face many challenges.

Reversing the Sixteenth and Seventeenth Amendments is unattainable, but ridding the executive branch of czars is within reason. Sequentially, presidents have continued with the rite of czars from Wilson to FDR, Nixon to Bush. Presi-dent Obama has appointed forty-eight and has another eighteen waiting in the wings. Thus, we have come full circle, Wilson and Obama, two Ivy League aca-demics, Princeton and Harvard respectively, who fundamentally believe that the country would be better off if it were simply left to their "elegant, academic" way of governing with no nasty and bothersome fingerprints from the legislative and judicial branches. They are policy men who have liberally appointed and continue to appoint constitutionally forbidden and unapproved czars.

Constitutional violations of this magnitude are dangerous and have the ability to be the tipping point that implodes the Republic. With no accountability regarding who is wandering around in the White House, the enemy is in our field. We have no way of knowing unless the czars are thoroughly vetted, as stipulated in our Constitution.

Along with the insurmountable debt, record-high unemployment, a great recession, and continual threats to our national security, the czar situation is equally as profound.

We the people have an obligation to hold our branches of government accountable.

Trepidation about czars is not a partisan issue. Democrats Russ Feingold and Dianne Feinstein questioned the wisdom, and Democratic Senator and constitutional scholar Robert Byrd (D-WV) expressed to Obama, "The rapid and easy accumulation of power by White House staff can threaten the Constitutional system of checks and balances. At the worst, White House staff have taken direction and control of programmatic areas that are the statutory responsibility of Senate-confirmed officials."

In September of 2009, the Czar Accountability and Reform Act of 2009 was introduced by Representative Jack Kingston (R-GA). The intent of the act was to curb the accumulation of czars by prohibiting taxpayer money from being used to employ "any task force, council, or similar office, which is established by or at the direction of the president and headed by an individual who has been inappropriately appointed to such position (other than on an interim basis), without the advice and consent of the Senate." However, the United States Senate Judiciary subcommittee on the Constitution concluded that appointing czars was acceptable. The issue was once again raised in the United States House in 2011 but has yet to make an impact.

We need to contact our representatives to seek the status of this bill and pressure them to persevere regarding this cause. We must also question any future presidential candidates about this issue. What are their intentions regarding czars? We need to know their perspectives on these unelected, unofficial, yet powerful and potentially dangerous positions.

Today, as we seek to chisel away at the enormity of the federal government that has besieged us and sucked the life out of our liberties, dignity, economy, and self-determination, dealing with the issue of czars is of paramount importance to our national security, the preservation of our country, and the future of Americans.

The czars are like stones in the scales of justice. One stone at a time, the perceptibility is minimal, but suddenly the stones will accumulate and the scales will break.

Janine Turner
October 18th, 2011
janineturner.com

Why Are We Selling American Liberty to China?

America would never sell her soul to China. Our liberty could never be bought. Right?

Wrong. America is mired with debt and steeped in political correctness. Both weaknesses are resulting in a dangerously naive embrace of the "new China."

Pro-China propaganda is as follows: China is emerging as a fledgling democracy and we need to support them. Brett M. Decker and William C. Triplett II substantially challenge this point and tackle the "New China Myth" in their book *Bowing to Beijing.*

Here are their most pressing points: China has no freedom of religion, press, speech, assembly, does not recognize private property rights, and does not respect the right to life, nor does it intend to do so. "Dissent is not allowed in the PRC, period," Decker and Triplett write.

Chinese novelist Murong Xuecun—pen name for Hao Qun—upon winning a literary prize, wrote an acceptance speech that was not only read by censors before presentation but forbidden to be delivered.

Murong walked on stage to accept the award, made a zipping motion in front of his mouth, and spoke not one word. Murong later referenced censorship in China: "Chinese writing exhibits symptoms of a mental disorder. This is castrated writing. I am a proactive eunuch, I castrate myself even before the surgeon raises his scalpel."

Chinese dissident Liu Xiaobo, a leader in drafting Charter 08, was awarded the Nobel Peace Prize in 2010 for his courageous demand for constitutional principles. Liu was unable to attend the ceremony because he had been arrested in 2008 and was given an 11-year prison sentence for his quest for human dignity. The award was presented to an empty chair.

Still, Americans do business with China, and President Obama holds a lavish state dinner honoring President Lu, complete with First Lady Michelle Obama in a sweeping red dress.

America is allowing China to swallow us up, investing in our banks, buying our property, and harvesting our resources. Even our universities are vulnerable, as Chinese government-regulated "Confucius Institutes" are being established to educate American youth about the virtues of China. Why? Money.

Universities are being paid $270,000 to $4 million to allow these academies on their campuses run by Li Changchun, CCP Propaganda Chief and the fifth most powerful man in China. The exchange of money allows only Chinese teachers, permitting no references to human-rights violations.

Alexandr Solzhenitsyn, the esteemed Russian writer who was imprisoned and exiled, commented on the temptation of the West to sacrifice liberty for material goods in his address to Harvard Class Day Afternoon Exercises in 1978:

> *The constant desire to have still more things and a still better life and the struggle to obtain them imprints many Western faces... the majority of people have been granted well-being to an extent their fathers and grandfathers could not even dream about.[...]It has become possible to raise young people according to these ideals, leading them to physical splendor, happiness, possession of material goods, money, and leisure, to an almost unlimited freedom of enjoyment.[...]So who should now renounce all this, why and for what should one risk one's precious life in defense of common values, and particularly in such nebulous cases when the security of one's nation must be defended in a distant country?*

America's vulnerability is predicated on financial gain. At some point, the consumer, corporations, and Washington, D.C., must reckon with this decision, which will come with fiscal sacrifice.

China is engaging in prodigious cyber-spying, seeking the ability to shut down the cooling mechanisms of our nuclear power plants. They are aiding and abetting our enemies in such places as Iran. They are curbing our ingenuity by stealing our patents and threatening our security by proliferating our military secrets. They are ravaging us with unfair trade deals.

At what price will America sell her soul? Confucius says, "He who will not economize will have to agonize."

Janine Turner
November 11, 2011
The Washington Examiner

House Leaders Should Enforce Constitutionality Rule

Republicans in the 112th Congress, under the leadership of House Speaker John Boehner (R-OH), had a good idea whose time had come. When they convened last January, House Rule XII was amended by adding clause 7(c): "A bill or joint resolution may not be introduced unless the sponsor has submitted for printing in the *Congressional Record* a statement citing as specifically as practicable the power or powers granted to Congress in the Constitution to enact the bill or joint resolution."

The crux of this amendment was that any representative who put a bill in the hopper had to prove from which article, section, and clause of the United States Constitution it received its justification.

Hence, no longer would a bill be considered, or reach the House floor, unless it was constitutional, yes? No. House Rule XII, Section 7(c) has proven to be a good idea in need of better execution.

Constituting America, the non-profit foundation which I founded and co-chair and which is focused on Constitutional awareness, published a report released last week on implementation of House Rule XII, Section 7(c), entitled "Constitutional Authority Statements: In Defense of House Rule XII." The report finds that many representatives sought due diligence and applied through justifications, while others listed seemingly deliberate nonsensical rationales.

"After a year, it's all too clear why the rule has become necessary, and that some (House) members should become more acquainted with the Constitution they have sworn to uphold," said Horace Cooper, who co-authored the report with Nathaniel Stewart.

A total of 3,865 Constitutional Authority Statements were submitted in 2011, with 660 of them simply referencing broad clauses that were not applicable, including the Preamble, which is simply an overview of the Constitution and not law.

A stunning 732 bills cited Article I, Section 8, Clause 3—often referred to as the "Commerce Clause" —as their constitutional justification. Case in point: Rep. Bill Pascrell (D-NJ) used the Commerce Clause when he proposed a bill to "encourage and ensure the use of safe football helmets…" It is a misnomer to insinuate that "use of safe football helmets" falls under the same category as regulating interstate commerce.

Many representatives listed "justifications" that were not valid, yet no method of operation was put into place to oversee such slights. The intentions behind House Rule XII, Section 7(c) were good but, without accountability, members have no incentive to take it seriously.

The dismal public approval ratings of Congress reflect that Americans are tired of good ideas that wither on the vine. Empty campaign promises and elusive governing sound bites are jeopardizing the Republic. Americans want action. Americans want responsible governing. There is no better place to start than with House Rule XII, Section 7(c), which requests a viable constitutional rationale behind the bills a representative puts forth. Execution, however, is the key. Suggestions made by Constituting America's report include:

- Allowing the Clerk to indicate if an Authority Statement does not satisfy the Rule's specificity requirement,

- Making sure that, at each step in the legislative process, the bill and its Authority Statement are attached and immediately available to House members

- Address the problem of attempts to amend an existing law that a House member believes to have been enacted without constitutional authority.

It is ironic that a rule has to be put in place to make sure that those who are sworn to preserve, protect, and defend the United States Constitution govern by the laws of such. It is disgraceful, and ultimately dangerous, that many still do not.

It is the responsibility of the House to maintain an adherence to its own rules. The House Rule XII, Section 7(c) was a good idea whose time had come. Now, it is time that it be executed.

Janine Turner
January 24, 2012
The Washington Examiner

The Real *Game Change* Isn't a Movie

Lack of honor is the most revealing aspect of the HBO movie *Game Change.* Yes, there is the horrific character assassination of Sarah Palin, much to the satisfaction of the Left. However, as the movie progresses, it becomes obvious that the blatant betrayal by members of Senator John McCain's (R-AZ) own staff is the culprit. After the film concludes, the permeation of this betrayal rises to intoxication. Palin is not the villain. The villains are two of McCain's staffers, Steve Schmidt and Nicolle Wallace.

I was prepared to write a piece about how the Hollywood Obama Machine twisted a damaging propaganda piece against Palin—who they thought would be making a substantial 2012 presidential bid—timing the release right after Super Tuesday.

I was prepared to write a piece about how liberals can't accept a strong, conservative woman because she threatens their coveted gender gap and their ironic big-government mainstay—keeping women dependent on Big Daddy.

I was prepared to defend Palin's character by pointing out the Left's attempt to thwart her impact on both the country and the 2012 race. However, what is most abhorrent about the movie is the betrayal of Republicans by Republicans. With friends like these, who needs enemies?

On *Fox News Sunday*, Chris Wallace asked McCain what he thought of Schmidt's words, "I regret playing a part in a process that yielded someone on the ticket who was not prepared to be president." McCain, with steely, somber reserve and flushed cheeks, replied, "I regret that he would make such a statement." Which leads one to wonder if Schmidt's passion is to protect the country or if it is passion fed by ego and vendetta?

Meg Stapleton, senior campaign advisor and spokesperson for McCain-Palin, said in the *Hollywood Reporter*, "Schmidt is infamous for lining up and destroying. He is abusive. He is abrasive. And he is nothing short of a world-class bully."

Jason Recher, who traveled with Palin on the 2008 campaign, told *The Hill*, "neither author of *Game Change* was ever present and that Schmidt was present on only five of two hundred bus or plane trips taken by Palin during her two months of campaigning."

Most haunting of all is the sobbing confession by Sarah Paulson, portraying Nicolle Wallace, revealing that Wallace just couldn't bring herself to vote for McCain because of Palin. This was the lowest blow. Could this be true?

Tellingly, Wallace has continued her attacks on Palin by writing a book, *It's Classified*, about a mentally unstable female vice-president. In a *Time* magazine article promoting the book she states, "The idea of a mentally ill vice-president who suffers in complete isolation was obviously sparked by the behaviors I witnessed by Sarah Palin."

It is easy for Wallace to sit back and make these accusations when she was not the one who had recently given birth to a baby with Down's Syndrome.

She was not the one with a son who was fighting in Iraq, with a pregnant teen-aged daughter, whose family was under attack, emails were being hacked, and who was being ridiculed nationwide.

She was not the one with a reputation and governorship to lose. Simply put, Wallace was not the one making the sacrifice.

Perhaps Palin was uncommunicative with Wallace and Schmidt because she did not trust them, and rightly so.

Shameful betrayals have inflicted damage on the Republican Party during a time when the country is on the edge of oblivion. They have tried to crush a woman whom many Republicans instantly loved and to demean a Senator America has long revered.

Yet, McCain and Palin have endured, emerging from it all with class, dignity, character, and love for country. Game change it is.

Janine Turner
March 13, 2012
The Washington Examiner

America's Hope That Obama Is Determined to Change

Newt Gingrich has found a new avenue of influence—the gas station. His campaign stop at a local gas station, holding the gas pump in his hand, decrying the lack of "algae energy," was brilliant.

He is correct. There is currently no algae energy available for America's massive demand, and thanks to President Obama, there is no fossil-fuel plan, either. He stifles coal. He stifles oil. He stifles natural gas.

Secretary of Energy Steven Chu wants gas prices to reach $8.00 a gallon, a la Europe, forcing Americans to switch. (Yes, he now disavows his statement from 2008, but it's a campaign year, so how seriously should that be taken?) But switch to what—the Chevy Volt? Only if you want to catch on fire.

The genius of the American people should not be underestimated. Americans did not blow out their candles before they had dependable electricity.

In response to Newt's well-armed fuel duel, Obama could only resort to snide comments, comparing Newt to a member of the "flat earth society." Obama's adoring crowd chuckled.

Will they be laughing when gasoline is $8.00 a gallon? Will they be laughing when Iran, backed by China and armed with nuclear capability, terrorizes the region and closes the Strait of Hormuz?

Will they be laughing when our economy crashes and China builds her attack upon our indebtedness to her?

Herein lies the problem. Obama threatens not only our livelihoods and our economy with his cavalier ideology but also our national security. He has put the cart before the horse. He has put his vision before America's best interests.

Most Americans would agree that energy alternatives are commendable, with emphasis on the word "alternative." Yet, we do not have dependable alternatives because Obama is giving tax money to losers like Solyndra and suffocating private enterprise with the EPA, heavy taxation, and political correctness.

Not only is it unconscionable and unconstitutional, it is also unsuccessful. Free enterprise and freedom to choose, not to mention freedom to innovate without government intrusion, are basic tenets of American rights and prosperity.

Obama's ostentatious insistence on going green, no matter the cost, is madness— especially when America is battling a national debt that is $15 trillion and rising.

To thwart America's rich and vast fossil-fuel resources is unreasonable. Hidden within the earth lies not only self-reliance but solvency.

Forbes contributor Peter Ferrara, quoting a recent Steve Moore piece in the *Wall Street Journal*, observes that, "In 1996, the U.S. Geological Survey estimated 150 million 'technically recoverable barrels of oil' from the Bakken Shale[...]In April 2008, that number was up to about four billion barrels, and in 2010 geologists[...] put it at eight billion. This week, given the discovery of a lower shelf of oil, they announced 24 billion barrels.[...]Current technology allows for the extraction of only about 6% of the oil trapped one or two miles below the earth's surface, so as the technology advances recoverable oil could eventually exceed 500 billion barrels."

In the same vein, Gingrich said "the number of recoverable barrels of oil estimated to be in the United States, waiting to be produced [is 1.44 trillion]. That's about the amount of oil the entire world has consumed since the first well was drilled before the Civil War. In addition, we have an estimated 2.744 quadrillion (a fifteen-digit number) cubic feet of natural gas."

Ferrara explains, "Gingrich notes the estimate of the royalties to the federal government from such oil and gas development at $18 trillion over the next generation. That is enough, he further notes, to pay off the current national debt of $15.5 trillion, without increased taxes."

Common sense dictates the harvesting of such vast American riches, yielding stabilizing independence. The statistics are startling in their breadth of hope, a hope that is denied by Obama's determination to change.

Janine Turner
March 20, 2012
The Washington Examiner

Does America's President Understand America?

Perhaps it is not surprising that President Obama, a president who grew up abroad and paints himself as an international man in his self-promoting books, does not identify with one of America's most fundamental and cherished tenets—religious freedom.

Deeply embedded in each American's spirit and psyche is the history and heritage of not only the freedom to worship as one chooses, but to do so without government intervention. The Obama administration's tone-deaf approach regarding the moral dignity of one's individual religious beliefs, and those of religious institutions, is vulnerable with dangerous denial.

Obama is attempting to violate one of our most treasured First Amendment rights by relying heavily on the ignorance and apathy of American citizens. The liberal media helps the president with the imbalanced attention it pays to only half of the religious-freedom clause in the First Amendment—keeping religion out of government entities.

Obama is banking on his hopes that most Americans have forgotten the other, more cherished half of the religious clause in the First Amendment that was the impetus for the pilgrimages that birthed America—keeping government out of religion.

President Obama's lack of reverence for keeping government out of religion expresses itself with such steamrolling techniques as Health and Human Services, as part of Obamacare, invading the sacred space of religion, religious affiliations, and religious people. He is mandating in forums where he does not belong and penalizing where he has no right.

Obama has not only taken on the Catholic Church, he has taken on all religion because he is redefining religion. Obama is dictating where a religious people are religious and where they are not, where they have a right to be religious and where they do not. According to President Obama, religious morality and compassion only exist in the temple itself. Catholic-initiated outreaches and missions extended in schools, colleges, hospitals, social-service institutions, and charities are not religious, according to Obama. This redefinition conveniently gives him the self-declared right to dictate how these Catholic institutions operate.

This is dangerous territory. This is an alarming precedent. With a thought process as this, Jesus would have been considered only valid and religious while teaching in the temple. His actions in the desert, at weddings, at lakeside gatherings, and on mountaintops would have been considered not religious teaching but simply a social service subject to government regulation. Even the Roman Empire did not define Jesus's teachings by his destinations of discipleship.

Yet Obama feels he can limit Christian outreach by redefining where that is allowed to take place. If Christians are ministering in any place other than the church building itself, then they and their outreaches are vulnerable to government definitions, mandates, restrictions, and penalizations.

By this definition, President Obama grossly misunderstands the Christian faith. The best works of Christ were, and are today, performed outside of the temple walls. Chancellor Jane Belford states, "Our faith is more than on Sunday. We practice our faith when we put it into action."

The new Health and Human Services law mandating that the Catholic Church provide abortifacients, sterilization, and contraception, a violation of the long-held Catholic tradition and faith, exposes the naiveté and reckless ego of the Obama administration, not to mention a grave misunderstanding of religious freedom.

Hence, Catholic institutions across the country filed massive lawsuits against the United States government on May 21, 2012.

To win public support of his penalization and violation of religion and religious entities, including but not limited to the Catholic Church, Obama is relying on a tornado-sized twist of truth—that women are being denied contraception. This can only happen if Americans fall into a deep sleep and enter the land of Oz. Women are free to get birth control all across the country, just not at the Catholic Church or its entities, because the Catholic religion believes it is morally wrong. This is their religious right; this is their religious freedom.

As Chancellor Jane Belford elaborates in a video, "This lawsuit isn't about contraception. With a prescription, birth control pills are readily available at major retailers for $9.00 a month and at no cost from various health-care clinics[...] This lawsuit does not challenge women's established legal right to contraception use nor does it challenge any employer's right to provide and pay for it."

The Catholic institutions that have filed lawsuits against the government have done so because of Obama's blatant violation of religious liberty and morality, his determination to redefine religion, and his petulant penalization of Catholic institutions. The Catholic Church is battling an attack on religious freedom not unlike those that launched a new world in the sixteenth century and a new nation in the late eighteenth. They are challenging a precedent that, if left unchecked, will open the gates of hell, unleashing a hungry government eager to control, manipulate, and persecute. It may seem subtle now, but the devil is in the details. The Catholic Church is protecting our great American legacy—religious liberty.

Janine Turner
June 1, 2012
pjmedia.com

You Should Never Despise Your Enemy

Sometimes it feels as if America is in the midst of a modern-day civil war. Instead of a battleground made of sod and stone, the battleground is in print and on television. Instead of guns and swords, the weapons are words and rhetoric.

It's a political civil war—a civics war—a war of politics and ideology.

America is divided. Americans are at odds—right vs. left, conservative vs. liberal, progressive vs. constitutionalist, religious vs. atheist, fiscal fitness vs. spending spree, unions vs. independence, corporate vs. government, executive branch vs. legislative branch, big government vs. small government, employer vs. employee, employed vs. unemployed, give me liberty vs. gimme gimme.

Everyone is touched by America's civics war.

George Washington predicted such a destruction in his farewell address. His concern was that the party system would be the demise of the Republic because people would care more about their party than they would care about America. They would self-identify as Republicans or Democrats instead of as Americans.

Americans have inherently strong wills, and Americans have intensely fought over the direction of our country since Adams challenged Jefferson and Federalists debated Anti-Federalists. However, a fundamental factor prevailed in 1787 that is presently missing—allegiance to the survival of the United States of America and the Republic for which she stands.

Only with a strength of mind and mission could a rag-tag militia filled with misfits overtake the most powerful country in the world. The hunger for liberty ran through ardent veins pumping for victory against incredible odds. The unity of souls with a Providential path prevailed over the weakness of human nature—individual, self-seeking angst. Wrapped within this modern-day warp of conscience is the antithesis to colonial unity. Harmony has been replaced by a wrecking political steadfastness rooted in creating an enemy nation within America's borders.

An enemy is now how brethren are treating brethren, spitting unreasoned sound bites into a citizenry who has forgotten the art of deliberation. Hate and ugliness have manifested in a biting duel of insinuations and innuendos.

The time has come for America to take her pulse and monitor the fever pitch in which venomous debate has thrust its evil talons. It's time to heed the age-old maxim based upon biblical verse, "Never despise your enemy."

We are, after all, all Americans. We are brothers and sisters living in a land pioneered by a tough, compassionate people compelled by the desire of a life free from tyranny. Presently, we are trapped in the tyranny of our own hatred of one another. We have become a nation where intellectual debate and rational reactions are obsolete.

Diverse opinions are rich and viable if they can be steeped in an avenue that leads to productivity. We, as a nation, are stuck in the mire of "me first" and "my way." We cannot survive as a nation with such selfish divisiveness. We must not despise our enemies. We need to respect our fellow Americans' desires and opinions without despicable behavior.

Love our enemies as we love ourselves. Respect our differences as we celebrate our similarities. Resolve our vivid and vast ideologies with a compassion bred by a shared heritage—we are all Americans. Forging the streams that concurrently challenge our differences is the bridge upon which we build our future. Acceptance of our uniqueness with a resolve to find commonalities is our only chance for survival.

Ironically, our enemies are within our own borders, as we are our own worst enemy. The resentments that reside in our hearts will ruin our resolve to be the people God made us to be, upholding the country God gave us to keep. America is a treasure. The America that is the hope of all mankind is best represented by people who are kind. May we not shatter ourselves with shameless ego.

During an election year ripe with divisions that cultivate civics war, may we not forget our national character. May we not despise our enemies but nourish our freedoms to be unique, culminating in an America that is steadied by her rudder of reason.

Janine Turner
June 13, 2012
pjmedia.com

"For Imposing Taxes On Us Without Our Consent"— The Declaration's Words

On July 4, 1776, the American colonists declared independence from an overbearing king and legislature that had imposed their will upon them without any regard for their petitions. "We have warned them from time to time of attempts by their legislature to extend an unwarrantable jurisdiction over us," states the Declaration of Independence. Sound familiar? A defiant president and a Congress controlled by Democrats granted themselves an unwarranted jurisdiction when they, the Democrats only, passed the Affordable Care Act, known colloquially as Obamacare.

"Our repeated Petitions have been unanswered only by repeated injury," the

Declaration states. Sound familiar? The United States Supreme Court repeated the Obamacare injury by upholding the Affordable Care Act as constitutional.

"A Prince, whose character, is thus marked by every act which may define a Tyrant, is unfit to be the ruler of a free people," the Declaration states. Sound familiar? President Obama is orchestrating his agenda like a tyrant king who is tone-deaf to the petitions of the people, and who is burdening the people with unfair taxes—the conglomerate of taxes that are in Obamacare. Aspects of the law have now been revealed, and legitimized, by the Supreme Court as the tax it always was.

On a hot, steamy Philadelphia day on July 4, 1776, discerning, brave, and brilliant men mutually pledged, with a reliance on divine providence, their lives, fortunes, and sacred honor in order to obtain independence from a tyrant king. Sound familiar? Today Americans are in a battle for their lives (health care), fortunes (taxes), and sacred honor (independence and dignity) from an overbearing and self-centered president and a legislature filled with partisan Democrats who are deaf to calls to redress the injuries.

One shudders to think what John Adams, Thomas Jefferson, Benjamin Franklin, John Hancock, and Samuel Adams would declare today, after a sweeping Supreme Court decision wiped independence off the United States of America's map and the individual American's manifest.

The Declaration of Independence includes a list of grievances against the tyrant king. One such grievance is "For imposing Taxes on us without our Consent."

A duplicitous president, who always knew Obamacare was a tax and who instructed his solicitor general to argue in front of the Supreme Court that it was a tax, has successfully imposed taxes upon us without our consent. Obama, the "Great Pretender," set the course of his agenda and legacy, the Affordable Care Act mandate, unpopular from the start, and led the great lie—that Obamacare was not a tax.

Upon this pretentious principle he built his socialist manifesto that robbed Americans and the states of their independence and renowned health care.

The Great Pretender cried at one town hall after another that Obamacare was not a tax. "Not one dime," was his declaration, promising no taxes would be paid to uphold Obamacare. That was yet another deception.

To accomplish this, the liberals had to build a legislation that was too thick for anyone to understand—two thousand seven hundred pages long. The liberals in the legislature pronounced to what they hoped was an ignorant populace that the bill was for their own good and sealed the deal with Nancy Pelosi's now infamous remark that they had to pass it to find out what was in it.

Obamacare was the biggest fraud inflicted upon the American people of all time until Chief Justice Roberts called Obama's bluff. Roberts came to the conclusion that Obamacare could be constitutionally upheld upon the premise of Obama's solicitor general's argument—that portions of Obamacare could be constitutionally legitimized as a tax. Chief Justice Roberts heard this argument and could rationalize the constitutionality of the law as a tax.

Regardless of the legal or fairness arguments, or even his true intent, the result is that Roberts exposed the Great Pretender. The Affordable Care Act is a tax—the largest tax hike in American history.

Media elites are debating whether Obamacare is a tax or a penalty. They proclaim that if you buy insurance then you are not taxed. However, the plague has not fully run its course. The bill is diseased with taxes—taxes on instruments, machines, probably even the Kleenex. Not to mention that the morgue will be filled with IOUs from anyone who makes $18,700 or more and defiantly doesn't care to pay the tax. The IRS pallbearers will be laden with the weight of unpaid bills.

The ultimate death is to American independence and to the American people whose health will inevitably suffer.

Obamacare is a tax. Obamacare is a government takeover. Obamacare is a usurpation of one-sixth of the American economy. Obamacare is the monster that will devour America's renowned medical genius and ingenuity.

Obama deceived America and Obama usurped the legislative branch with his great pretend—that Obamacare was not a tax. Upon Obamacare will be the fall of America unless it is overturned by the people.

Hence the greatness of the United States Constitution, one of the three miracles that made and kept America—the bravery of the men who designed and signed the Declaration of Independence, the victory of the men who won the American Revolutionary War, and the genius of the men who orchestrated the United States Constitution.

Due to the separation of powers and the three branches of government, Americans can save the Republic with their vote in November. The buck does not stop with the Supreme Court. Americans can reclaim their independence from executive usurpation by reclaiming their voice in the people's branch—the legislative branch.

"They too have been deaf to the voice of justice and of consanguinity," declared our Founding Fathers in the Declaration of Independence. Sound familiar? Now all three branches of government have been deaf to the voice of justice for the American people.

It is time to declare a new independence—an independence from the Democrats and progressive liberals who have put us in this place, and a call to action to limit bills in Congress to thirty pages so that the American people can understand their legislation and hold their representatives accountable. Otherwise why have a republic? Perhaps this is the agenda of the left—confusion to defy accountability.

Chief Justice Roberts just made Obama accountable. If Republicans win in the executive and legislative branches in November, then Roberts's gamble will have been worth it. If not, we are doomed.

"…appealing to the Supreme Judge of the world for the rectitude of our intentions, do, in the Name, and by Authority of the good People of these Colonies, solemnly publish and declare, that these United Colonies are, and of Right ought to be Free and Independent States…," reads the Declaration of Independence. Sound familiar?

Freedom and independence cannot be upheld with devastating debt and dubious leadership. We must declare ourselves free and independent from the nanny state and an overbearing, intrusive government. The Affordable Care Act is a paradox that carries with it the fatal debt that robs us of our independence. We must declare independence. We must act. The election in November is our Revolutionary War.

On this July 4th may we read the Declaration of Independence at our festive gatherings. May we ponder our Founding Fathers' wisdom as we watch the fireworks in the sky.

"Think what you do when you run into debt; you give to another power over your liberty," said Benjamin Franklin

Happy 4th of July. God bless our republic.

Janine Turner
July 4, 2012
pjmedia.com

A New Definition of War

The Boston bombings have awakened a new reality in America. Just as the casual glance in the sky at an airplane or a skyscraper was forever altered by 9/11, an outdoor sporting event or gathering has been altered by the Boston bombings.

The real new awakening, however, if American liberties are to prevail and Americans are to survive, needs to be a new criminal and constitutional standard to deal with terrorists engaged in the modern-day definition of war. There is such a war that is now menacing the American homeland: *jihad*, a "holy war."

The prevailing thought has been that terrorism is only an "act of war" if attached to a foreign country or foreigner. However, after the Boston bombings a new precedent has been established as it should have been after Fort Hood. Yet it seems as if the Obama administration and many Americans, in defense of political correctness, want to deny the new rules of engagement.

The new definition of war is not whether an attack is attached to a foreign country or aliens from a foreign country. The new definition of war is in the name of radical Islamic *jihad*. This type of war is defined by anyone who engages in evil acts of terror, death, and destruction in the name of jihad's ideological fanaticism.

The Boston bombings were not an act of wayward, confused, misinterpreted, bomb-building, pot-smoking, naturalized Americans from Chechnya. The murders in Boston were an act of war carried out by jihad's soldiers. It was an act of *jihad*. Coming to terms with this new definition of war as a "holy war" by the radical jihadists, who use religion as a cover for their vengeance, and the acceptance that their soldiers, whether American citizens or foreigners, are enemy combatants are an absolute must if America is to endure and remain safe.

The jihadist movement has come to our shore. The enemy is in the field, and the movement that was once confined to radical foreigners has now elicited our vulnerable American youth to perpetrate their war, be their "troops," and to both carry and shield their evil. There is a reason they are doing this.

The radical jihadists know America's innate goodness, inclusiveness, and our structure of government better than most Americans do, especially the rising generations. They intend to use our own Constitution and rules of law to riddle our society with death and destruction. They want their network and plots to elude detection by hiding behind Miranda rights. American citizen soldiers are their best assets.

We are at war with radical Islamists, and these recent terror attacks—including the failed underwear bomber, the Times Square bomber, the successful Fort Hood attack, and Benghazi attacks—were acts of war. The Boston bombing was an act of war. It was an act of *jihad*, a holy war self-proclaimed by the alleged perpetrators themselves.

Obama adviser David Axelrod was quick to state that perhaps the Boston bombings occurred because it was "tax day." This is an insult to Americans. It appears that there is an attempt by the Obama administration to deny the reality of *jihad* on our shores, within our borders. The reluctance to tell Americans the truth is a dangerous game played at the expense of American lives. With every Fort Hood denial, Benghazi denial, Boston bombing denial of a jihadist "holy war" is a gleeful snicker from our enemy and an emboldened foe.

The jihadists are beating us at our own game. We are being outsmarted. Our enemies are relying on the Obama administration's remarkably stubborn lack of faith in its people. The Obama administration seems to think that Americans are not capable of both handling the truth and remaining vigilantly unbiased. Yet the collective American common sense knows the difference between a peaceful Muslim religion and its people and radical jihadists and their soldiers, foreign and domestic. Americans also know a war when they see one.

The United States military oath states, "I do solemnly swear (or affirm) that I will support and defend the Constitution of the United States against all enemies, foreign and *domestic*." The initial oath in 1789 under President George Washington declared that the military was to defend the Constitution as well as to "solemnly swear or affirm (as the case may be) to bear true allegiance to the United States of America, and to serve them honestly and faithfully, against all their enemies or opposers whatsoever…"

We need to remember that our enemies are both foreign and *domestic* and that our president is sworn to protect us "against all [of our] enemies or opposers whatsoever."

An attack on the American people in the name of *jihad* is an attack on America.

America's survival depends on the wisdom and wise decisions that permeated her founding. The new reality is that jihadists are now wrangling Americans to be their soldiers because they believe their American shield to be foolproof—the American citizen jihadist protected by the United States Constitution. Now it is time to define a new criminal and set a constitutional standard to deal with American citizen-terrorists engaged in *jihad*. It is time for the rules of engagement to change.

Janine Turner
May 2, 2013
pjmedia.com

Sound the Alarm: The Little Black Box Is Coming

Never has your voice been more important, and never has your voice mattered more. Your voice is necessary. Your voice is needed—now. Engineers have created a vast array of exciting and pertinent technologies that have revolutionized the way we communicate, work, and play. Yet they have also opened gaping loopholes for tyranny. What's the latest one? The little black box.

On a daily basis, we are discovering the invasions of the federal government into our private lives. They are using the very tools we crave, value, and refuse to relinquish: cell phones, emails, Google searches. The government now listens to what we say, reads our emails, harvests our email contacts, and analyzes our Google search habits. Even retailers target our shopping habits, thrusting delegated ads onto our screen. A dinnertime conversation at a restaurant isn't even safe. With every bite we chew, we are vulnerable to strangers who may be videotaping us.

Our freedom to talk, freedom to socialize, and freedom to communicate via the marvels of these new technological wonders have ironically cast the very net for our own capture. We are, quite simply, being watched, monitored, and analyzed with our own permission. We sign the social media "agreements" because if we don't, we can't have the social media we seek. Does anyone really read the "agreements?" We are blindly forging into mass communications, which allows Big Brother to monitor our behavior and navigate our private lives.

We do this because we still relatively trust our government and because we innately think that we are not the bad guys. However, define "bad." How can we possibly know all of the laws and abide by them, or know if we are breaking them, if we can't understand them? We are being hoodwinked by our own naiveté.

But, be aware. Be warned. There is something coming that marks the diving point of no return. The little black box. Now the greedy government, both at a state and federal level, wants to monitor your car. The government wants to monitor your driving habits, the number of miles you drive, and where you drive. Why? Taxes and control.

This latest tyrannical act, the black box, will be put on your dashboard to count the number of miles you drive so that you may be taxed accordingly. You will no longer be free to drive and travel as you wish without being constantly observed and punished. The more you drive the more you pay. Unbelievable. Frightening. Tyrannical. This little black box will be a window into your privacy, your life, your liberties, your freedoms. If this tax passes through state or federal legislatures, due to a lack of rebellion, then your freedom to travel privately will soon be irreparably impeded and your American way of life finished.

The environmentalists like it, of course, because they want you to drive less. Better pick up a pony then, and install a windmill. Buy a feather pen, ink, and paper, and hire a courier too, because if you want liberty from an oppressive government it will be the only way you can get it. (Every piece of mail that goes through the government post office is photographed, hence the courier.)

These taxes could easily be collected at the gas pump and circumvent the blatant invasion of privacy, but the purveyors of this project prefer the little black box.

To achieve their goal they are going to make it deviously appealing. They are going to add gadgets to the device, such as creating capabilities to monitor traffic speeds in order to alert the driver of congested routes. Buyers beware.

Our only hope is that since it is a visible, tangible object sitting on our dashboard, watching, Americans may balk. Ironically, we have black boxes watching us now monitoring our emails, social media, and Google searches—we just can't see them. Ignorance is not bliss. Knowledge is power. This is what our government knows, and they are depending on our ignorance and apathy.

Invasive and frightening is the little black box that counts miles, tracks movements, and sends data back to Washington, D.C. Even if they say it will not track the locations or send information back to Washington, D.C., the boxes have that capability, and that's the danger. It is time to sound the alarm. It's time to express our voice now because if we don't stand up for our First Amendment rights, who will? Not the government.

Once this gadget gets glued to our dashboard, we will be trapped. It will be the mire of our own making if we don't raise our voices now. Your voice is essential.

Janine Turner
October 29, 2013
pjmedia.com

The Gate Called Beautiful— How Common-Sense Compassion Heals

ACTS 3: 2 *Now a man who has lame from birth was being carried to the temple gate called Beautiful, where he was put every day to beg from those going into the temple courts. 3 When he saw Peter and John about to enter, he asked them for money. 4 Peter looked straight at him, as did John. Then Peter said, "Look at us!" 5 So the man gave them his attention, expecting to get something from them. 6 Then Peter said, "Silver or gold I do not have, but what I do have I give you. In the name of Jesus Christ of Nazareth, walk." 7 Taking him by the right hand, he helped him up, and instantly the man's feet and ankles became strong. 8 He jumped to his feet and began to walk. Then he went with them into the temple courts, walking and jumping, and praising God. 9 When all the people saw him walking and praising God, 10 They recognized him as the same man who used to*

sit begging at the temple gate called Beautiful, and they were filled
with wonder and amazement at what had happened to him.

A lame, dependent man was begging for money. This unfortunate man thought that money was the only answer for his particular plight. Peter and John looked at the vulnerable man. They saw his situation. They asked the troubled man to look at them—to see another way. Peter told him that they had no money to give him but that they had something even better to offer: a healing, a way for him to find his own peace, his own money. The man was willing, and he gave his attention to Peter and John, who, through the power of Christ, healed him. Peter and John provided a way for him to walk on his own two feet. He rose and started jumping and praising God. It was beautiful.

The healing power of God is the obvious message. However, upon reflection, there is both a secular and political application.

Today, under the helm of the Democrats' rudder, historic numbers of people are on food stamps.

According to PolicyMic.com:

> *2013 has seen a surge in the use of food stamps, which are now at*
> *historical records. Currently, a record 47.8 million Americans are en-*
> *rolled in the Supplemental Nutrition Assistance Program (SNAP).*
> *Enrollment in SNAP has increased 70% since 2008 and currently, an*
> *unbelievable 15 out of every 100 Americans are on food stamps.*
>
> *Consequently, the U.S. spent a record $74.6 billion (slightly less than*
> *the combined budgets of the Department of Homeland Security and*
> *the Justice Department) on the SNAP program in 2012 alone. That*
> *expense has more than doubled since the start of the "Great Reces-*
> *sion," increasing $40 billion dollars since 2008 ($34.6 billion).*

There are two political perspectives as to how to handle this problem. The Republicans, the Libertarians, the Constitutionalists want people to have the opportunity, the knowledge, and the tools, to independently seek the gate called Beautiful. They believe this can only be done with a limited government that abides by the enumerated powers in the U.S. Constitution.

The Democrats and liberals want to hand out government money, convincing vulnerable people that dependence on big government is the answer. The trap is set and the weak are caught. The gate called Beautiful shut.

The media, the culture, and the president tell the vulnerable people, and all Americans, that it is not only socially acceptable but a social responsibility to rely on the government. Yet, polls indicate that Americans are angry and unhappy with the government. They are unhappy because this trend in America not only goes against the independent nature of all Americans; it also goes against their moral compass.

Americans do best when they help one another find their way to the gate called Beautiful. Americans are happier when the government stays out of the way. However, the current popular, knee-jerk reaction is for the moral compass to point toward the government as the healer of all society's ills, and those who want big government perpetuate this myth.

In this respect, Americans have lost control of the very charitable, find-our-own-way mentality that is in their DNA. Every turn toward the government is a turn away from liberty. It is a snare, a trap, a prison gate.

The easy money that the Democrats promulgate, with no accountability personally or fiscally, has led to debilitating dependencies, a nation crippled in debt and a people who are just plain unhappy. Vulnerable Americans are paralyzed at the gate that leads to a better life. Always seeing but never attaining.

Democrats believe that easy money equals easy votes, votes that progress their ideology. There is no accountability to the true welfare of the person or to the true welfare of the country. Dependent on the Democrats' dime, they are stifled and become simply a statistic. This is an abuse of power, keeping the vulnerables vulnerable.

It is not coincidence that, during a time when an historic number of people are on government-assisted food stamps, Americans are terribly unsatisfied. In a recent *Washington Post ABC Poll* when asked, "Do you think things in this country are generally going in the right direction or do you feel things have gotten pretty seriously off on the wrong track?" 68 percent said "wrong track." When asked, "Do you approve or disapprove of the way the U.S. Congress is doing its job?" 85 percent disapproved. President Obama has hit an all-time low approval rating at 39 percent in a recent Quinnipiac University Poll.

Thus, urgent is the call for the anti-progressives to rise up, get loud, and be law-abiding, respectful rebels. It is time for politicians and citizens to grab the megaphone and shout out the truth about the ills of government dependency. Knowledge is power and reason is vital. The anti-Democrats need to make their message clear, crisp, loud, and pervasive because those who are perplexed, dependent, unhappy, and angry are only hearing the propaganda machine of the liberal elites.

The vulnerable are taught by these elites that Republicans are cold, heartless, and uncompassionate to those who are suffering monetarily. They are constantly bombarded with deceptive imagery about the Democrats as warm, big-hearted, and compassionate. However, the D in Democrat stands for dependence.

The ones who really care about the vulnerable and their destinies are the ones with commonsense compassion—Republicans, Libertarians, and Constitutionalists. Commonsense compassion calls attention to the ill-fated trap of government money, even if it isn't sexy to the voters.

The only way to walk through that gate is to be independent and to seize the opportunities to learn, to adapt, and to grow through a crisis. Only a government with commonsense compassion can offer this type of hope.

Private charity and free enterprise were a remarkably successful aspect of the American way of life in the post-Revolution early nineteenth century, as noted by Alexis de Tocqueville in *Democracy in America*. He was mesmerized by Americans' lack of desire for government assistance and lack of tolerance for an overbearing government. Their compass pointed to themselves and each other, not the government.

Peter and John had no money to offer the ailing man. They only had healing, a healing that enriched him far beyond what money could do—his ability to provide for himself. If Peter and John had given this lame man money, he would have spent all his remaining days lying by the temple gate called Beautiful begging, putting his sustenance and fate in the hands of others. They decided to give him commonsense compassion. Peter and John lifted him out of his mire by making him self-sufficient, independent—whole. With this new life, he had the dignity to choose his own path. He might succeed or he might fail, but he was free—jubilantly jumping. He had gained his life, his liberty, and his ability to pursue his own happiness, whatever that may be.

Everyone has a low in life at one point or another, and some may need a financial helping hand, but true compassion is instigating and inspiring one to reach their full potential and purpose in life independently. Constitutionalists see the miracle of human dignity in the Declaration of Independence and the preservation of such dignity in the checks and balances of the U.S. Constitution.

Peter and John provided a pathway for the lame man. They blessed him with a miracle—the ability to walk through that gate on his own two feet. This benevolence, this commonsense compassion was beautiful and the promise of a fulfilled life.

Janine Turner
December 2, 2013
pjmedia.com

Legislators Are Digging Their Own Graves and Taking Us Down With Them

The number-one threat to our republic is not the debt, not the entitlements, and not invasion from another country. The number-one threat to our country is lust. It is not a sexual lust. It is a lust for power. Since time began, the lust for power, and its ruthlessness, has ruined liberty, derailed democracy, wrecked republicanism, crippled nations, and killed millions. The paths have been many but the goal singular—lust for power.

Our Founding Fathers knew firsthand how the lust for power corrupted human rights. They knew that, to quote James Madison, "men are not angels." Thus, they created a government of checks and balances that would keep tyranny at bay. According to the Constitution, one branch of government can never usurp the other, and no one branch can be autonomous.

There has been, and is, a faction amongst us that wants to change the fundamental structure of these checks—the progressives. Progressives don't want a multi-tiered, self-checking, and self-limiting government. They wanted an all-powerful, singular nexus of decision-making in the executive branch, free from checks and balances.

American progressives are savvy and cunning. They know that Americans will never willfully accept tyranny or a lustful tyrant. Hence, progressives set forth, over one hundred years ago, to accomplish their goals in an underhanded manner—slowly, steadily, stealthily. Their mission is to eradicate the potency of the U.S Congress, thus eliminating the utterly crucial check on executive power. They accomplish this by diminishing the reputation of the legislative branch and thus crippling its power and effectiveness. Our legislators fell for this in 1912. They are falling for it again, and they are taking the American people with them.

Progressives had astonishing results in 1912 and 1913 with the Seventeenth Amendment. Progressives managed to convince the state legislatures and U.S. senators that they were, themselves, corrupt. They convinced them to vote for their own demise. In the late 1800s, patient and premeditative, progressives had planted a negative public-relations campaign against the Senate to germinate into the nucleus of the culture. With political comments such as "The Senate is corrupt," progressives fanned the flames of destruction.

They manipulated a masterful coup in the Senate, denying states' rights, with a simple message—"The Senate is controlled by special-interest groups." Sound familiar? It was simply stunning. Henceforth, U.S. senators would no longer be appointed by the state legislators but by the people. With this singular, monumental sweep of states rights, the Constitution, which they conveniently believed to be outdated, was thrown off kilter.

Be aware, progressives are not finished. They are enacting the same campaign today. Now instead of the Senate, the entire legislative branch is the problem. "The legislative branch prevents all good from taking place." "The legislative branch is corrupt." "The legislative branch is a bother." "The legislative branch never gets anything done." "The legislative branch is corrupted by special-interest groups." By beating down the legislative branch, the executive branch rises.

What is their goal? Progressives want the legislative branch to be beholden to the executive branch. However, constitutionally, the executive branch is to be beholden to the legislative branch. Only with this process can the people truly be protected. George Washington knew this well. George Washington knew that as general of the Continental Army he was beholden to the Congress. He also knew that as president he was beholden to the Congress. Alexander Hamilton at one point wanted Washington to coerce the Congress to bend to Washington's will. Washington refused, reminding Hamilton that he, as president in the executive branch, was beholden to Congress—the legislative branch, the people's branch.

This is not what permeates the culture today. Most Americans consistently rate Congress much lower than the president. Why? Americans are being brain-washed because they essentially do not understand the United States Constitution, and because legislators are digging their own graves.

Here is the crux. The American people do not understand what their congressmen and women are saying. Simply put, the legislative branch is legislating the American people out of their favor with bills that both they and the American people cannot understand. Legislators need to understand their own bills. The American people need to understand the bills. The American people want to understand. Currently, the president is more appealing and more trusted than Congress because his message is simpler. The president's message, delivered in friendly, fatherly sound bites, is comprehensible to the people. It is clear, concise, and easy to understand. Congress's message—with bills ranging from 1,200 to 2,700 pages—is simply incomprehensible and unfathomable. Consequently, legislators are deemed untrustworthy by the American people.

Legislators in the legislative branch need to act, and they need to act quickly, very, very quickly. They need to pass rules that limit their own largesse in order to prevent progressives' "Legislators are corrupt" campaign from succeeding. They need to save our country by returning the people's house to the people. They have let it be run by lawyers. They have leveled American's trust with legalese.

Legislators need to simplify, simplify, simplify. They can start by reducing the number of pages in their bills and by summarizing their objectives. Comprehensive bills are compromising our republican form of government. The executive branch, the president, is the branch that is most vulnerable to tyranny and corruption. Ironically, the American people are trusting the branch that can enact the most uncensored control over them if left unchecked.

The progressives' plan is working, and legislators in the Legislative Branch are playing right into their hands, just as they did in 1912 with the Seventeenth Amendment. If we lose this last battle, then progressives, in their subtle form of sorcery, will have succeeded in radically changing our government. The American people in turn will be denied the only thing that protects our inherent rights: our limited, checked government.

Our legislators need to introduce and pass the TRUTH ACT. They need to reduce the page numbers of their bills to thirty pages. This was the norm until the past couple of decades. Our legislators need to read and understand the bills they write. The need to convince the American people that they actually know the bills' true intentions and repercussions before they vote on them. They need to read these bills to the American people and have the bills available to the public in many forums. Legislators need to give the American people the respect they deserve by letting them have due time to explore the bills before the vote takes place. In short, legislators need to return the people's branch to the people.

As Thomas Jefferson stated, "A great number of laws had been cast violating, without any apparent necessity, the rule requiring that all bills of a public nature shall be previously printed for the consideration of the people; although this one of the precautions chiefly relied on by the constitution against improper acts of legislature."

It is absolutely imperative that to maintain our democratic Republic the American people turn their trust and attention first and foremost back to the legislative branch and understand that it is *their* branch. It is time for legislators to earn this trust, and quickly, or they will be reduced to irrelevancy and take the American people with them, all of which will culminate with the demise of our experiment in self-government. We will be leaving our children in the hands of a lustful, tyrannical form of government that will focus all power to one executive, or one man, and their liberty and inherent rights will be forever lost.

The writing is on the wall. The pages of history tell the tale. Let us pay heed.

Janine Turner
April 18, 2014
pjmedia.com

The TRUTH Act

The TRUTH Act—it's time to ACT for TRUTH

It is time to reclaim our legislative branch of government. It is our branch. We need it. It represents *us*. It protects us from tyranny. It protects us from the usurpations of the executive branch. It protects us from the tyranny of big government. Well, it is *supposed* to protect us from the tyranny of big government.

Across the air and television waves, politicians and pundits complain and explain—in vain—the issues of the day that are crumbling our Republic. They are constantly deviating from the real problem. It's as if no one sees the real issue.

Government is too big because the bills are too big. Government is incomprehensible because the bills are incomprehensible. Government is out of control because our representatives don't know what's in their own bills.

Why do they not know what's in their own bills? It is not because they *do not* read them; it is because they *cannot* read them. Our own legislators cannot understand what's in the very bills they are orchestrating because the bills are written by lawyers. Consequentially, lawyers, or our representatives' aides, are having to interpret for our representatives their very own bills. This is not only a sad state of affairs, it is a dangerous state of affairs.

The state of affairs in our legislative branch is leaving us vulnerable to the enemy that is in the field. Thus it is of no avail for us to elect men of our own choice. Our Republic is quickly becoming a sham. The answer is not to dissolve or disregard the legislative branch. We need it. Our democratic Republic depends upon it. Without our legislative branch we are left with an executive branch that will quickly rear its ugly head, and, like a fire-breathing dragon, torch our liberties.

It is time for us to stand up and take action regarding our legislative branch, not disparage it. We need to save it! It is time for us to demand truth. It is time for my TRUTH ACT.

I met with many representatives on the hill regarding my TRUTH ACT, and to my surprise, many of our representatives agreed with the sad state of affairs. Many of them explained to me how incomprehensible the bills truly are, adding that when these bills are amended, they become even more innocuous because the amendments are not notated. Our representatives, many of them, welcome the TRUTH ACT.

It can be done, and it has been done for the majority of our Republic. Only recently, because "we the people" have not been vigilant, have bills become so out of hand. Chairman McCaul (R-TX) recently achieved this with H.R. 1417, Border Security Results Act of 2013, which was twenty-six pages long.

To address this crisis in our government both on the state and federal level, we need to curb the voluminous and incomprehensible bills with my TRUTH ACT.

T   —Limit the pages of the bills to single subjects and Thirty pages.

R   —Our representatives must Read the bill. Bills should be written and summarized in a manner so that our representatives and the majority of the American people can read them.

U   —Our representatives must be able to Understand the bills before they vote on them. This can be achieved for them and the American people by writing bills that are simple, limited to one subject, with legal codes accessible in the margins, and with amendments both highlighted and duly noted.

T   —Our representatives must Testify under oath that they have read and understand the bills before they vote on them.

H   —The American people must be able to read the bills and Hear the bills, which are to be read online, at least thirty days before the vote takes place, in order that the people may have ample time to respond.

To join the mission please, visit my website at www.janineturner.com and sign the petition. "We the people" will prevail, and our republic will survive, but only if we are not complacent. We will survive if we take action. It is time to ACT for TRUTH.

James Madison said in Federalist 62,

> *It will be of little avail to the people, that laws are made by men of their own choice, if the laws be so voluminous that they cannot be read, or so incoherent that they can not be understood; if they be repealed or revised before they are promulgated, or undergo such incessant changes that no man, who knows what the law is to-day, can guess what it will be to-morrow. Law is defined to be a rule of action; but how can that be a rule, which is little know, and less fixed?*

Janine Turner
April 3, 2012
janineturner.com

Chapter Four

The Manipulation and Mission of Women in Politics

These are the times in which a genius would wish to live. It is not in the still calm of life, or the repose of a pacific station, that great characters are formed. The habits of a vigorous mind are formed in contending with difficulties. Great necessities call out great virtues. When a mind is raised, and animated by scenes that engage the heart, then those qualities, which would otherwise lay dormant, wake into life and form the character of the hero and the statesman.

—Abigail Adams

Preface

Herein lies the conundrum. Conservatives who are pro-life seek to show pregnant women the ultrasound of the babies, prodding them to keep the God-given miracle of life, but they do nothing to combat a public-relations campaign that condemns the single mothers of these children as godless and immoral for making this choice. They cradle the mother until she cradles the child, and then they let her walk into the world, where she has to hear the bullet fire of grim statistics and sure-fire damnation shouted from none other than conservatives, the same conservatives who told her to keep the child.

—Janine Turner

Women are still sex symbols to the Democratic Party. So much for burning the bras. No "I am woman, hear me roar" from the Democrats' camp. It is sex and reproduction, sex and reproduction. Sex is the sexist target of the Democrats.

—Janine Turner

Women are currently perched upon a precipice of paramount importance in both our culture and our country. At no other time has the woman's influence and vote been more vital to the survival of a republican form of government. Consequentially, massive manipulation attempts, and successes, are being waged on the woman's psyche. Without an education about the bigger impact of our vote and voice, the future of our Republic is in dire straits.

Women, of all people, have a masterful sense of intuition. We, and our daughters, need to be able to read behind the words, see behind the curtain, and think beyond political, force-fed falsities. Women have been striving for years to be independent. Why then are so many of us depending on the government or insisting our sisters be dependent upon the government? Let us educate one another and not be mired in political naïveté.

Some of my select opinion editorials included in this chapter deal with the needs of women, the branding of women, the crisis in the Republican party regarding women, and how to talk to a woman who, in the political realm, has a differing political perspective, even sometimes a forceful and unyielding one.

Barack Obama: President of Replicants

President Barack Obama lives in a pretend world. He sees things through the eye of a kaleidoscope, and all of the pretty pieces of glass are his "composites." He peers through his illusionary tool at his "composite people" and plays with the frailties of life. As the shattered flecks, or figures, morph into his fantasies, he envisions his life, the lives of others, and the governing of the American people as shapes and variations that mirror his own private, pervasive, and presidential ideals—regardless of reality or reason, or if it's best for Americans or America.

It is Obama's world. Who is the real Barack Obama? Not only is Barack Obama a mystery, but so is the basis of his governing. Currently, he is proposing to the American women, whose votes he desperately needs to win, the he will govern them on the basis of his composite woman "Julia." Life will be like the glasses of his kaleidoscope, beautiful and transfixed. Vote for Obama and your life will be like Julia's.

Perfection works in the realm of make-believe. If you are a Replicant, as in the movie *Blade Runner*, or an imaginary "Julia," you can be blessed by Obama's world. Replicants and Julias are blank sheets of paper on which Obama can write his manifesto.

In reality, however, women have feelings, spirits, complexities, and inborn American yearnings for self-determination. Turning women into cookie-cutter images doesn't work any better now than it did in the days when communism in the USSR attempted to homogenize the human soul and mind. Communism leads to tragedy and demise, cruelty and bitterness, as recently reflected in the cries from Chinese-rights activist Chen Guangcheng for asylum in America.

Obama paints an ideal world where the "wealth is spread around," the taxpayers foot Julia's bill, and the end goal for women is to volunteer in the community garden. The "Julia" manifesto presents picture-perfect scenarios. There is no mention that Julia spends her life dependent on the government.

> *Under President Obama: Julia is enrolled in a Head Start program to help get her ready for school. Because of steps president Obama has taken to improve programs like this one, Julia joins thousands of students across the country who will start kindergarten ready to learn and succeed.*

There is no mention that some tenured teachers are contributing to the demise of the American education system. There is no mention that Obama will *never* stand up to the unions.

> *Under President Obama: for the past four years, Julia has worked full-time as a web designer. Thanks to Obamacare, her health insurance is required to cover birth control and preventive care, letting Julia focus on her own work rather than worry about her health.*

There is no mention that birth control costs about $10.00 a month. There is no mention that it is not the responsibility of the taxpayers to pay for Julia's birth control.

> *Under President Obama: As she prepares for her first semester of college, Julia and her family qualify for President Obama's American Tax Credit, worth up to $10,000 over four years. Julia is also one of millions of students who receive a Pell Grant to help put a college education within reach.*

There is no mention of the national debt, because Obama wants us to believe that there is a pot of gold at the end of his Obamabow. There is no mention that the debt clock runs up so quickly you can't even write it down fast enough. The number as of this writing is almost 16 trillion: $15,705,864,699,709.00.

> *Under President Obama: Julia enrolls in Medicare, helping her to afford preventive care and the prescription drugs she needs.*

There is no mention that Medicare is essentially bankrupt. There is no mention of an Obama reconstruction plan to save Medicare. There is no mention that Obamacare actually robs Medicare to help pay for the overbearing, insurmountable health-care overhaul. There is no mention that the U.S. total debt is $57,451,655,210,000.00.

In Obama's world, women blissfully volunteer in a community garden at the end of their life. Note that the garden is not their *own* garden.

Women should be smarter than this. Women are smarter than this. Ironically, the women of the Democratic Party are allowing themselves to be patronized and dependent all over again. Deep in their hearts, women know that they are not "Julia" Barbie Dolls. Women are living, breathing human beings who have minds, unique determinations, and quests for independence.

The real Obama may not reveal himself, but the real women's voice should. Women should balk at being forced into an Obama mold. Not all women aspire to culminating their life and legacy in the community garden. First it was the kitchen, now it is the garden.

The Democrat Party is the women's party? Think again. It was the Republican majority that presented and ratified the Nineteenth Amendment. It is the Republican Party that recognizes, propels, and propagates women's independence.

Obama wants women who are reliant replicants, not self-sufficient women who reason.

Janine Turner
May 9th, 2012
pjmedia.com

Pro-Life in the Womb But Not Pro-Life in the World

During this election year, when it is imperative that conservatives garner every vote from Obama, it seems prudent to step back and assess the mixed message conservatives serve to women in the media.

Conservatives struggle with ideals of limited government, moral rectitude, and pro-life missions. They want both sides of the argument to be their victory, but it cannot be. There is a dichotomy in the works—a clash of ideals.

Even though statistics prove that social issues win elections for conservatives, the party of "father knows best" still needs to bridge the gender gap to win [in 2012]. This is proving to be complex. The pressing issues are the pro-life stance and the single-mother taboo.

How can one simultaneously be pro-life and support the single mother while appeasing the principles of the Republican Party? Single mothers, after all, are touted as irresponsible drags on society, both morally and financially.

Herein lies the conundrum. Conservatives who are pro-life seek to show pregnant women the ultrasound of the babies, prodding them to keep the God-given miracle of life, but they do nothing to combat a public-relations campaign that condemns the single mothers of these children as godless and immoral for making this choice.

They cradle the mother until she cradles the child, and then they let her walk into the world, where she has to hear the bullet fire of grim statistics and sure-fire damnation shouted from none other than conservatives, the same conservatives who told her to keep the child.

This blatant disregard for the life of the woman who chooses life, and for the life of her child, is duplicitous. Do conservatives not see that they are sending less brave pregnant women and terrified pregnant girls straight to Planned Parenthood for an abortion?

Conservative doublespeak in the media regarding the pro-life stance sends women running to the less judgmental Democratic Party. This begs the question, where are the pro-life men and women in the media who should be defending the brave single mothers who choose life?

Though many conservatives work behind the scenes to support these single mothers, in front of the camera they close up like clams.

This is why so many women choose abortion. They are afraid of the stigma. They hear conservative men and women spouting off statistics about how their children will be strippers, drug addicts, or become incarcerated, and how they, the single mothers who birthed the children, are disdained by society.

Conservative candidates do occasionally pander to the single mother by calling her heroic, but in the next breath they spout words like "child out of wedlock" and "illegitimate" and speak only of the woes the world has to offer her and her child. They insinuate her immorality as part of "deviant modern times."

Not every pregnant woman is simply looking for a handout. Not every single mother wants to live off of the government. Not every single mother is immoral and ignorant. Not every single mother seeks a life without the father. Not every single mother is faithless.

Speaking of the father, where is he? He is held relatively blameless by the press. He lives blithely carefree and unscathed.

Are conservatives considering the political ramifications, if not the moral ones? Their message in the media can be summed up as this: "I am pro-life. Abortion is a sin, yet woe to the single mother and her child. She is a modern, immoral matriarch, and her child's life is doomed."

This is the paradox presented to the conservative movement. Morally, how does one support the child yet alienate the mother who supports the child? How does one who cares for life set that life up to fail from the very beginning?

Politically the conservative movement cannot win the women's vote with a message such as this.

For those who are pro-life, the message of hope and emotional support should not stop within the private walls of the shelter. The burden is on the pregnant woman who has to walk out into the world and hold her head high. The burden is on the child, destined by God to be here, who has to prove his/her condemners wrong.

Like Jesus's message of love, a language of compassion does not endorse alternative lifestyles. An act of public support simply blesses the "life"—the child conservatives sought to protect and his or her mother—with an act of inspiration and hope.

To win elections and to win with life, the pro-life conservatives in the press shouldn't consistently drop the single mother and her child into a pronounced destiny of despair and ill repute, no matter what the statistics.

If they continue to condemn, then they are pro-life in the womb but not pro-life in the world.

Janine Turner
February 22, 2012
janineturner.com

Will Women Sacrifice Our Republic for Sex?

As the polls continue to reflect, female voters have significant sway in the election process and in election results. Women proved to be the final contributing factor in Terry McAuliffe's victory as the new governor of Virginia Tuesday night. The margin was incredibly slim, yet it was women who carried the day for McAuliffe and for the Democrats' agenda—an agenda that ironically handcuffs women and the women's movement. The Democrats' promise of independence for women is an empty promise.

As we approach two pivotal elections in 2014 and 2016, it is rather vital for the survival of our democratic Republic that women pay heed to the fact that not all forms of independence stem from the womb. This womb-jerk reaction in the voting booth is a response upon which the Democrats rely. They hold the baby rattle over women's heads to distract them from the true intention of the party: dependence. This is a deception dripping in irony because women have fought for centuries for independence of mind and spirit.

Democrats are ignoring women as a complete soul—one of intellect, courage, talent, and leadership—and focusing on the age-old tradition of treating women as sexual objects.

Haven't we been trying to prove for centuries that we are more than our bodies? Yet this is the sole focus of the Democrats' campaign for women—because it's the only one they have.

Women are still sex symbols to the Democratic Party. So much for burning the bras. No "I am woman, hear me roar" from the Democrats' camp. It is sex and reproduction, sex and reproduction. Sex is the sexist target of the Democrats.

Amazingly, women fall for these antics. Like a blind man on a tightrope, women who vote for Democrats fall prey to the seduction of voting solely for sexual independence.

Yet independence is varied and complex, and to the complete woman it reaches beyond—way beyond—sex.

What good is sexual freedom if all other freedoms are sacrificed in the process?

There are many battles for freedom that women should be fighting. Battles that have huge implications not only for themselves, but also for their families and their country.

Who offers freedom from unemployment for themselves, their husbands, and their children? Not the Democrats. They want socialism, which crushes the economy and free enterprise.

Who offers freedom from crushing federal regulation that keep women from opening their own businesses and being their own bosses? Not the Democrats. They want big government and over-reaching control, which make start-up businesses almost obsolete, especially for women.

Who offers freedom from federally mandated school curricula that prevent kids from reaching their full potential? Not the Democrats. They are against school choice and charter schools, and they oppose state sovereignty.

Who offers freedom from the Obamacare fiasco, which will ruin the best healthcare system in the world? Not the Democrats. Obamacare prevents women and their families from using their doctors of choice, at the time of their choice, with the plan of their choice.

Who offers freedom from the exorbitant national debt? Not the Democrats. They are in constant denial of the impending fiscal collapse, and they refuse to deal with it.

Who offers freedom from high gas and electric prices? Not the Democrats. They want to shut down America's natural resources, forcing us to rely on foreign countries and jeopardizing Americans' safety and financial solvency.

Who offers freedom from entitlements and crippling dependency, which are especially high among women? Not the Democrats. They want apathy because dependence is their sustenance.

Who offers freedom from an unaccountable federal government? Not the Democrats. They believe the Constitution, which limits power, is irrelevant.

Who offers freedom from tyranny? Not the Democrats. They crave a bloated government that is secretive and coercive. It is tyranny, and it is the demise of a republican form of government. Only a constitutional republic and a small limited government protect Americans' inalienable rights.

Freedom.

Women's sole focus on the womb and perpetual denial of the necessities of other pertinent freedoms will be the cause of our Republic's demise and America's implosion. When this happens, women will lose not only their social rights but their First Amendment rights, and when they pull themselves up from the collapse of their country, they will suddenly realize that it was the Democrats who returned women to square one—silenced, imprisoned, impoverished.

Janine Turner
November 7, 2013
pjmedia.com

Stop Singling out the Mother

Democrats are masters at public relations. This is one of the areas where Republicans falter. Democrats are masters at re-inventing the message. This is one of the areas where Republicans falter. Democrats are masters of imaging themselves as loving, helpful parents. This is one of the areas where Republicans falter (the Republican's image is one of angry, judgmental parents). Democrats are masters at making villains out of Republicans. This is one of the areas where Republicans falter—Republicans make villains out of Republicans.

The time has come for Republicans to join the street fight, challenge the bully Democrats, and win. How? Republicans need to step back, analyze their image, challenge their messaging, and get into fighting form.

One place to start is with single mothers. No matter what the statistics, no matter what the number, the constant barrage of attacks on the single mother as a culprit of America's demise is lethal, especially in an upcoming duel with Hillary Clinton. How do Republicans triumphantly deal with this issue in the arena with Hillary Clinton? They need to master the re-imaging of their single-mother messaging.

Instead of singling out single mothers, they need to put the emphasis where it really belongs—single *parents*. It takes two to tango. For every single mother, there is a single father. There are single parents.

As a single mother and a Republican, I deal with this barrage of constant negative messaging. Here's the bottom line: Republicans will not win, politically or socially, with this mean-spirited, biased message, and it is certainly not helping the single mother or her child. Republicans need to stop living in the problem and start living in the solution. One way to do this is to watch the verbiage and the unfair, stereotypical attack on single mothers—the single mothers who are actually raising their children.

Instead, Republicans need to actively acknowledge that for every single mother there is a single father. Republicans need to bring single fathers onto the playing field. For many single mothers, especially those who are actually taking care of their child, there are many single fathers not only missing in action, *but being held to zero accountability by Republicans and the Republican party.* This reeks of chauvinism—a chauvinism I don't believe exists in the Republican Party, but the current message is chauvinistic. Where is the focus on single fathers?

There cannot be a single mother without a single father. Single parents.

Not only should the wording be addressed but, along with it, the thought process. Republicans need to thoroughly think through the following: a) if one is pro-life, if the GOP is the party of pro-life, then it shouldn't be attacking the mother who *chose life, to have the baby;* b) the judgment heaped upon single mothers is making pregnant women run to the abortion clinic. Even religious, pro-life families send their daughters to abortion clinics to avoid slanderous attacks. This is a tragic irony and one that needs to be addressed by the pro-lifers, Republicans, and the Republican Party.

Where is the compassion?

Hillary will have heaps of it in 2016.

Yes, there needs to be an action taken to bring awareness to the intrinsic value of healthy families that include both parents, but these actions need to be taken with compassion.

Yes, many children who are being raised by single mothers are in dire straits. Yet they are not all just poor welfare types in dire straits. There are many unique situations that encompass all communities, all religions, all demographics—the rich, the poor, and the in-between.

Yes, there needs to be a way to worship God, the God of the student's choice, within the school walls.

Yes, there needs to be a moral compass within the communities—all communities, all demographics—one of which should be to help the fathers learn to be accountable.

Yes, there needs to be an aggressive campaign in the culture. The culture needs to be infused with works that represent love, forgiveness, acceptance, and values that lead to a safer, better, healthier, more successful way of life.

As an actress, I think this can be done with a wide spectrum, not a narrow one. As an example, these qualities can be found in movies like *Juno* and *The Christmas Candle*. The messages of love, compassion, overcoming trials and tribulations, and dealing with doubts and fears come in many different types of passion plays.

The bottom line—for the sake of single mothers, their children, and the fate of the Republican Party—is that the publicity campaign, the imaging, the wording, the messaging, and the true intent need to shift focus from single mothers to single fathers to single parents.

Stop the blame game. Stop attacking women, or giving the perception of attacking women.

The issue at hand includes two people—parents. Stop singling out the mother.

Janine Turner
October 23, 2013
pjmedia.com

Dialogue with My Mother, Janice Agee Gauntt

Your father, you know, was in strategic air command and he had to go to work every other week and stay near the runway to be ready to jump in his plane and go if he needed to. And then every other month, he spent a month overseas somewhere. He had traded with someone to be on alert for him so he could be there for you when you were born. But that replacement fell in that first snowfall and broke his leg and your father had to go on duty after all. But he was there the moment you were born. That was something, because the first time, when your brother was born, he was not there. That's the Air Force for you, you know.

—Janice Agee Gauntt

My mother. My mother is my mentor and my best friend. My mother is one of those mothers that is there for you whenever you need her, at any moment. My mother is devoted, full of love, and can illuminate the room with her presence and laughter. My mom, though she denies it, is of pioneer stock. Don't mess with mama bear. For my 51st birthday, my mother called me on my radio show and we reminisced down memory lane. It was a moment to treasure. Family is still the lifeblood of existence literally, emotionally, and figuratively.

Janine: That'll get your feet tapping. There you go. That's good music for my mom. That music's got a good vibe, very energetic. Oh, so it's a birthday song. That's funny. It's talking about birthday. Mom—my mother is our special guest today. Janice Gauntt—Janice Agee Gauntt, my mom. Mom, welcome to *The Janine Turner Show*.

Janice: Well, thank you, and happy birthday to you.

Janine: Well, thank you, Mom. You know, it was funny because Edie, my friend Edie Waterhouse—I was talking about this in our earlier segment—told me when it was Juliette's birthday, "Well, tell Juliette 'happy birthday,' but it's your birthday too, because you birthed her." And then, that same day, her birthday, I popped into an AT&T store because I had to get something and I felt really guilty getting it because it's my daughter's birthday. The woman who was helping me said, "Honey, you birthed her. It is your birthday, too." So Mom, it's your birthday too, because you birthed me.

Janice: Well, you were born on the first snowfall in Lincoln, Nebraska—

Janine: Yeah.

Janice: It was such a moment, but you know what? I was thinking about your birthday, and you've had birthdays all over the world. You've had them in many, many states. New York, California, Seattle, Texas, Arkansas, Florida, even China, so it's nice it's in Texas this year.

Janine: My favorite is to have my birthday in Texas. You know, Juliette's birthday is such a big deal, so by the time we roll around to mine, when people ask "So what do you want to do?" I used to answer "I want to eat pizza," but now, I can't because I can't do gluten or anything. We used to have a lot of birthdays where we just sat around in our PJs with comfy socks and had pizza. That's a pretty good birthday, actually. A lot of fun for me.

Janice: That's one time, but like I said, you had the one in China and also, when you were in middle school, we had a come-in-your-pajamas birthday party and we awakened you when the guest arrived. That was fun.

Janine: You did. And I was in my curlers. I was in my pink curlers, as I recall. You always did great birthday parties. Mom made little tiny quiches, Mom, a home-economics major from Trinity University in San Antonio, a beauty queen. How many pageants did you win, Mom?

Janice: Oh, I don't know, thirteen or sixteen. It doesn't matter anymore.

Janine: Thirteen or sixteen (laughs).

Janice: What a way.

Janine: Of course, it matters. And you were in the top ten of all female students in college—tell me that again.

Janice: It wasn't in America, but this is your birthday. We're talking about you.

Janine: Okay, but I like bragging about you. You birthed me. Anyway, Mom made these little tiny quiches, I remember. Little tiny mini-muffin quiches for that birthday. And Mom would always make—Mother, do you remember? She would always make these doll cakes where you take a Barbie doll and make a cake for me. Those were so much fun.

Janice: Well, it's kind of an American tradition with a Barbie doll. (Laughs)

Janine: Yeah.

Janice: And the cake is just, you know, embellishment on that, but you know, a birthday is special and it needs to be joyfully received every year that you're lucky enough to have one. And people who think birthdays aren't worth celebrating are just wrong, in my opinion. It was all the celebration you could do. And one thing about you, I was thinking about it, is that it gets better as each year goes by and you are able to reinvent yourself every year that you seek more challenges and more opportunities. You were born beautiful, but it appears you were also born smart.

Janine: (Laughs) I get it all from you, Mom. And I certainly get that industrious quality, that business sense from you. My mom—I'll tell you what, my mom is an Energizer Bunny. Even Dad admitted to that. We were sitting somewhere, I remember I was young, and this person asked Dad "where did she learn to do this?" I was probably sixteen or seventeen, you know, out there just banging on the doors trying to get work. And Dad looked at this person and said, "from her mom." (Laughs) "Her mom is a businesswoman—her mom's a go-getter business person."

Janice: Well, you know, it's ingrained in you to do your best and go for it. So—

Janine: It's that pioneer spirit. It's that pioneer spirit.

Janice: Well, I recommend to live life to the fullest and go for the goal, or go for the prize, or go for the zest. That would what I would say, go for the zest.

Janine: Well, you've always worked really hard, Mom. You were plucked out of Trinity University to marry Dad, who arrived at your door all handsome in his West Point military uniform. But you reinvented yourself. You served our country because Dad was in the Air Force. How many times did you move in one year, Mom?

Janice: We moved thirteen times in eight years—

Janine: Thirteen times in eight years.

Janice: —in the Air Force. Mm-hmm.

Janine: Right, and you talked how you made all the curtains, didn't you, when you arrived in all these new places on Air Force bases?

Janice: Oh, yes, we made them like home. And you know, that's what people need to do, whether it's your home or somebody else's, while you're there it's yours and you need to make it as pretty and as comfortable as you can. Whether it belongs to someone else or not. While you're there, it's yours. And you were born on Morningside Drive in a little blue house, and in the fall we had peonies clear across the backyard that were exquisite. That's one of the things I remember about Nebraska and where you were born, is the peonies. They're a Memorial Day flower, so I try to send you those when they're in season, which they're not all year. You remember peonies.

Janine: Well, I do and they're a type Memorial Day flower, which is always around my second birthday, when I got sober. So that's when you usually sent them to me, isn't it?

Janice: That's right.

Janine: Well, you were also in Garden Club. I remember Garden Club. I remember going to all the Garden Club events with you, and you had to arrange the flowers, but then you decided to enter real estate. Dad encouraged you. He had a Red Carpet Realty franchise that he had purchased. So how old was I, like fifth, fourth grade?

Janice: You were in second grade.

Janine: Second grade. And then, Mom, you started selling real estate and of course became a powerhouse in real estate, and gosh, I still think you should write a book about your stories. Recently, Juliette and I were talking about my carpet at the ranch on the stairs that I really want to get it replaced 'cause it's just a mess right now. And as I'm walking out the door, I looked at Juliette and said, "my memory of early childhood is my mother being on the telephone, which was attached to the wall, which did not have voicemail or call waiting, and she'd be saying, 'Oh, it's a wonderful little house. It has wall-to-wall carpeting.'" I must have heard wall-to-wall carpeting a thousand times. That FHA loans, or whatever they are—are they FHA loans?

Janice: Well, FHA is one kind, yes.

Janine: Yeah, I remember hearing that on the phone, but wall-to-wall carpeting, I remember hearing that.

Janice: Well, now, everybody wants hardwood floors, so it goes in cycles, you know.

Janine: It does, but you've become the star realtor over the years, Mom. I'm so proud of you. And thanks for birthing me. Of course, in those days you really didn't get to enjoy the experience, they just knocked you out, right?

Janice: Well, you were there when I came out of it. (Laughs) And your father, you know, was in strategic air command and he had to go to work every other week and stay near the runway to be ready to jump in his plane and go if he needed to. And then every other month, he spent a month overseas somewhere. He had traded with someone to be on alert for him so he could be there for you when you were born. But that replacement fell in that first snowfall and broke his leg and your father had to go on duty after all. But he was there the moment you were born. That was something, because the first time, when your brother was born, he was not there. That's the Air Force for you, you know.

Janine: Yeah, so true. So true, that's so true. So many women are serving in the Armed Forces today, too, and leaving their kids as well, so it's such a sacrifice. People who serve in the Armed Forces and the families that are there for the journey are real heroes, I thank them for what they do. But yeah, I was born on the first snowfall. Recently, we were on our 6,200-mile road trip across America for Constituting America, my foundation that I started with Cathy Gillespie. There are so many people who bring Constituting America to life. Mom, you're on the Board. And Maureen is now with Constituting America as well. But we drove through Nebraska on our road trip. We went out of our way to go find that Morningside Drive, and there was the house, Mom. And wasn't it blue? Because see, I loved the color blue in that blue barn when we lived in the blue barn in Euless. Now my barn at the ranch and my roof at the ranch is blue. But Morningside Drive, wasn't that house blue?

Janice: Yes, it was blue. It had more frame up there whereas we have a lot of brick and stucco in Texas, but in the east and the Midwest, they have a lot of frame. You know, you build what surrounds you.

Janine: And it was blue, blue frame, I think, yeah.

Janice: Mm-hmm, it's blue.

Janine: Yeah, we had to go find the house. Well, Mom, and we've got Maureen on, so before I close, here's Maureen, my best friend of twenty-seven years.

Maureen and Mom and I have done a lot of fun things together. Maureen, do you remember when we drove the little red corvette to Florida—to Destin, Florida—and we met Mom there and we rented that house—

Maureen: Oh my goodness. And, hi Janice.

Janice: Hi.

Janine: We rented the house for what—a week or something? I just remember we would watch movies. What movies were we watching? The movies with Judy Dench and all. Do you remember, Mom, the name of the movies we would watch? Some—

Janice: No, I don't.

Janine: Oh it was—

Maureen: I do remember we were all so relaxed. We would walk around that huge house and just go back out in the sun and I remember your mom, 'cause she made the best sandwich I think I have ever had.

Janine: Sandwiches are always better when your mom makes them, I find. And I—

Maureen: It was the best. It was with alfalfa sprouts—

Janine: Oh wow.

Maureen: —and wheat toast and you put it in the oven, and I remember we took it to the beach and it was hot initially. You toasted it perfectly. I just couldn't get over this sandwich. You're a great cook.

Janine: Oh yeah. I just remember we're—

Janice: Thank you.

Maureen: It's the simple things that I remember. We were walking around and we all finally looked at each other and said, why do I feel like we're in *Remains of the Day*?

Janice: Well, yes.

Maureen: We were so mellow.

Janine: Oh, yes. Yes, yes, yes. And I just remember we were all sitting around and my mom said, "Maintenance," 'cause we needed maintenance. "Maintenance!"

Maureen: Right, I love it.

Janine: Well, Maureen, I've got to hop off and—and, so Mom, I just want to thank you. I had to bring Maureen in because she's been such a big part of our lives for twenty-seven years. It's over half my life, but Mom, thank you for bringing me into this world.

Janice: Well, it was my distinct pleasure. My distinct pleasure and just keep celebrating life and reinventing yourself every year as you continue to do and living life to the fullest.

Janine: Well, I have to tell you something, my mom's a Taurus, so she's Taurus the bull. She's very, very determined, but Mom, you have always been there for me, no matter what time of day; no matter what's going on; no matter where I am in the country, you are always there and you'll come and you'll do whatever—you are the most amazing mom ever, so thank you on this day of my birth. I believe too that we pick our parents, so I picked you and Dad. Did you know that?

Janice: Well, I was waiting (laughs).

Janine: I believe Juliette picked me, too. I really believe in that. And Juliette would always talk when she was a baby saying, "I miss God" and "I want to go back and see God again." On 9/11 she said, "Mom are we going to see the face of God today?

I believe we are in heaven and we looked down and we'd have a little chat with God and He'd ask, "Are you up for this?" I'd say, "I want to go be with them." And He said, "Okay." So there you go, so I picked you, Mom.

Janice: Well, thank you, and I'm glad to have you. (Laughs).

Maureen: And Janice, real quick, I want to thank you for bringing Janine into the world and we love you, love you, love you. Celebrate, celebrate.

Janine: Well, happy birthday to you too, Mom. (Laughs).

Janice: Well, happy birthday to you and many more.

Janine: All right, many more. Love you. Thanks for coming on the show.

Janice: Bye-bye.

Janine: Bye, love you. (Kiss). Okay, so we're going to be back with the closing inspirational segment on *The Janine Turner Show*.

The Janine Turner Show
December 6, 2013

Chapter Five

Contending with and Countering the Culture

The moment you give up your principles, and your values, you are dead, your culture is dead, your civilization is dead. Period.

—Oriana Fallaci

Preface

Hollywood is a surreal and pretend world whose way of life is actually ruthless free enterprise—it is called show business, after all. Hollywood is where stars, movie producers, writers, and agents actively seek glamour, money, power, and fame; where they covet fast cars and face-lifts and fly in private jets. They drink fine wines and insist on free spirits. They are the ultimate connoisseurs who insist on living liberty at large. Somehow, the inhabitants gag at the very thought of capitalism going on elsewhere.

—Janine Turner

Other such over-achiever kids were George Washington, John Adams, Thomas Jefferson, Abraham Lincoln, and Martin Luther King, Jr. Today, they would be considered "Super People." Today, they would be muted and shamed for their desire to speak their thoughts, acknowledge their God, seek seemingly attainable goals, and, God-forbid, win. Today, they would be labeled Mama's boys, demeaned as privileged, constrained as prejudiced, or taunted as eggheads. Yet just imagine America without them. Without them, there would be no America.

—Janine Turner

The culture. The culture. The culture. Powerful. Persuasive. Perpetual. The culture reigns today as the primary source of our teaching and, even more dangerously, of our children. The big question—who is teacher?

Like a silver foil screen that's fiery hot from the absorbed sun, we are absorbing the dictates of the culture, and it's frying our brains. It moves at lightning speed and destroys in a flash. How will America and her children survive the wizards who are pulling the strings of America's cultural outlet?

Mass media has become our moral compass, our primary coping skill, and our chosen form of communication with one another. This alters reality, negates personal one-on-one human relations, and stifles emotional compassion.

Our culture is our modern-day form of pagan worship. How do we deal with today's scientific marvels, yet maintain the integrity of the human spirit? These are just some of the issues I address in this chapter, along with Hollywood, virtue, faith, success, race, and Madison Avenue.

Success—A Social Crime

Success has become taboo. Leadership has become unfair. Reason has become politically incorrect, and money has become malevolent.

Monochromatic is the theme. Mute is the desire. Mundane is the mission, and control is the goal.

Where do we live? America?

In a recent *New York Times* article, James Atlas ridicules the "Super People." The students who have worked hard and achieved much are taunted in his article. According to Mr. Atlas, the "Super People" are only successful because of frustrated helicopter moms or because they stretch the truth on their applications. "Super People" are super weird. The "Super People" made great grades, excelled in sports and/or music, and contributed to country and society with social service. Losers. Oh, and they only succeeded because their mother made them do it, or they were rich—the 1 percent.

Where do we live? America?

We are a country that was built on true grit, hard work, and a desire to soar on eagle's wings. Invigorated by freedom and free from the chains of tyranny, immigrants were inspired to reach for the sky and seek success. They labored and toiled, passionately pursuing their dreams. Liberty was a gift from God. Talent was admired. Success was revered. Public service was not only a virtue but inherent.

Children from broken homes, poverty, and despair had the opportunity to reach and seek higher ground. Our history is filled with examples of young students who studied meticulously, read voraciously, and worked many jobs at the same time. Exertion and perseverance were synonymous with American pride and dignity.

Candice Millard brings to life a stunning example of such attributes in her biography of the often-forgotten president James A. Garfield. He was born in a log cabin and fatherless by the age of one. He worked many jobs to put himself through school. At preparatory school, he studied so diligently he was promoted from janitor to assistant professor. At age twenty-six, he later returned to be the school's president and passed the Ohio bar in his free time. His adult life mirrored his youth with ardent service to his country and countrymen in combat, Congress, and as president.

Other such over-achiever kids were George Washington, John Adams, Thomas Jefferson, Abraham Lincoln, and Martin Luther King. Today, they would be considered "Super People." Today, they would be muted and shamed for their desire to speak their thoughts, acknowledge their God, seek seemingly attainable goals, and, God-forbid, win. Today, they would be labeled Mama's boys, demeaned as privileged, constrained as prejudiced, or taunted as eggheads.

Yet just imagine America without them. Without them, there would be no America. Is the design of the liberal elite? No America?

We are dangerously on the brink.

James A. Garfield was taught by his mother to "walk with his shoulders squared and his head thrown back." He was proud to be an American. America gave him the opportunity to achieve his destiny.

Today we teach our kids to hide their heads in the sand like ostriches.

Our children are taught to hold their head down in silence and shame. "America is not exceptional." "God is not good." "Winning is self-indulgent." "Succeeding in business is unfair." "Be the 99 percent."

Is this America?

Janine Turner
October 13, 2011
janineturner.com

How Liberals Become Cover Girls in the Capitalist System They Oppose

A 2011 Gallup poll found that 40 percent of Americans consider themselves conservative and only 21 percent consider themselves liberal. So why does the advertising community—a.k.a. Madison Avenue—and their clients continue to hire outspoken liberals for their advertising campaigns?

While I was waiting outside an office the other day, I picked up a magazine. On the back was on outspoken liberal actress in an ad for a cosmetic cream. I sighed as I continued to flip through the magazine and saw another liberal activist actress who was recently spotted leading chants at Occupy Wall Street events. She was in an ad for a wholesome drink. Are Occupy Wall Street events wholesome (defecation, urination, public acts of sex, rape, drugs, violence)?

As I returned home and turned on the television, it was more of the same. I was barraged with liberal thought and actions in sitcoms, dramas, and reality shows. I received no reprieve during commercial breaks. I saw hair flipping around in a hair color ad by an actress who recently held a fundraiser for Obama in her home and did a pre-Obama PSA. Would an actress who was pro-Bush or is pro-Romney get this same opportunity?

Before I could blink, the next commercial flashed more outspoken liberal actors. Liberal are the ones who rant against Wall Street, big business, and banks. Yet liberals are the ones doing ads for—you guessed it—Wall Street, big business, and banks, those same money-making entities that liberals say are so evil.

Question: Would any of these liberal actors be doing the cosmetic, hair, credit card, and drink ads for free? You can bet not. They have big-time agents negotiating big-time deals that pay them millions. To quote Peter Roff, the businesses are being persuaded by liberal advertising companies "to feed from the hand that bites them."

Where is the reason in all this?

Ironically, in a country where more Americans identify themselves as conservative than liberal, Americans are being peddled goods by outspoken liberals. Businesses are being influenced by Madison Avenue to hire celebrity spokespersons with outspoken liberal political beliefs to sell their products. Why are they not hiring conservative celebrity spokespersons who actually rally for free enterprise, which benefits the buyer?

This is just another avenue for liberal bias and a progressive attempt to influence the buyer politically, even with blatant hypocrisy. It's an underground movement whose motives the liberal advertising companies are hoping will not be noticed.

There is nothing wrong with liberals being hired to do commercials, but there is something wrong with conservatives not being hired because they are conservatives.

Why is this important? It is important because of the influence apathy gives Madison Avenue. It is important because of the sheer magnitude of power indifference gives the media over our minds. Americans are letting their thought processes and instincts be manipulated by their lack of action. It's time to vet the nanny who is raising our children and influencing our own minds: the culture (i.e., the press, media, sitcoms, dramas, reality shows, music, and advertising).

I've heard it said that conservatives will buy products peddled by liberals (because they have no other choice) but liberals won't buy products peddled by conservatives. If this is true, then it is time for conservatives and independents to wake up and smell the ads. If we want change, then it's all in the pocketbook.

We are all Americans. I don't mind seeing liberals in ads, as long as there is no hypocrisy in their actions. However, the playing field should be leveled. Conservative Americans should not be shunned and conservatives should be duly represented.

The time has come for advertising companies and their clients to spread the politics around and for the American buyer to demand it.

Janine Turner
June 29, 2012
pjmedia.com

We Should Reject the Race Card as King Did

Have we rejected the race card?

Dr. Martin Luther King, Jr., was in jail. From that Birmingham, Alabama, jail, he wrote a letter:

> When these disinherited children of God sat down at lunch counters, they were in reality standing up for what is best in the American dream and for the most sacred values in our Judeo-Christian heritage, thereby bringing our nation back to those great wells of democracy which were dug deep by the Founding Fathers in their formulation of the Constitution and the Declaration of Independence.

As Americans honor the dignified life of King this week, it is fitting to reflect upon his great courage, wisdom, faith, and vision. King spoke of God's grace, of healing the nation's people, of the values inherent in our founding documents, and of a peaceful process to unity.

King's message is one we should seek today. He is the type of leader we should seek today. Do we? King believed in a God who sees no man or woman of color but only His children.

King's niece, Dr. Alveda C. King, who lived through the bombing of her childhood home and her father's church and who lost both her uncle and father to violence, says, "Our nation is not yet past racism because our nation has not yet understood that there is one race: human."

There is only one race: the human race. Ironically today, when America has her first African-American president, the issue of race is being used as a source of divisiveness primarily by his own administration and his own party, instead of putting the issue to rest. The race card has not been rejected. It has been revitalized. This was not King's dream.

King envisioned a nation that would be healed from the rift of race. He sought an America where race would no longer be a point of differentiation. Today, many organizations perpetuate the difference of color instead of embracing the similarity of souls. "There is only one race: human."

True unity can only begin when Americans see themselves as Americans, not Caucasian or African-American, Chinese or Hispanic. True unity can only begin when we pause to recognize that we are not Democrats or Republicans but Americans.

Dr. Alveda C. King expresses it best: "Today, I tell people in every party God is not a Democrat, God is not a Republican."

King believed the United States Constitution and the Declaration of Independence were the "great wells of democracy" dug deeply for all people.

Today, many denigrate the bedrock of American principles as antiquated. King, however, understood the power of the founding documents and that through the amendment process the will of the people would and could be heard and respected.

Most importantly, King understood the power of unity. He understood the power of peaceful and positive action. He knew that bitterness and a perpetuation of racially based agendas only creates division.

America and American unity are best served when positive action defies race by being blind to race. We are all a part of the human race. God sees no color. God sees no party. God sees only His proposed purpose in the lives He creates. It is up to us to find it and to deliver it.

King fulfilled his God-inspired purpose. His legacy calls to us today. He held his head high. He knew God saw no color. He knew that when people used color to create friction, they were only using it as a means for their own selfish ends.

King reflected the true essence of God—love, peace, grace, and acceptance. Dr. Martin Luther King had a dream. Are we, as a nation, honoring that dream today?

Janine Turner
January 17, 2012
The Washington Examiner

Virtue and the Pursuit of Happiness

As the midterm elections heat up, candidates from the Democratic Party will beat the "economic unfairness" drum. They will declare that their constituents' "pursuit of happiness" is being thwarted by corporate evil, an evil championed by Republicans. Once again the airwaves will echo that the 1 percent, even though it is fluid and open to all Americas, is closed to the rest of the 99 percent of "hard-working, unfairly treated" Americans.

Obama's 1 percent campaign was a phenomenal success that rendered him a second term in office. However, the 1 percent campaign is a balloon of hot air, and the only instrument that will burst it is an educated populace who truly understands what life, liberty, and the pursuit of happiness really means.

Aristotle examines happiness in his *Nicomachean Ethics*. He states, "the human good comes to be disclosed as a being-at-work of the soul in accordance with virtue … ." Washington stated, "There is no truth more thoroughly established than that there exists in the economy and course of nature an indissoluble union between virtue and happiness."

Democrats and progressives want to redefine the "pursuit of happiness" as the "pursuit of money," coupled with the institutionalization of the belief that Americans are automatically guaranteed this "happiness." The Democrats' efforts are like the Wizard of Oz. This great orchestration, the illusion behind the curtain, is really a manipulation. They do not want Americans to rediscover that virtue and the pursuit of happiness are intertwined because if Americans revive their virtue, then all hope is lost for the Democrats whose principles are both self-serving and false.

How far Americans have strayed from the true intent and knowledge of what "happiness" really is. Is this any surprise? Recent generations have been educated in public schools and colleges that deny students knowledge of the fundamental principles upon which "happiness" is built—God and virtue. God is absent from the schools, as is the focus that virtue leads to a purposeful, productive life both as a person and as a citizen. Our Republic, a country that embodies and operates upon the principles of inherent rights, cannot survive without educating our nation's children about "Nature's God," and that happiness begins within one's own character.

Our culture and our schools have incubated and birthed the new "principle"—that we are "owed" happiness and that society "owes" happiness to others. This fallacy has been promulgated by a progressive movement—a movement that has been unchecked by a lazy citizenry.

If we are to survive as a truly charitable people and a free, good society independent from government, then we have to honor and understand why principles matter. We have to immerse the culture in a non-judgmental way with a message that virtue is the compass for happiness and that it is not simply an old, prudish characteristic pushed by conservatives. The correlation between virtue and the pursuit of happiness is non-partisan.

Without a doubt, there must be checks and balances in all regards, but as a nation we need to quit pointing the finger at others, blaming and judging, and instead point the finger at ourselves. The answer is not "out there"—owed to us. It is "in here"—inside our own souls and dependent upon our own virtue.

As we start the New Year, it is a perfect time to discuss virtue at the dinner table with our kids. For as Ronald Reagan said, "All great change in America begins at the dinner table." Our nation's kids no longer learn about Providence or Nature's God—God has been deemed offensive in schools. There is not enough time in the curriculum for virtue, and Constitutional values are not endorsed, as they subscribe to the belief that it is an outdated document. Thus, it's all the more vital that those of us who understand these necessities discuss them at the dinner table— that God and virtue are crucial to the *personal responsibility* of pursuing happiness.

Janine Turner
January 16, 2014
pjmedia.com

Pope Francis's Actions Speak Louder Than Words

Pope Francis, *Time* Man of the Year, is captivating. He is humble. He lives in a hostel instead of the papal palace, and he drives an old Ford instead of the papal Mercedes. He is accessible. He has been known to cold-call people in need and takes part in selfie photographs with his followers. He is a man who doesn't just talk the talk but walks the walk, Pope Francis is a breath of fresh air.

Amidst the praise and awe around the globe, Pope Francis is also garnering criticism. This duality is to be expected of a man who is stepping out of the norm. Aristotle said, "To avoid criticism, do nothing, say nothing, be nothing." Pope Francis is most assuredly doing something.

One corner of criticism is from conservatives. According to *Time*, conservatives bemoan that in his exhortation he mentions abortion only once. This censure is astonishing when one looks at Pope Francis's actions. Pope Francis offered to baptize a divorced woman's baby (whose married lover wanted her to abort it). He has also admonished priests who won't baptize children born out of wedlock for their "rigorous and hypocritical neo-clericalism." Actions such as these are sanctifying life and giving courage to pregnant women, who, free of condemnation, choose life.

Actions such as these emulate Christ's mercy. Actions such as these value not only life but the quality of the life and soul of both the mother—who chose life—and the child. Pope Francis's actions speak much, much louder than his words. His compassion for the single mother and child is a stellar example of Christ's love. What good is it to speak of the sanctity of life and then not value the life once life is born?

Pope Francis, famous for the words "Who am I to judge?" strikes the proper tone of a humble servant of the Lord dedicated to the souls he has been commissioned to heal. Should this not be a message to ponder in our social and political atmosphere here in America? Many conservatives isolate the single mother, the woman who made the courageous, Christian choice of life, by harping on the traditional family as the only way to raise healthy, happy children. There must be a way to uphold the intrinsic importance of the traditional family without making the mother who chose life feel condemned for not being in one.

To show us the way is Pope Francis, who warns us of rigorous hypocrisy. Compelling the single mother to choose life is only the beginning of her and her baby's story. Mercy and compassionate guidance need to follow them for the rest of their days. Pope Francis's actions spoke louder than his words. He saw the woman and child as Jesus would see them. He saw them as children of God. Shouldn't we?

Janine Turner
January 8, 2014
pjmedia.com

GOP Candidates Should be Trumping Obama

Donald Trump is pop culture. He is pop culture with a spin. He is smart, really smart. He is flashy, media-savvy, and epitomizes the American dream. More importantly, he appeals to a wide demographic of Americans.

He is exactly why the Republicans need to capture the "cool" buzz, and heaven knows the Republican Party needs some "pop and sizzle."

The Trump debate on December 27th is a gift to the Republican party and vital to Republican candidates. It is an opportunity to expose the mainstream culture to the Republican cause.

Yet, the Republicans have balked. They have reneged on a cheeky chance to garner a wide berth of potentially new recruits—the autopilot liberals.

Many align with the Democratic Party because it is "hip." The liberal elite presents the Republicans as stuffy and boring. Younger generations are vulnerable to the subliminal, perverted message that only the Democrats care for the poor, the environment, the teachers, and the firefighters.

To them, the Republicans are rich, wealthy, selfish characters who simply want to trample on the less fortunate and ruin the environment.

Ironically, what better way to contradict this myth than with an iconic entrepreneur who has the ears and eyes of the mainstream populace?

Trump, with his star quality and mesmerizing arrogance, is willing to offer the Republican candidates a paparazzi paradise showcasing their reasonable, hardworking characteristics and that they, too, care about the poor, the environment, the teachers, and the firefighters, not to mention the economy and national security.

To a new audience, they can present their ideas and solutions for America and Americans instead of preaching to the choir on Fox News. Disappointingly, all but two of the Republican candidates have passed on the Trump debate.

Gingrich and Santorum are the only ones who have the compelling willingness to jump into the ring. Their courage exhibits inherent American qualities: true grit and determination.

The other candidates' refusal to attend reflects poorly upon their confidence and it begs the question: if they cannot hold their own with Donald Trump, how can they hold their own with Barack Obama? Trump is a walk in the park in comparison to Obama

The Republican Party has slipped into amnesia. How quickly they underestimate Obama's absolute genius at capturing and manipulating pop culture.

Obama's uncanny knack for harnessing the power of persuasion is unparalleled, as is his ability to blitz the media, and subsequently the minds of Americans, with his toothy smile and modish manner. The only one who can match his intrigue is Trump.

Someone within the Republican Party and the Republican campaigns needs to wake up and smell the smolder. Obama is winning the race with his masterful sound-bite campaigning with Truman and Teddy tried-and-trues.

Donald can trump Obama at this own game of media manipulation and sound-bite genius. The Republican candidates need to step up to the plate and join the debate.

Janine Turner
December 12, 2011
The Washington Examiner

A Generation of Robots—What Godless Schools Create

We need God back in the schools. It is of no use to educate our children, creating active, imaginative, and smart minds, if we send them out into the world with no coping skills and no moral compass. We are spitting kids out of America's school system like new cars from an assembly line—robotic, scientific, empty vessels.

We are creating socially challenged generations who are discovering it is hard to cope in the cold, cruel world, not to mention during their challenging school years. Why? They need the foundation of faith—a faith of their choice—during their formative years. They deserve the freedom to discuss God at school, especially since many do not get this opportunity at home.

We are doing a great disservice to our nation's children, and our nation in general, if we do not give our children a designated time during every school day to reflect, reason, and hear basic tenets from religions of their choice. It is through these tenets that children learn how to treat others, even those with whom they disagree, with dignity and respect, not to mention learning how to navigate life's trials and tribulations.

It's time for those of us who believe in freedom of religious discussion in schools to stand tall and take action. We are letting the social left dictate whether a few moments of soul-searching—from any faith or no faith—can take place during school. For those who believe in the First Amendment—"Congress shall make no law respecting an establishment of religion, or prohibiting the free exercise thereof" —it's important to understand that our children have this right, deserve this right, and are inherently born with this right. We can reclaim this right for them.

Contrary to popular belief, the Supreme Court is not the final say on matters in our country. Just because the Supreme Court keeps making erroneous decisions about separation of church and state, such as *Reynolds v United States* (1879) or *Everson v Board of Education* (1947), based not on the Constitution but on a wildly misinterpreted letter of Thomas Jefferson to the Danbury Baptists, it doesn't mean it cannot be addressed again through the legislative branch.

Let's break that down for a moment. We should not make judicial decisions in our country based on random letters of Founding Fathers or founding presidents or any president. That was never our Founding Fathers' intent, nor should it be ours. Our Founding Fathers did not want one man's opinion dictating the rights of Americans. They considered this to be tyranny. That's why our Founding Fathers wrote a specific, enumerated Constitution—the first of its kind. They wanted specificity. Our judges are sworn to make judicial decisions based on our United States Constitution, not on handwritten personal letters or social trends (even Thomas Jefferson wouldn't have wanted this).

The United States Constitution states, "Congress shall make no law respecting an establishment of religion, or prohibiting the free exercise thereof." These are the first words written in our Bill of Rights—the very first words—hence their paramount importance. Our Founding Fathers knew that upon this freedom to exercise religion, and the unparalleled importance of a faith of one's choice, rested the cornerstone not only for life, liberty, and the pursuit of happiness, but for the survival of republicanism itself.

Yet the Supreme Court ripped faith, an intrinsic freedom and a vital coping skill, from our children's developing years based on a letter from a Founding Father who wasn't even at the Constitutional Convention. This decision, which resulted from the deliberations of nine Supreme Court justices, single-handedly took away the very essence of human spiritual development, and a basic Constitutional right, from our children.

And we just let it stand. We said, "Oh well, that's the final decision." Defeatism, especially based on fallacy, is the downfall of our Republic and our citizenry's ability to cope, co-exist, and maintain equilibrium.

By no means should a government-run public school mandate a religion upon a child, but on the other hand, by no means should a government-run public school deny a child the freedom to seek the God of his or her choice at school.

Children are not robots. Children are humans with souls that need to be nourished and guided. Our nation's children deserve a routine time in their school day to enter into a discussion about the God of their choice, or no God, voluntarily. Fifteen minutes a day, kids should freely be able to congregate to the room of their choice, to the God of their choice, or to no God at all. This is their freedom to exercise their First Amendment right.

It is a mission that will take years, yet it can only be achieved one day, one person at a time. Accumulatively we can accomplish this goal. We must not rest on our laurels. We must seek one another and unite. This basic human right can be re-established either through the legislative branch or, better yet, through state sovereignty. States need to declare, and practice, autonomy in this area.

No child should be forced to worship a God in school and no child should be forced to deny their God in school.

This is their First Amendment right. Let's get it back for them.

Janine Turner
November 4, 2013
pjmedia.com

Living Amid Hollywood Hypocrisy

I had to listen to it for years on sets, at dinners, in rehearsals, in the make-up chair, and at award ceremonies. The judgmental, hot, mostly uninformed rants of Hollywood liberals breathed down my neck and sucked all the air from the room. Usually the rants were so hostile that I was afraid to speak up, or so ridiculous that I thought it futile to reply.

The liberal Hollywood elite, who stand firmly on their right to be heard, their right to express, their right to persuade through art, arrogantly deny that same freedom to anyone who may disagree with them. And like most liberals, they have a blind spot for their own intolerance.

I remember one Emmy ceremony in particular for its incessant anti-conservative, anti-Republican diatribes—one after another. I remember sitting, slumped in my chair, just counting the moments until I could be released from the lions' den. There I was—a captive, a hostage to their narrow-minded and condescending point of view, expressed in a vacuum.

I couldn't wait to leave Hollywood. I always felt like I was in a bubble when I lived there—in a stifling, tropical snow globe. It was like that fabulous scene in *The*

Truman Show where Jim Carrey leaps from his boat and beats his head against the sky on the set of the world, wanting to get out.

In Hollywood, people think America is inherently bad—a world embarrassment—even as they gorge themselves on the American dream.

Hollywood is a surreal and pretend world whose way of life is actually ruthless free enterprise—it is called show business, after all. Hollywood is where stars, movie producers, writers, and agents actively seek glamour, money, power, and fame; where they covet fast cars and face-lifts and fly in private jets. They drink fine wines and insist on free spirits. They are the ultimate connoisseurs who insist on living liberty at large.

Somehow, the inhabitants gag at the very thought of capitalism going on elsewhere.

In Hollywood, they deplore censorship. However, they embrace tyrants such as Hugo Chavez who use power to censor opposition. They sneer at Wall Street even as they fall all over themselves running to see how many millions their movies have grossed. They think Obamacare works nicely for poor people in the "flyover states," yet they would never accept anything but the top doctors for themselves.

They think socialism is a novelty—a nicety whose time has come. How odd to imagine their lot under a Chavez or a Castro or a Stalin. Just picture the collapse of Hollywood's playground—the redistribution of their wealth, the despotic squelching of their free speech, and the strangling of their rights and riches.

They would howl like lone wolves do in westerns. They would beg like Scarlett O'Hara. They would scream like the Wicked Witch of the West. But instead of screaming, "I'm melting! I'm melting!" they would scream, "Not me! Not me!"

Janine Turner
September 9, 2011
The Washington Examiner

The Republican Dilemma Exposed

The uniqueness of our American Revolution was not that we overthrew a tyrant or established a new nation. The uniqueness of our American Revolution was that we cultivated, declared, and obtained a new set of ideals, never before proposed in such a manner. "All men are created equal." God gives us rights. We are born with them. They are inalienable, and with these rights we have life, liberty, and the pursuit of happiness. These were the declarations that inspired a rag-tag army to beat the most powerful nation of earth. These were the declarations that consequentially changed and ennobled the world.

In 1776, our brilliant forefathers laid out the principles and ideals that were truly unique and truly American in our Declaration of Independence. Being born with inalienable rights, given to us by the Supreme Being, our government would govern by the consent of the governed.

Hence the American mantra: If God gives us our rights, as the Declaration declares, then only God can take them away. But if government gives us our rights, then government can take them away. Do modern-day Americans understand this basic American precept upon which our liberties lie?

Today, Republicans believe that God is the basis upon which our rights prevail. Democrats believe that God doesn't give us our rights, and that only government can adequately shepherd the governed. Democrats believe that the "people need the consent of the government," instead of a "government who needs the consent of the people," as the Republicans believe.

This explains the glazed look upon the Democrats' faces when the Constitution, which upholds the principles set forth in the Declaration, is mentioned. The Constitution establishes limits on the power of government with a checks-and-balances system to prevent tyranny, thus protecting our God-given rights. Democrats do not want a limited government, as they do not believe government should be limited. Democrats believe that they know best and that only they, being omniscient, should provide for the people.

Republicans believe that only God is perfect and that humans are fallible, thus men must be checked. "Men are not angels," wrote James Madison in *The Federalist*. Democrats believe that humans can be perfected with the right amount of guidance and governmental control because their government is all-powerful.

This is the major theoretical dividing point today—God gives us our rights (Republicans) versus government gives us our rights (Democrats).

The Republican mission: educating Americans on the principles that our rights are inalienable, given to us by God—a Supreme Being, and that this belief preserves our equality, maintains our liberties, and keeps our self-governing republic in the hands of the people and free from tyranny of big-government tyrants.

The Democrats' mission: inconspicuously convincing Americans that the Constitution, and all of this God stuff, is outdated. As they are posing as a party who upholds the Constitution, they surreptitiously remove God from schools and governing ideals. They empower government as all-knowing under the guise of "we're looking out for you."

What the Democrats don't say is that the bottom line is an open door for a tyrant or for the tyranny of a massive government that renders the governed paralyzed by ignorance, stifled by regulations, and, eventually, through feelings of powerlessness, apathy.

The tension between God-given rights versus government-given rights is the seesaw upon which popular conviction will dominate our future—liberty or tyranny. Republicans need God, and herein lies the Republican dilemma exposed.

Republicans need Americans to understand and choose our God-given principles and rights in order to preserve our self-governing republic. They are, however, driving much of the populace away from God, and hence to the Democratic Party, with the perception of a God who is not loving, a God who is judgmental, a God who is exclusive. Many Americans feel, and pop culture depicts, that the God of the Republicans and the Founding Fathers, documents, and principles only apply to people who are pro-life, heterosexually married couples, and traditional parents.

This perception and mostly misconception has led many Americans to choose the Democrats' "government is God" instead of the Republicans' belief that "only God is God and government is beholden." By default, Americans are choosing a government who governs the people instead of a government who governs by the consent of the people. It's a knee-jerk reaction to the Republicans' judgmental God. Most people more than likely agree with the Republican belief that God gives us our rights, but they are repulsed by the Republican Party rhetoric.

This is a serious problem that must be addressed and quickly. I am a pro-life devout Christian, and a Republican who believes that our rights are God-given. However, as a single mother I can uniquely feel and relate to what is driving many Americans to the "government gives us our rights" Democrats instead of the "God gives us our rights" Republicans because of the insistence on the "traditional family".

The same sort of scenario is taking place with same-sex marriage and same-sex rights issues. Herein lies the Republican dilemma. The judgmental messages in the media and in the Republican primaries by certain candidates are threatening our republican form of government, dooming a government based on the consent of the governed. Where is the Republican message of non-judgmental acceptance, forgiveness, and the love of a caring God—the same God they are asking people to acknowledge who has given them their God-given rights? It exists but it needs to be louder, and all Republicans need to coalesce around the big picture—

maintaining our God-given rights and self-government—which can only be done by winning the hearts, minds, and votes of the populace. The divide within the party will create the fall of the party and our republic.

The ironic reality is that the all-accepting "government gives us our rights" Democrats will ultimately keep that single mother in poverty, or at least on a government-probated allowance from which she and her children can never rise. The ironic reality is that the same-sex married couple will be stripped of their rights to speak, petition, and assemble when the "party of government gives us rights" Democrats decide to take them away – which is inevitable. Their rights will be removed by either the tyranny of a big, out-of-control, unchecked, financially broke government and the apathy it induces or by the blatant take-over of a feel-good, non-judgmental, come-to-Daddy tyrant.

Here's the bottom line, the tyranny of the "government gives us our rights" Democrats will win if the "God gives us our rights" Republicans do not wake up and see the perception and consequences of the judgmental God they are depicting.

As it stands now the perception among much of the populace is that the Republicans are the party of rejection, pushing away, and the Democrats are the party of reception, drawing in. This is the challenge, one example of the brilliance of Ronald Reagan, is that he stood by his convictions but presented them in a way that was gentle and loving—like a grandfather. He presented them like the Godly man he was with the realization that all Americans, being unique and different, cannot be pigeonholed into one box. His demeanor was of acceptance with a twinkle in his eye.

God is forgiving. God is of love. My job as a Christian is to let God be the judge. Only God knows people's hearts, heartaches, and destinies, and I am not God. In America, the young woman who has an abortion is still entitled to the "God gives us our rights" form of government, as is the single mom and the same-sex couple. Even though Republicans *do* believe that all Americans are entitled to the "God gives us our rights" form of government, this is not what a frightening number of Americans feel from the Republicans. They feel rejected by the very people who bring forth the message that within the Declaration of Independence and the U.S. Constitution lie the principles that they are entitled to—that they are protected by a loving God who gives them their rights.

There is no moral test in our founding documents. God is good and God loves us. God wants us to be free from tyranny, which is evil. It is this God who spoke to our forefathers. It is this God of whom our forefathers spoke. The God who gives us our rights is a good God and a loving God.

The American people need to feel it, which can only be accomplished with a loving God brought forth by the Republicans. Then the American people can see that Republican ideals are the best way to preserve life, liberty, and the pursuit of happiness and our rights to govern ourselves.

Our rights are secure because God gives us our rights. If government gives us our rights, then government can take them away. If the general populace doesn't feel and see this fundamental truth, then there will be no rights for anybody anywhere, and the experiment of self-government that blazed from the paths of Plymouth will flicker and the American ideals that were once the hope of all mankind will meet their demise.

Janine Turner
July 7, 2013
janineturner.com

Town of Greece, NY vs. Galloway: With Victory Comes Responsibility and Respect

For those Americans who believe in the sanctity of freedom of speech, religion, and the First Amendment's words, "Congress shall make no law respecting an establishment of religion, or prohibit the free exercise thereof," the Supreme Court's 5–4 decision in *Town of Greece, NY vs. Galloway* upholding these rights in local government is a victory.

As Justice Kennedy states in his decision, "The First Amendment is not a majority rule, and a government may not seek to define permissible categories of religious speech. Once it invites prayer into the public sphere, government must permit a prayer-giver to address his or her own God or gods as conscience dictates."

These words give guidance, and permission, to prayer-givers. When asked to pray at local government gatherings, prayer-givers now have the blessing, so to speak, to pray to their own God. Many prayer-givers have been disconcerted about how to pray at a gathering of diverse people on a local level. Should they be generic or true to their own convictions? How does one not "offend"? According to the recent Supreme Court decision, the prayer-givers have the right to pray to their God of choice.

This great liberty, fought and bought with blood, sweat, and tears, is accompanied by great responsibilities, however, from the local government, the prayer-givers, and the community of citizens. Today's America embodies a wide swath of religions, thus *local governments* carry the responsibility of incorporating a comparable scope of prayer-givers that encompasses varied religions. The *prayer-givers* have the right to be honest to their convictions, honoring their God, but also have the responsibility to craft a prayer that does not force their beliefs on others. The prayer-giver's prayer should refrain from using prayers that "threaten damnation or preach conversion," states Justice Kennedy. The *community of citizens* has the responsibility to be respectful to the prayer-giver and to the local government, sustained by their right to believe in the prayer or not.

An expression of one's religion by the prayer-giver, who was invited by the local government, does not equal an establishment of a religion forced upon a community. Thus, the right of the local government to call the meeting to order with a prayer should be respected. The inherent freedom of speech and religion in the prayer-givers' prayer should be respected, and the diversity of religions within the community of citizens should be respected.

What makes America great is the ability of her citizens to honor the laws whether they agree with them or not. This honor stems from the innate knowledge that Americans rule through the Republic, which is sustained by the United States Constitution. Americans' rights and laws are crafted, executed, and judged indirectly by the people. American laws are not forced upon the populace by a tyrant, dictator, or monarch. They are established by a rule of law within the confines of a republican form of government.

Americans have freedom. However, Americans are only as free as they are responsible, respectful, and involved. In this respect both parties are winners in the *Town of Greece, NY vs. Galloway* Supreme Court Case. It embodied an active citizenry and a resilient local government. Only passivity brings true defeat.

Responsibility and respect—federal, state, local, citizenry—rules the day and preserves freedom of speech and religion. One truly cannot exist without the other.

Janine Turner
May 6, 2014
janineturner.com

John Quincy Adams Says It Best

My friend Cathy Gillespie gave me an antique for Christmas. It is my favorite genre of antique—an antique book. Couple this with the fact that it is a book based on my favorite topic—history—and she scores a home run in gift-giving. This antique book is written by one of my favorite American presidents, John Quincy Adams. John Quincy Adams, John Adams's son, was, like his father, a great American patriot and dedicated servant of America. He started his service as a young lad as secretary to the Russian embassy, followed by service in posts such as ambassador, United States Senator, secretary of state, negotiator of the last peace treaty with Great Britain, president of the United States, and then as a congressman in the United States House of Representatives. He died on the floor of the house, as he rose to give a speech, at the age of eighty. A true American hero.

As I reflect upon his greatness, I realize that it was not so much the list of accomplishments that make him heroic, but the dignified and virtuous way he lived his life. All of his decisions were influenced by his faith. Upon this moral compass he, armed with earnestness, confidence, and the passion of God's guidance, made enormous decisions that changed the destiny of human dignity and became the beacon of hope for all mankind.

In a book of letters to his son (*Letters of John Quincy Adams to His Son on the Bible and Its Teaching*) he dedicates each letter to teaching his son the disciplines of faith that he had learned from his father and mother. John Quincy, writing from St. Petersburg in September 1811, tells his son how he awakens early in the morning and reads the Bible for one hour. He describes how hard it is to absorb it all and how the daily aspects of life rush to compete with his meditation. He reflects about how he makes it a mission to routinely read the whole Bible in a year because "... every time I read the Book through, I understand some passages which I never understood before." He hearkens, thus, to not only reading but absorbing and utilizing the words he has read.

John Quincy decides that it would be mutually beneficial in improving both his comprehension and his son's to study aspects of the Bible together. Hence, the letters in the book. He stresses how vital it is that his son should not only have a formidable foundation of faith, derived from the written word of God, but also the clarity of application. He states, "It is essential, my son, in order that you may go through life with comfort to yourself, and usefulness to your fellow creatures, that you should form and adopt certain rules or principles, for the government of your own conduct and temper. Unless you have such rules and principles, there will be numberless occasions on which you will have no guide for your government but your passions."

As I read this I am in awe, not only of his self-discipline, but of his astuteness as a father to recognize the necessity of taking it upon himself to teach his child these basics of life. He did not leave it to his child's schoolmasters or to his friends. He undertook the task himself. Even a Sunday School or a regular church service did not equate to the one-on-one time of principled study.

Hence, an affirmation of what I already deeply believe—no one will have a bigger impact on my child's moral compass than me, not only by what I read with her and teach her, but by how I respond to situations, how I apply these principles. Currently, Juliette and I are reading C.S. Lewis's daily meditations in the morning, followed by scripture from the Bible, and then finishing with a quote from *24 Hours A Day* about how to cope with the world in a sober way. If the mornings are crazy then we do this in the car on the way to dance. I must admit that John Quincy is correct, I absorb more of God's word when I study it with my child.

In a secular world of instant gratification and a flood of information and communication, where is the time for God? It is our impulse to turn on the television, read our Facebook and email, and check our text messages before we reach for God. We have a great challenge before us. There are so many distractions clamoring for our attention.

We must ask ourselves this pivotal question: Who is clamoring for our children's attention?

Really, life was not different in his day. John Quincy was an extraordinarily busy man who was never idle. Yet, he made the time. The choice was his, and the choice is ours. What we put before our God we lose. Are we willing to lose a generation of children? Are we willing to lose the future of our country?

John Quincy states it best: "It is no use to discover our own faults and infirmities, unless the discovery prompts us to amendment."

Janine Turner
December 29, 2010
janineturner.com

Chapter Six

Conversations from the Janine Turner Radio Show

Well, Janine, it underscores why I am running. I mean when I was a kid, and my dad used to say to me over and over again, "When we faced depression in Cuba, I had a place to flee to. If we lose our freedom here, where do we go?" And it's an incredible blessing to be the child of someone who had fled oppression because you understand just how fragile liberty is. And if we don't stand up and defend it right now, we are at risk of losing it.

—Senator Ted Cruz (R-TX)

Well, a lot of people are disappointed in the president because even if you're a liberal and you thought he was going to be a good liberal but at least maybe he will support the First and Fourth Amendments. Now it turns out that he has targeted reporters [whom] he disagrees with. He has gone after reporters and used the bully nature of government to go after them. Now it looks like he's abusing people's privacy by looking at millions of records. It's not exactly what you would expect from a liberal who says "Oh, I'm gonna defend your civil liberties." He's not really engendering a lot of confidence in his ability to lead.

—Senator Rand Paul (R-KY)

Preface

Even FDR never really expected it [Social Security] to remain the public entity. I think he expected it to be more privatized at this point. It just makes sense; it's just reasonable that we do these kinds of things. And I agree with you, we need you up there to help us get these things done. I love your [Ted Cruz's] thoughts on all of this, on the free enterprise, the government regulation, taking the government out of even big businesses. You know what, the government has sort of grown around all of this like an octopus.

—Janine Turner

On fire with enthusiasm from my constitutional fortitude and political opinion-editorials, I launched my radio show, *The Janine Turner Show*, from my home, which led to yet another genre of writing: monologues. I used my phone as a microphone and my computer as an editing tool. I merged my political opinions with my Hollywood storytelling and was off to the races. I would gather my monologues, stories, and interviews with prominent political figures, and promote them on the Internet. This show was first picked up by KLIF in Dallas/Fort Worth as a Saturday night show, then by KPRC in Houston, and it is now currently distributed by Clear Channel and heard on iHeart, the wave of radio future.

Both my opinion-editorials and my radio show caught the attention of Bill O'Reilly. This led to a year's worth of regular Friday night appearances on *The O'Reilly Factor* debating the political topic of the day. Talk about challenging! Some days I was quaking in my snake boots. (The television shots on these types of appearances are from the waist up, so, often, I would have on my jeans and snake boots on the bottom half and my dressy blouse on the top half.)

These efforts naturally progressed to my next field of writing: speeches. I love to write speeches. Like a traveling salesman, I have been traversing the country delivering speeches, including a stop in Tampa to speak at the Republican National Convention in 2012. I still ride the circuit giving speeches to audiences whose ages range from eight to one hundred and eight. Maybe that's why when I was on Chris Wallace's *Fox News Sunday* as Power Player of the Week, he said, "Like a modern-day Paul Revere, (Janine) Turner will keep spreading the word about our founding principles."

In this chapter I have included a rare, long conversation with Ted Cruz (when he was running for Senate in the Republican primary) and Rand Paul, the senator from Kentucky. Radio is a joy for me. What a gift to be able to have conversations with such great minds and devoted patriots.

Senator Rand Paul

When our Constitution was written, we were worried about British soldiers having general warrants where no one was named and they willy-nilly go into anyone's house. This is sort of equivalent in the digital age. Nobody [is] just named in this, no one has probable cause that you've committed a crime, and yet the government's trolling through millions and millions of your records, and what bothers me about it is, also, I think it is a bad way to combat terrorism.

–Senator Rand Paul (R-KY)

The Wild-West Texan in me has an appreciation for Senator Rand Paul. I am a believer that very few Americans can be pigeonholed into one political party. Rand Paul obviously has a bit of libertarianism in his political fervor, as do I. Like most Americans, my heritage is a mix of different countries and cultures: British, French, Scottish, and Native American. My political perspectives are equally as varied. It is exciting to have Senator Rand Paul on Capitol Hill. He is shaking things up and stirring the pot. This needs to happen. I had the great pleasure of speaking with Senator Paul on my radio show on June 6, 2013 on KPRC.

Janine: Now we have, I'm so excited, the one and only Senator Rand Paul. He's fighting for our freedoms and liberties and what's best for America every day in Washington, D.C. Senator Rand Paul, welcome to the Janine Turner Show.

Senator Rand Paul: Well thanks for having me on, Janine.

Janine: I really do appreciate your service. You know, you're up there in the middle of such drama today and such critical issues, and I'm just glad you're there.

Senator Rand Paul: It's sort of a pit of evil. I need to go home on weekends just to feel clean again.

Janine: Right. (Laughing) It's not funny actually. Where do we begin? I think the first question I would like to ask you—it's in the news today, where the NSA has a top-secret court order to get average Americans' phone records. What do you think about that?

Senator Rand Paul: You know I think we ought to be concerned. You know Franklin said if you give up your liberty to have security, you may end up with neither. So it is a real concern. When our Constitution was written, we were worried about British soldiers having general warrants where no one was named and they could willy-nilly go into anyone's house. This is sort of equivalent in the digital age. Nobody [is] just named in this, no one has probable cause that you've committed a crime, and yet the government's trolling through millions and millions of your records, and what bothers me about it is, also, I think it is a bad way to combat terrorism. We need to have good police work. Like the Tsarnaev boys who had done the Boston Marathon bombings, we didn't know they had gone back to Chechnya and returned. We didn't know anything about them. They should have been on a list, because the Russians gave us their names. We should have been aware of their movements. Instead we're searching the phone records of trillions and millions of Americans, and we lose sight of the ball. We lose sight of the good police work that needs to occur because we're just wading through everybody's phone records. There really is an expectation of privacy, and you shouldn't give it up just because a third party is holding your records.

Janine: It's pretty frightening. My e-mail was hacked this morning. And the new big National Security Agency complex, I believe it's in Utah, where it's just building after building to sort through all of these records.

Senator Rand Paul: Well, Janine, you are definitely on the list. I would just go ahead and acknowledge you're on the list.

Janine: (Laughing) So scary. Oh dear. You know what this is? It's like an illegal search. It's interesting to see the Boston scenario, because there they were just blasting into people's houses with their guns, not literally firing, but the search they did looking for the Tsarnaev brothers was a bit concerning.

Senator Rand Paul: Well, my biggest concern over that whole thing is... number one, we're letting too many people here on asylum status. We have admitted sixty thousand people from Iraq in the last two or three years. A bunch of them settled in my hometown, of Bowling Green, and we caught two of them trying to buy stinger missiles to do terrorist attacks in this country. Fortunately they were trying to buy them from undercover FBI agents. But my question is, why are we bringing so many from the Middle East here under refugee status? We discourage them from working. We sign them up for every program under the sun. They are all in government housing and on Medicaid. We have exemptions. You get easy access if you're a refugee. I don't mind giving people shelter who are coming from dictatorships, if your church wants to sponsor them. My church has sponsored people, and that's great. You sponsored them, you get them a job, and you take care of them. But don't get them all here and say, "Oh I'm a great person because I brought them here and signed them up for welfare." The Tsarnaev brothers got over $100K in welfare. They got all of this money. I don't know why they hated Americans so much. Americans were taking care of them.

Janine: That is a great lead-in to immigration, but before we get there I have another question. What do we do about the threat that we're under? Do you have any ideas about how we remain informed to make sure that we aren't attacked without jeopardizing people's liberties and privacy?

Senator Rand Paul: Well, I think you need to do a more targeted approach. You know, after 9/11, we had a program that looked at student visas from the Middle East. That's who attacked us, people from the Middle East and people on student visas. So wouldn't you think that would be the number-one priority for the government? So we did look closely, and we actually sent 13,000 people home after 9/11. But President Obama just recently completely defunded the program and it's gone now, so we have no more scrutiny because he thought it was unfair to scrutinize twenty-five countries. But these are twenty-five countries that have a significant population of Islamic jihadists and people who hate America. Wouldn't you think that's who you would be careful about admitting into your country? And for goodness sakes, if they say they're coming as refugees, you can't believe what everybody says. We have people joining the Afghan army [who] are our allies who say they want to work with America, and then when our soldiers turn away, they shoot our soldiers in the backs. We do have to be careful, and we should apply extra scrutiny to the people who have historically been attacking us.

Janine: Instead of taking the phone records of millions of Americans.

Senator Rand Paul: Yes, and I think that by doing that, it's sloppy too. We have so much audio. I read somewhere that we have like 25 million hours of audio, and we've only been through 1/3 of it. So we overwhelm ourselves. I'm not against getting some audio and phone records of people who you have probable cause to believe they're associated with terrorism. But that's police work. And I'm not against intelligence and counter-intelligence and all the stuff that we need to prevent people from attacking us. But just willy-nilly combing through everyone's phone records is the wrong way to go. Congress actually invited this because Congress gives the phone companies limited liability. They said to the phone company, "We know you made a privacy arrangement with your customers not to share their information, but we won't let them sue you." So right now if you're part of Verizon, which I am, I can't sue them for turning over my records to the government and breaching my contract because the government gave them an exemption.

Janine: Wow, that's very interesting information. That's pretty disturbing. We have a Bill of Rights that says you have to be very specific about who you want to search. You have to have a reason why you want to search. You have to search a house, and not the whole block. This is like the days of a monarchy where they search towns.

Senator Rand Paul: That's the whole point. Our Founding Fathers didn't want this. They wanted it to be specified. They wanted the warrants to be specific to the person, place, and items you're looking for. The Fourth Amendment is very detailed and specific on this front. But, we have been letting it slip away from us for quite a while. Starting in the 1970s, the Supreme Court ruled that when you gave up your records to a bank or the Visa Card Company, or any kind of third party such as an internet service provider, that your expectation of privacy and Fourth Amendment protections were out the window. I disagree. You cannot live in this age without having a lot of stuff that third parties hold for you. So I think we really went the wrong direction, but particularly with the technological advances we need to revisit those cases. I would love to see those re-taken up. I have introduced amendments here and had votes. Unfortunately I haven't won any of those votes yet. But I have had the Senate put on record whether or not the Fourth Amendment applies to third-party records. I think we got twelve votes in favor. Apparently the people up here haven't figured out that the people do want some privacy.

Janine: So it's up to us to speak up. I feel like Americans are just bombarded right now. On this show, I try to live in the solution and not the problem. I'm like, "call your representative, call and tell them" and yet pick an issue, pick a scandal. There's so much going on right now. I heard you comment recently that the president lost his moral authority to lead. It's just amazing to me. Even the American people, at some of the polls, think, "Well maybe the Obama administration is doing all of this, but I shouldn't hold Obama responsible."

Senator Rand Paul: Well, a lot of people are disappointed in the president because even if you're a liberal and you thought he was going to be a good liberal but at least maybe he will support the First and Fourth Amendments. Now it turns out that he has targeted reporters [whom] he disagrees with. He has gone after reporters and used the bully nature of government to go after them. Now it looks like he's abusing peoples' privacy by looking at millions of records. It's not exactly what you would expect from a liberal who says "Oh, I'm gonna defend your civil liberties." He's not really engendering a lot of confidence in his ability to lead.

Janine: No. Well, we have about forty-five seconds left here. With the IRS scandal, the AP situation, today's story about the Verizon seizure, Benghazi, EPA, immigration, what's the hope here? Other than you, because I believe there's a lot of hope with you up there leading us, Senator Rand Paul, what's the hope here?

Senator Rand Paul: I think the hope is that we have an incredibly great country. You know, our founding documents are awesome. Our economic system has created such wealth. We keep fighting for it and we say it's so important that we're not going to let the president infringe upon it, we hold him in check, we hold him accountable, and we fight on for another day, knowing that our country is too important to give up on.

Janine: That's right. If we study history, America has been through a lot of ups and downs over the years. We certainly have prevailed.

Senator Rand Paul: We'll survive. We'll do better. But we can't just [let] him run roughshod over the Bill of Rights.

Janine: No, and I don't see much changing there in the way they're operating. Hang tough in there, Senator Rand Paul. I thank you so much for all you're doing. Thank you.

Senator Rand Paul: Thanks, Janine.

Janine: Senator Rand Paul, wow. I really do appreciate his service to America. He's a Republican, but also a Libertarian. I'm a Constitutionalist. When you can back away from the partisanship and look at things from a standpoint of reason, there's a little more light at the end of the tunnel, and there [are] more solutions.

The Janine Turner Show
June 6, 2013
KPRC Houston

Senator Ted Cruz

Any politician who says he or she is going to balance the budget without entitlement reform is lying. Right now, the federal government borrows forty cents of every dollar that it spends. Entitlements and interest on the debt constitute two-thirds of the federal budget, which means you could shut down the entire federal government, you could fire the Army, the Navy, you could shut down the FBI, you could close every federal park, and the federal budget still wouldn't balance.

—Senator Ted Cruz (R-TX), during the Texas primary for US Senator

It was recommended to me that I have this relatively unknown candidate on my radio show back in 2011, four months before the Texas Republican primary election. His name was Ted Cruz. I did, and instantly I knew he was the man for the job. At the time, my radio show was on Saturday nights on KLIF, and during the week I had my weekday radio show. I did this weekday show in podcast format. I sat in a cubicle in my friend's State Farm office in Dallas. I operated all of the controls myself. This venue, and Ted Cruz's new-man-on-campus status, gave me the opportunity to have an extended, relaxed conversation with him. Now that Cruz is a senator, this type of interview would be virtually impossible. Thus, this interview is one (out of the three we did) of my favorites. Cruz is brilliant. He is committed to principles. He is like the men who formed our nation—men built of intellect, education, and fortitude. He reminds me of Patrick Henry, one of our most dedicated, outspoken, and gifted Founding Fathers. William Wirt described Patrick Henry as "A spirit fitted to raise the whirlwind, as well as to ride it." This is a perfect way to describe Senator Ted Cruz.

Janine: Okay, Mr. Cruz, are you there?

Senator Cruz: I am.

Janine: Welcome to *The Janine Turner Show*. This is so much fun.

Senator Cruz: Well, thank you. I am really glad to be with you.

Janine: Oh, I have to tell you, people are raving about you, I have got to say. Great buzz on you, Mr. Cruz.

Senator Cruz: Well, that's great to hear. We are working very hard, and we have been seeing just incredible excitement and enthusiasm and momentum.

Janine: Well, it says here you were featured on the cover of the *National Review* where they called you—I just have to brag on you, right?—"The Next Great Conservative Hope." That's really big, "The Next Great Conservative Hope," and columnist George Will called you a "Candidate As Good As It Gets."

Senator Cruz: Well, it's been very, very encouraging. We have seen a lot of excitement, and I think the reasons are that the stakes in this election are higher than I think they may ever have been.

Janine: Certainly they are for the country, I know that.

Senator Cruz: Yeah. No, I mean President Obama is so radical that we are really facing crossroads. If we don't get strong conservative leadership in Washington to turn this country around, we have got a real risk of following the path that Greece and much of Europe are following.

Janine: You know, I agree. I just kind of have this irritation in my gut today when I read the news that comes along about the lack of leadership within the Senate and the House. We have to get a new president in the office, a 2012 Republican president. But I am a little disturbed about what happened in Ohio with the collective bargaining and with the unions and whatnot, are the people going to be willing? We want candidates that are going to make tough choices. So let's say we elect you to go make tough choices, just like they did in Ohio, and then nobody backs you. Nobody backs the representatives or senators or governors when they do make the tough choices. And I am a little bit worried about the people, we the people, it ultimately relies on us, doesn't it, to a certain extent?

Senator Cruz: Well, it is certainly a tough challenge, although I tell you, Janine, I am really optimistic. I have been spending just about every day on the road, traveling all throughout Texas and all throughout the country. And people are energized and have a passion to retake our country in a way that I have never seen before. Obama has been so radical that it has sparked a great awakening that leaves me tremendously optimistic about the future.

Janine: Well, I do believe that. I write op-eds for the *Washington Examiner* and one was published this week, it was actually yesterday. I talked about the magnanimous majority versus the Occupy Wall Streeters and all these union people. I believe that the people of retirement age deserve their retirement and their Social Security, they have earned it, they deserve it, but the tenor of the AARP commercials is really off where they say things along the lines of, "We are 50 million strong," "We are voters," and "Don't change our entitlements." I thought, well, there is a magnanimous majority in this country, and it's going to be people who would join this movement crossing all generations, young and old, that are going to pull this country together by making sacrifices. And of course, our Founding Fathers really believed in the genius of the people, according to Alexander Hamilton. So I am glad you are seeing it out there.

Senator Cruz: Well, and I think what it's going to take is a new generation of leaders. I think a lot of the guys [who] have been up there for a long time in both parties, they frankly just don't get it. And one of the most exciting things in 2010 we saw all over the country was a tidal wave of new strong conservative leaders, candidates like Marco Rubio and Mike Lee and Rand Paul and Pat Toomey getting elected, strong, principled, free-market conservatives. Republicans had really lost their way. I mean we needed fresh blood that wasn't just reading from talking points but actually believed in individual liberty and the Constitution.

Janine: Now let me ask this question because I am a big believer in free enterprise and less government regulation. Yet, there was something I was reading yesterday talking about the government subsidizing businesses. I guess it started in the nineteenth century with the government giving to the railroads and the government giving this and that. But we are in this big myth. How do we even begin to pull out of the government funding all these big businesses that really want them? They say they don't want regulation, but they want the money. How do we address that?

Senator Cruz: Look, it's an enormous problem. And one of the biggest lies in politics is the lie that Republicans are the party of big business. The truth of the matter is big business does just great with big government; big business inevitably gets in bed with big government; they have armies of lobbyists, and they get bought off.

Janine: So we are talking about—

Senator Cruz: In my view, I think as conservatives we should be the party of small businesses, of entrepreneurs, of the next inventors starting a business in his or her garage that's going to take out the giant businesses of today. I mean that's what's provided the creative destruction, the spark that's led to unprecedented prosperity and what it's going to take. I think I am opposed to bailout across the board. I don't think government should be picking winners and losers; we shouldn't be subsidizing anybody. But what it's going to take is new leaders [who] are not just desperate to stay in office. Part of the reason you see it is the guys in Washington, all they want to do is get reelected, and there are not—a lot of them [who] have been there a long, long time, these career politicians, they are just looking to buy votes. And I think we have got a unique moment in time with the people energized and engaged to elect leaders [who] are willing to lead the fight, to dramatically shrink the size, power, and spending of the federal government and get us out of the business of picking winners and losers and bailing anybody [out].

Janine: How do you do that, though? How do you begin? There are so many areas in this country with the 70 percent pie of entitlements and the super committee of twelve. I don't know what's going to be accomplished there. But how do you begin? Yes, we want to encourage people so they don't need the government. They don't want the government. Liberty and freedom were truly represented in the Revolutionary era, that's what they wanted. But how do you begin to chisel away from these big businesses that are so dependent on it? I mean I think the new call of the day for so many Americans is "give me liberty and give me give me." [Laughing]

Senator Cruz: And that's certainly the call of the Occupy Wall Street folks. I mean you listen to them when they are interviewed, and all they want is more free stuff.

Janine: Right, like in Ohio, this initiative that was just—

Senator Cruz: Um huh. In terms of how we get it done, I think there are a couple of things. One, I think the Senate is really the tipping point. There are five or six strong conservatives in the Senate who are vastly outnumbered, and I think one of the most important things that's at stake in 2012 is can we grow that core of five or six strong conservatives to ten or twelve. If we do that, it will radically transform the senate. If we have ten or twelve strong, principled conservatives willing to lead the fight to dramatically shrink the size, power, and spending of the federal government, it will change the heart and soul of that institution, and we are very, very close. Now the second piece, as you rightly pointed out, is you can't get any of this done without the support of the American people, and we need leaders [who] can go and make the case, just as Ronald Reagan did. Ronald Reagan made the case to the American people that the serious words in the English language were, "I am from the government, and I am here to help," and he made the case. We right now have a real shortage of leaders [who] can effectively champion liberty, can explain how free markets and individual liberty produce unprecedented opportunity and prosperity.

Janine: Yeah. Look what happened at the turn of the century or turn of the nineteenth century. It was amazing what happened.

Senator Cruz: Well, and I often tell the story of—in my personal family, my dad is from Cuba, and he was imprisoned and tortured in Cuba as a teenager. And he fled Cuba, and when he came to Texas, it was 1957; he was eighteen years old. He didn't speak a word of English; he had nothing but $100 sewn into his underwear. And he got a job as a dishwasher making fifty cents an hour and worked his way through the University of Texas. And I have said many, many times, thank God some well-meaning liberal didn't come, put his arm around my dad, and say, "Let me help you. Let me put you on the government check. Let me make you dependent, and whatever you do, don't learn English."

Janine: Yeah because Democrats, they depend on the dependents, don't they?

Senator Cruz: That's exactly right. They want a captive political class that will keep voting them into power, and that would have been the most destructive thing they could have done is if you make someone dependent, you destroy their self-respect—

Janine: You take away their dignity.

Senator Cruz: That's exactly right.

Janine: Even Roosevelt said that. There is even a quote from FDR about that. I don't have it in front of me, but he even just talked about that, ironically.

Senator Cruz: Yeah, and that's what works. So I mean the only way anyone has ever climbed the economic ladder is by pulling himself or herself up one rung at a time. And we need to be championing policies that encourage individual responsibility and taking care of yourself and your family. It's the old line, give a man a fish, you feed him for a day; teach him how to fish you feed him for a lifetime. We need to be teaching people to fish.

Janine: Well, this should start in the schools, too, don't you believe? I mean the culture—

Senator Cruz: Yeah, absolutely.

Janine: Cathy Gillespie and I have started a foundation called Constituting America to educate kids, but we try to reach them through the culture with "best short film," "best song." But the culture of the schools, the judicial branch even to a certain extent, and the liberal press, I mean it's just permeated everywhere. Thank goodness for the tea parties, is all I have got to say [laughing], they really helped change things around.

Senator Cruz: Oh, yeah, no, I mean it really is incredible, and it's millions of Americans standing up and really concerned about the direction of our country—

Janine: Well, we really need to start with this. The bottom line of my show is "Where is Reason." But the youth of our country are being taught one way and that's the only way, especially for so many liberal professors in college. If they can have both perspectives, they can at least reason and have a basis of reasoning that's not just one sided. You can't reason if you are just force-fed a particular message, like Biden going to those school kids and saying that their problems are because the rich don't want to pay their taxes. Did you see that?

Senator Cruz: Yeah. And the young people are being fed a bill of goods. I have two daughters, a three-year-old and a one-year-old, and both of them were born into the world owing $50,000 a piece. And young people, we are saddling them with crushing debt because their parents and grandparents can't live within their means, and it's fundamentally immoral. None of us would do that to our kids in our own lives, and yet, that's what our country is doing to our kids.

Janine: Yeah, so it's kind of big. So what about these mandatory spending entitlements? [How] do you feel about that?

Senator Cruz: We have to take on entitlement reform. Any politician who says he or she is going to balance the budget without entitlement reform is lying. Right now, the federal government borrows forty cents [on] every dollar that it spends. Entitlements and interest on the debt constitute two-thirds of [the] federal budget, which means you could shut down the entire federal government; you could fire the Army, the Navy; you could shut down the FBI; you could close every federal park, and the federal budget still wouldn't balance. The only way to bring our government spending under control is fundamental entitlement reform. Now the problem is whenever you talk about that, the Democrats demagogue the heck out of you. And yet, I am convinced that the people are ready for serious leadership on these issues now, and I will tell you I mean I am campaigning on entitlement reform.

Janine: Do you like Kay Bailey Hutchinson's new Social Security plan?

Senator Cruz: I don't know that I have seen the elements of her plan in particular. I have very strong views on what I think should be done to Social Security.

Janine: Okay. So what do you think should be done to Social Security?

Senator Cruz: I think any reasonable reform should have four elements. Number one, for seniors on Social Security or near Social Security [age], there should be no change whatsoever, and I think that is a commitment that they have made, planned on, they have expected, and we need to carry through with that commitment. But for younger workers—I mean I am forty, for people of my generation, most of us don't think Social Security is going to be there in the first place.

Janine: Right, that's so true, [Laughing] yeah.

Senator Cruz: And there are three simpler reforms you can do that can save Social Security. I mean the truth of the matter is the Democrats, if we continue on the path we are on, Social Security is headed towards bankruptcy. You have got to have fundamental reform to save Social Security. And the three reforms that I would do is number one, gradually increase the age of eligibility. When FDR put Social Security in place, the average life expectancy was sixty-two, the age of eligibility was sixty-five.

Janine: Doesn't that amaze you?

Senator Cruz: It's incredible how things change, but the math doesn't work. It was initially designed to be in the very tail years of life. Now we have got life expectancy up at seventy-eight. And if you gradually increase the eligibility age for younger workers who have time to plan on it, time to save, that's step one. Step two, right now, Social Security benefits grow about 1 percent more than inflation. If you simply (overlapping)—

Janine: Isn't that called COLA?

Senator Cruz: Yes. If you simply have [to] match inflation rather than grow more than inflation, those two changes make Social Security solvent. The third piece that I think is critical is to allow younger workers to use a portion of their tax money to go to a personal account that they own and that they control that can earn market interest rate and that when they pass away, they can pass on to their kids and grandkids.

Janine: I like that; I like that a lot.

Senator Cruz: And I think people are ready for leadership on these issues. I don't think the Democrats are going to succeed in demagoguing these issues the way they have in the past.

Janine: Well, thank goodness we need strong leaders like you up there to take care. I like that plan a lot because I am forty-eight, I don't expect to see any Social Security either really [Laughing]. And I have a thirteen-year-old, soon to be fourteen-year-old daughter, and I would love to see her be able just to do what you said. That was your third step, I guess, about putting in account to do it. That just makes more sense, wouldn't you say?

Senator Cruz: Yeah. No, I mean it has grown out of control. And in the last three years, we have galloped further and faster towards government control of the economy in our lives than anytime in history, and we have got to stop. And I will tell you, the stakes in the Senate race, the entire fight in Texas, is the Republican primary. The primary is on March 6th—it's just four months away. And at this point, my principal opponent is Lt. Governor David Dewhurst. So the lieutenant governor is a perfectly nice, decent man, but his record as lieutenant governor has not been conservative. He has proposed the State of Texas should have an income tax; he has flip-flopped on issues like sanctuary cities, like in-state tuition for illegal aliens; he has flip-flopped—he killed the bill this last session that would have prohibited the TSA from groping you at an airport. And to my mind, this race is going to come down to two simple questions, will the next senator from Texas be a strong conservative and will the next senator from Texas be a fighter. And I think Texas is too conservative of a state for us not to be leading the fight. The four strongest conservatives in the U.S. Senate right now are Jim DeMint, Mike Lee, Rand Paul, and Pat Toomey, and I am incredibly humbled and honored to be the only candidate in the country who all four of them are supporting.

Janine: Oh, that's great.

Senator Cruz: Because they need reinforcement; they need a conservative and a fighter who is willing to take on the squishy leadership in our own party and address this brave economic and fiscal crisis.

Janine: Well, and hold the executive branch accountable. I can't believe that Obama goes out saying, "We can't wait for that legislative branch." If there was ever an example of why the Constitution is so incredibly vital and relevant, it's that. I mean I think that President Obama is the one who would dissolve the legislative and judicial branches in a minute if he could. I think the Senate and the House have passed so many things that actually hurt them in the long run; they gave too much power to the executive branch. It comes back to bite us.

Senator Cruz: And this is a president who has just been lawless, I mean yeah, this is the president who creates czars seemingly every day.

Janine: Oh, I know, I wrote an op-ed on that too, the czars. Okay, I am so glad you brought that up because I have an op-ed about czars, and I really, really am concerned about czars and the amount of them. I think Obama has like forty-something with eighteen waiting in the wings. What's your position on czars? And I don't need to let you go.

Senator Cruz: I think we have to restrain the unconstitutional actions of this president, and he has just disregarded the law, whether it was the offshore drilling moratorium. I represented the U.S. Chamber of Commerce in twenty-nine chambers of commerce challenging the offshore drilling moratorium in federal court, and the Federal Court of Appeals agreed with us that the moratorium was contrary to federal law, and this president essentially ignores that. Or if you look at something like "Fast and Furious," which is another just disgraceful program where you had all federal law enforcement officials deliberately selling guns to violent criminals who in turn used the guns to murder innocent people.

Janine: And nobody knows about it, of course. I didn't know about it.

Senator Cruz: This is an administration that admitted to a radical leftist agenda expanding government power of every aspect of our lives, and they are willing to pursue it by any means necessary.

Janine: Well, it's just going to bring down our country, because if you look at Europe, socialism obviously does not work, and it's not working. And I love reason, and I don't think there is any reason behind even proposing socialism in this country, without this Obamacare and all this. Obviously we can't sustain it with that $15 trillion. When did we hit that, like today or tomorrow or something, the $15 trillion or have we already?

Senator Cruz: Yeah, I mean we are right there. And you are right, the math just doesn't work. They can disregard a whole lot of laws, but one law they can't disregard is the law of arithmetic. You are right, socialism has been a dismal failure; everywhere in the world, it's been tried, and yet, that's the direction where you are barreling towards under this president and under Harry Reid in the Senate.

Janine: Well, it would just absolutely destroy our country; it will bring it completely down because we can't sustain that; it's not sustainable. And when you run out of money, then tyranny can come, and people get—there is a big depression. I think it jeopardizes a republic in a form of government, almost worse than a war or a tyrant. I mean I know security is huge, dealing with terrorism and all that, but debt is a kind of a tyrant within itself, don't you think, because of what it can—

Senator Cruz: The chairman of the Joint Chiefs of Staff told Congress that in his opinion, the single greatest national security threat to the United States is our out-of-control national debt.

Janine: Well, there you go.

Senator Cruz: As Margaret Thatcher put it, "the problem with socialism is eventually you run out of other people's money."

Janine: Right [Laughing], so true. Well, you are just awesome. I am so glad we have the opportunity to meet over the radio. I look forward to meeting you in person. Let me brag on you a little bit. You are the former solicitor general of Texas; you are the first Hispanic solicitor general in Texas, the youngest solicitor general in America, and the longest to hold the position in Texas. That's pretty impressive. You are currently a partner at the law firm Morgan, Lewis, & Bockius, where you lead the firm's U.S. Supreme Court and national appellate litigation practice. You are an adjunct professor of law at the University of Texas School of Law, where you teach U.S. Supreme Court Litigation. But, get this, you earned your BA from Princeton University and your JD *magna cum laude* from Harvard Law School. That's impressive.

Senator Cruz: [Laughing] Well, I will tell you anytime I am in West Texas, and it comes up that I went to Princeton and Harvard Law School, I immediately have to say, "I have got an awful to apologize for."

Janine: Yeah, exactly, but that's impressive, that's really—and you are a second-generation American, I guess. Your father is the one who came—

Senator Cruz: Yeah. My dad came with nothing back in '57.

Janine: See, that's the American promise; that's the dream of America that we don't want to extinguish, that great flame, the great hope of America.

Senator Cruz: Well, Janine, it underscores why I am running. I mean when I was a kid, and my dad used to say to me over and over again, "When we faced depression in Cuba, I had a place to flee to. If we lose our freedom here, where do we go?" And it's an incredible blessing to be the child of someone who had fled oppression because you understand just how fragile liberty is. And if we don't stand up and defend it right now, we are at risk of losing it.

Janine: I agree with you; I could not agree with you more. Somehow, I have had a love for the Founding Fathers since third grade, I don't know why. It's strange. John Adams is one of my all-time favorites, and Alexander Hamilton and George

Washington and all of them, Jefferson. But they knew tyranny; they knew what it was like, and we are spoiled in this country; we don't know what it's like. But as you say, there is a great hope; there is a promise in the genius of the people—they believed in the genius of the people—and I think that a lot of us understand that more than Washington, D.C., gives us all credit for [Laughing].

Senator Cruz: Now I think that's exactly right, and I think there is a great awakening. I call it the second great conservative awakening. The first one was in 1980 with the Reagan Revolution, and the second one is happening right now. And I will tell you in our campaign, we have seen and are seeing a conservative army coming together all across Texas and all across the country.

Janine: Awesome. Well, I can see why. I think you are very, very impressive, and I am thrilled that you took the time to be on *The Janine Turner Show* today. And I look forward to meeting you. I am a Texan; I am right here in Texas. So I have longhorn cattle. That fits in with UT.

Senator Cruz: Fantastic.

Janine: Yeah, Tiger Bud, he's kind of orange.

Senator Cruz: My dad was UT class of '61.

Janine: Oh, really? Oh, my gosh. My nephew is at A&M. I am sorry to say, but I love UT, just as well.

Senator Cruz: Well, I have got Longhorn blood in me, but I am actually—I love the Aggies, too. They are a fearsome crew, and they are fighters.

Janine: They are, so true. Well, listen, thank you for your time. I look forward to speaking with you again, and God bless you in all that you are doing. We need you; we appreciate it so much.

Senator Cruz: Well, thank you so much, Janine. It's really great to be with you.

Janine: All right, thank you. Bye.

The Janine Turner Show
Originally aired on janineturner.com
Re-aired on KLIF Dallas

Chapter Seven

Seeking and Keeping Sobriety

It's a great advantage not to drink among hard-drinking people.

—F. Scott Fitzgerald

Preface

If I am an alcoholic, then I must be weak.
If you are an alcoholic, then you have a disease.
I will not be able to cope.
You will be given coping skills.
I will lose all my friends.
With friends like that, who needs enemies?
I will lose all my passion.
You will realize how monochromatic your life has been.
It's impossible to never drink again.
You will not drink again one day at a time.
I will lose my best friend.
You will lose your worst enemy.
I will be dishonored.
You will be envied and respected.
I will be worthless.
You will be a hero.

A Classic Conversation between an
Active Alcoholic and a Sober Alcoholic
—Janine Turner

Sex, drugs, and rock 'n roll. Beer, wine, pot, and pills. We as a nation are inebriated by quick fixes. Not everyone is an addict or alcoholic, but many, many, many are. And once the drug or drink is picked up, only an infinitesimal percentage can ever recover and stay recovered.

Alcoholism is a cyclical, hereditary disease—an allergy. If both parents are alcoholics, then their child has a 100 percent chance of becoming an alcoholic. If one parent is an alcoholic, then their child has a 50 percent chance of becoming an alcoholic—tragic consequences. Jails are filled with good people who were "blacked out" from alcohol or drugs. Families are ruined, lives devastated.

In these pages I discuss in various genres how I stopped drinking at twenty-three years of age, how I've coped with life as a sober woman and mother, and how I've dealt with the social, moral, and parenting effects. These many stages have been mostly poignant but never easy. That's why I have learned to "Let go and let God."

If I Have You

THE CHILLING winds of adversity may blow,
  Life's turbulent waters may flow

And though my eyes be wet with
  sorrow's tears
It's having YOU that always cheers

Me along life's oft uneven road,
And when cares are heaviest—
  always YOU lighten my load.

Then when life flows smoothly
  along,
YOU add beauty to it, with your
  cheerfulness and song

So today as we sing Songs of joyous
  Christmas cheer,
The most that I can ask Him for
  is that I may have YOU from
  year to year!

–Copyrighted 1927
Richard H. Burgess
My great-grandfather Burgess

My Spiritual Walk

My desire is to walk with God every day.
My desire is to live His will for my life.
My desire is to let go of my ego and let in His direction.
My desire is to remember that all I do should glorify Him.
My desire is to be a forgiving, non-judgmental person.
My desire is to continually nourish my soul with His word.
My desire is to stand up and brush myself off when I make mistakes, and ask for forgiveness.

janineturner.com
2003

Grandpa J.B.

Years ago my dad gave me a massive book documenting the Gauntt family lineage. It sat on my shelf for quite a while. One day I was flipping through it, and I was astounded by journal entries of James Bass Gauntt, my paternal great-great-grandfather, in the back of the book. One of the entries was about his withdrawals from John Barleycorn. I was awestruck by the evil, his torment, and his vivid imagery. He painted a complete and thorough picture of the tribulation. Equally as mesmerizing was the dire warning he proclaimed to his progeny—stay away from John Barleycorn. I knew nothing about this episode in his life. I, coincidentally, have not only heeded his warning, but I also have preserved his humble homily in a song. Here is his recounting and the subsequent lyrics I wrote in 2009. Recently, I glanced through his entries again, and I have a newfound appreciation for his political views. He was a character!

Boys, Stay away From John Barleycorn

Written by John Bass Gauntt, my great-great-grandfather, on November 12, 1922

I am writing the following experience for the benefit of any boy or young man that by chance they may read these lines: Following is the only experience the writer ever had with a well-developed case of delirium tremens; had been drinking for three or four days, was confined to a private room for a few days, after the last drink. (Then is when they come on from twelve to twenty-four hours from the last drink). In the afternoon and just before night the scenery began to come and go; saw some of the most beautiful sights my eyes ever beheld; some of the prettiest little snow-white children come before me, one little girl especially, snow-white complexion, with auburn hair, and sparkling blue eyes; beautiful landscapes and mountain scenery would come and go, and the writer was wide awake while all this was going on; demons with awful faces would appear and disappear between midnight and day; beautiful birds by the million began milling and circling around under what appeared a vast upturned plain. They kept this up till daylight, accompanied by all the above scenery... Just at the dawn of day I noticed some fine Plymouth Rock chickens pearched (sic.) on the foot of my bed (this was not a dream—was wide awake) they were gentle and perfectly satisfied, apparently. The next scenery was a bunch of carrion crows sitting around on my bed, I could see them bat their eyes and would walk around over the bed, when one came toward my head I would grab at him but failed to catch him, but he was there all the same and black as an imp itself and while these things were romping around over my bed something resembling a big long-nosed black possum with cripped-up ears and black keen eyes came crawling from among the chickens and carrion crows up across my body, could feel his crawling and almost hear him breathing; I made a dive at him but failed to get him and while this was all going on everywhere I would turn my eyes about the room I could see big snakes come slipping down the walls toward me, and they would come from under the bed and from under a piano sitting in the room and big black wharf rats would come from under the bed and piano and chase around over the floor while this was taking place; in a certain place on the wall there was an imp hanging by his hind legs every time I would look at him he was fixing to jump on me; he was about as large as a grey squirrel, cold black, with sharp ears, and black keen eyes. Another portion of the wall, there was a covey of quail, some small, to natural size running around the wall; another place on the wall hung a picture of a beautiful little girl and her dog, and the little girl would shake her head, bat her eyes and make mouths at me and the dog did similar acts. (This picture was real, but the little girl and dog made fun of me all the same.) I saw many other demons and devils too numerous to mention. I stood this awful ordeal to about 9 A.M., and could stand it no longer; I left that room and went into the room where the family was, but the demons kept after me, snakes and rats would come from under the stove and beds and I could look out across the street and see men some with white shirts on, working around a work train and tried to show them to some of the family but they could not see them ... Boys don't never tamper with no kind of John Barley Corn, for he will drag you down into disgrace and degradation."

(first and last time) J.B. Gauntt

Grandpa J.B.

I wrote this song based on my great-great-
grandfather J.B. Gauntt's letter.

(Verse)
It started as snowy white children
One girl with red auburn hair
Beautiful birds by million were milling
Around my lonesome straw chair.

(Verse)
By dawn the Plymouth Rock chickens
Perched at the foot of my bed
Turned to crows, batting their eyes
Soaring all over my head

(Verse)
Out came a possum attacking
Black as a wild, evil imp
Breathing beside me, tearing my veins
He dodged my feeble attempts

(Chorus)
Boys, stay away from John Barleycorn
Listen to Grandpa J.B.
My wits and my ways are ransomed
And he won't let me see or be me

(Verse)
Slipping down walls racing at me
I see snakes, and wild, red-eyed pigeons
And the girl with her dog in the painting
Shakes her blonde-headed piggy-tailed ribbons

(Verse)
No, no, she says, eyebrows knitted
You ruin your chance at redemption
As long as you stay on the liquors
Your heart will no longer listen

(Verse)

I scold her and tear at her image
Hearing cries from the very next room
I pause and hear my sweet family
Weeping from the feelings of doom

(Chorus)

Boys, stay away from John Barleycorn
Listen to Grandpa J.B.
My wits and my ways are ransomed
And he won't let me see or be me

(Verse)

What started as fun, harmless frolic
Beer with boys on wild Friday nights
Has turned into frightful reliance
On spirits that drown out my light

(Verse)

Men in white coats stand there laughing
Pointing and starting to seize me
I scream at the ghosts of my haunting
Demons of barley made whiskey

(Verse)

I cry out for help and forgiveness
I seek freedom from John Barleycorn
I hear now my father's recounting
The sickness that starts with just one

(Chorus)

Boys, stay away from John Barleycorn
Listen to Grandpa J.B.
My wits and my ways are ransomed
And he won't let me see or be me

Alcoholism is Ancient

I accepted the opportunity to speak to Houston's Council on Alcohol and Drugs after it was procured by my beloved cousin Robert Gauntt. Robert and I never met as kids, even though we were both raised in Fort Worth, Texas. By Divine Providence, I met Robert indirectly. On a Braniff flight, returning home to NYC in 1987, I made a choice that I now know was prompted by God, to sit in the wrong seat. (The plane was half full and it was pre-9/11). I inadvertently sat by Robert's NYC roommate. He asked me if I was related to his roommate Robert Gauntt. I said, "I don't think so." I gave Robert's roommate my number anyway. Robert promptly called me and we met for lunch. We discussed our mutual heritage. We were related! Our great-great-grandfather was Grandpa J.B. Our fathers' grandfathers were brothers! All of us were of the lineage to whom Grandpa J.B. warned, "Boys, stay away from John Barleycorn." At our lunch Robert was amazed that I was only drinking iced tea. I shared my sobriety with him. He consequentially got sober shortly thereafter. Robert, who today has twenty-seven years of sobriety, and I, who have twenty-eight years of sobriety, have remained very close. We often guide one another through the life lessons of sobriety, still marveling at God's divine purpose in bringing us together. God wanted me to share my sobriety with Robert, which never would've happened if I hadn't sat in the wrong seat on that flight to NYC.

Speech to Houston's Council on Alcohol and Drugs

"Who has woe? Who has sorrow? Who has strife? Who has complaints? Who has needless bruises? Who has bloodshot eyes? Those who linger over wine, who go to sample bowls of mixed wine. Do not gaze at wine when it is red, when it sparkles in the cup, when it goes down smoothly! In the end it bites like a snake and poisons like a viper. Your eyes will see strange sights and your mind will imagine confusing things. You will be like one sleeping on the high seas, lying on top of the rigging. 'They hit me,' you will say, 'but I'm not hurt! They beat me, but I don't feel it! When will I wake up, so I can find another drink?'"

I love this passage because I believe it sums up alcoholism. It is timeless. It is absolutely accurate and spellbinding in its description. Do you know from where this passage comes? Would anyone like to guess? The Bible. The Old Testament. From King Solomon, the wisest man who ever lived. From the time period around

970 BC. This passage is from Proverbs 23:29-35. I read the Bible in a year in 2002, and when I read this proverb I was both amazed and comforted by the fact that the Bible would reference alcohol in such a way.

Alcoholism. Alcoholism is ancient. Alcoholism is present. Alcoholism is prevalent, rampant, insidious, genetic, cunning, baffling, debilitating, frightening, disruptive, evil.

It rips souls apart, families apart, lives apart, children apart. It creates wounds, scars, disfigurement of mind, holes in the body, lineages of heart-rending devastations—like the waste of a nuclear bomb. It creates generations of cyclical behavior that leaves children and grandchildren and great-grandchildren to see their destinies reflected in pools of dysfunction, denial, and violence. They are left nursing deep wounds filled with years of tears and blood and alcohol. They are dazed and confused and on a path for destruction laid for them by the train tracks of history, by the cycles that spin and spin like a ravaging tornado, spinning lies and deception, spewing blame and shame in its wake. The wake of wine poured, champagne ordered, beer foaming, martinis shaken, brandy sniffed, scotch on ice clinking—over and over and over again. Over and over again. And the devil laughs.

I have seen my reflection in those pools. I have nursed those deep and disturbing wounds. I have lain in the devastation of the nuclear bomb. I have raced upon those train tracks. I have been ravaged by the tornado, and I have writhed on the wake of its destruction.

And I have survived, and I am here to tell you today that I have seventeen years of sobriety. The devil did not win with me. By the grace of my forgiving and loving and generous God, I was lifted out of the mire and given a second chance. And I feel no shame. I only feel the deepest sense of gratitude.

I was twenty-three years old when I decided to surrender my will to God, not even totally grasping what that meant. I only knew that I was free from the bondage of denial, that I was choosing to challenge my haunts. I was tapping them on the shoulder and challenging them to a duel. One day at a time. With wobbly legs I ventured into this new journey, which at times felt like a marathon. Strength came only with prayer, persistence in seeking help in all of the right avenues, and showing up. I learned that one has to show up for sobriety and one has to show up for life. No more hiding. No more running. No more escaping. Raw. Raw. Raw. I have learned that vulnerability and willingness don't ruin you—they actually heal you. I have learned that humility reaps many rewards: clarity, compassion, passion, discipline, forgiveness, hope.

God has graced me with sobriety, and sobriety has both strengthened my character and shaped my talents. Daily I am reminded of my faults and my fears, but daily I strive to overcome them. When times are tough, when times are confusing, when I am experiencing fear, I exercise something I never had before: coping skills. I drop to my knees in prayer, I try to promptly initiate calm and clear communication, I express my feelings through writing, I read the Bible, I exercise, and I take a hot bath! Believe it or not, a hot bath does wonders!

Sobriety has many promises, many gifts. The most meaningful gift of sobriety that I have received besides my daily, deepening walk with God is the fact that I am able to show my daughter both the joy of sobriety and that we no longer have to ride the train tracks of history. No matter what accomplishments I have achieved and will achieve, the greatest accomplishment of my life is that my daughter will walk through her life fortified with the knowledge and the example of a life lived fully without alcohol. The cycle has been broken.

My assistant told me a true story the other day about a friend of hers who had an alcoholic father who was also an atheist. She had been praying for years for her father's sobriety and salvation. His years of alcohol abuse resulted in a coma. She prayed over her father's bed as he lay in a coma. After much deliberation, the family finally decided to pull the plug. So they did. They all gathered around his bedside and the plug was pulled. After the plug was pulled, there was silence, and then he woke up. He woke up and looked at this daughter and said, "I have been dreaming. I have been dreaming that I was on a battlefield of good and evil and then a hand reached out and touched me and said, "Do you want to be a hero?" And I said "Yes," and I woke up. He looked at his daughter and said, "I want to be a hero."

I believe that this story is not only miraculous but relevant. The fight for sobriety is like being on a battlefield of good and evil. The armor of alcoholism is fear of shame and stigma. The sword of alcoholism is denial. The armor of sobriety is awareness and acceptance. The sword of sobriety is action.

This battlefield spans across all societal boundaries and affects people of both genders, every ethnic group, and people in every tax bracket.

These are some of the battles that are being waged:

- There are more deaths and diseases in the US from substance abuse than from any other cause.

- About 18 million Americans have alcohol problems.

- More than half of all adults have a history of alcoholism or problem drinking.

- Heavy drinking contributes to illnesses in each of the top three causes of death: heart disease, cancer, stroke.

- Our nation's children and teenagers are not immune to this problem. About 6.8 million Americans between the ages of 12–20 are binge drinkers, and 2.1 million are heavy drinkers.

The battlefield, the arena, *per se*, is played upon perception. The Department of Health and Human Services made the following analysis:

> *Alcohol advertising overwhelmingly associates drinking with positively valued activities and consequences such as romance, sociability, and relaxation, and creates a climate in which drinking is presented as normal, appropriate, and benevolent. More subtly, the use of alcohol is linked to happiness, wealth, power, prestige, sophistication, success, maturity, athletic ability, virility, romance, creativity, sexual satisfaction, and other positive images. Adolescents who are heavily exposed to advertising were more likely to agree that drinkers possess valued characteristics such as being attractive, athletic, and successful.*

These images perpetuate the lie. It is cool to drink. It is hip to drink. Life is great as long as I can drink. I will only have friends if I drink. I can't do business without a drink, I can't be sexy without a drink, and so on and so on. To equal the playing field, what if the ads showed the other side of drinking? What if the ads showed drinkers holding their drinks as they were falling off their barstools, incapable of walking, slurring their speech, sobbing on the sidewalk, sleeping on a park bench, sobbing in hysteria, shouting obscenities, throwing up over toilets, choking on their own vomit, dying in a hospital bed, having a fist fight with their best friend, passing out on the floor, driving their car into a pole, raping innocent women, stabbing their enemy, denying their family, getting killed in a car accident, killing others in a car accident, hitting their spouses, hitting their children, verbally abusing, burning in a fire, getting HIV, shooting their lover, shooting themselves?

Awareness, acceptance, action. Awareness is the first step. In order to level the playing field, the American public must be made aware of the trials and tribulations associated with drinking alcohol. Facilitating more public service announcements is paramount, and it will require both funding and fighting for more air space on the networks.

The most fervent battle, however, lurks and lingers in the alcoholic's mind. Denial is truly the devil's doing. Here is a classic conversation that an active alcoholic would have with a sober alcoholic.

> *If I am an alcoholic, then I must be weak.*
> **If you are an alcoholic, then you have a disease.**
> *I will not be able to cope.*
> **You will be given coping skills.**
> *I will lose all my friends.*
> **With friends like that, who needs enemies?**
> *I will lose all my passion.*
> **You will realize how monochromatic your life has been.**
> *It's impossible to never drink again.*
> **You will not drink again one day at a time.**
> *I will lose my best friend.*
> **You will lose your worst enemy.**
> *I will be dishonored.*
> **You will be envied and respected.**
> *I will be worthless.*
> **You will be a hero.**

Awareness, acceptance, action. These are all things that the Council on Alcohol and Drugs Houston is seeking to establish and communicate throughout the community. Their goal is to reach one million alcoholics by December 2004. What a momentous mission. What a worthy goal. All of you here today have contributed to this vision. The battle will be won because good always defeats evil, one day at a time, one alcoholic at a time.

I close with a verse from Proverbs 24: "By wisdom a house is built and through understanding it is established, through knowledge its rooms are filled with rare and beautiful treasures."

May God bless the alcoholic, may God bless the council, and may God bless you.

Janine Turner
2004
Speech to Houston's Council on Alcohol and Drugs

Dialogue about Sobriety with Maureen Quinn

That's exactly what keeps me coming back, is the laughter. It's not an ugly world sober. We understand how blessed we really are. We laugh because we have escaped great tragedy, we laugh because we are in the lifeboat, we laugh because we have cried, not because we are clowns. We know how blessed we really are.

–Maureen Quinn

In 1986, when I had 37 days sobriety, I attended a Hollywood meeting. Out of the corner of my eye, I saw a young woman who looked a lot like Candice Bergen throw her head back in laughter, cascading her Wella Balsam blond hair in a dramatic fashion. I had yet to see such happiness in sobriety. She had a smile that lit up the room. Upon her countenance she shared her joy with a wisdom born of obvious trials and tribulations. It was both her depth and her contagious zeal for life that drew me across the room to meet her. I wanted what she had. I related to her dualities. As Kahlil Gibran said, "The selfsame well from which your laughter rises was oftentimes filled with your tears." I could relate!

Her name was Maureen Quinn, and she had a year-and-a-half of sobriety. We became fast friends and have remained so for over twenty-eight years. We have traveled the United States together and weathered many storms, and I don't mean rain—more like the thunder of the soul. Together, we tackled our torments with a lasso of humor. In the past, we wrote screenplays together. We also envisioned a coffee shop where people could sit and chat, because we would wander around New York City and Hollywood desperately seeking a sober place to hang! Starbucks ring a bell? We joke about how we thought of it first!

Now, coincidentally, both of us are single mothers, and we are reunited as a writing partners. We also share two segments on my radio show. I'm including two of our segments together. One is about how we continue to cope with life in a sober way (below) and the second is about holidays and sobriety. By the grace of God, I currently have twenty-eight years of sobriety and Maureen has thirty years of sobriety. My, how time flies when you're having fun!

Maureen: "Days of wine and roses." This is from a movie classic. Did you ever get a chance to see the movie, *The Days of Wine and Roses*?

Janine: Is that about alcoholism?

Maureen: Yes, yes, it is, and Jack Lemmon was brilliant in the movie [with] Lee Remick. Major classic. It's *The Days of Wine and Roses*, about alcoholism, and this is the scene where he is recovering and his wife can't stay sober and the baby girl is in the crib and the wife comes in and he has this chat with her and says, "You remember how it really was, you and me and booze, a threesome. You and I were a couple of drunks on the sea of booze, and the boat sank. I got hold of something that kept me from going under, and I am not going to let go of it, not for you, not for anyone, If you want to grab on, grab on, but there's just room for you and me, no threesome."

Janine: That is such a great line!

Maureen: Isn't that?! And you know what I love about it? The movie is so believable and there is the little girl in the crib, then the next line is of course he goes on to say, "There's a little girl in this crib who would love to wake up and see her mother here." And he says, "All you have to do is say the right words." You know it's alcoholism, and it touches just about everybody's life in one way or another. And she just can't do it, that's the disease. She says, "The world just looks too dirty to me when I'm sober." When she's sober, she just can't deal with that reality. You think of all the great actors and writers who died of alcoholism and what they *could* have done. You know, when I was teaching, I told my students to imagine what these great actors and artists who died of alcoholism could have accomplished had they stayed sober. A lot of people think "Oh, I'll get into drugs and alcohol," and I say, "No, no, no, think what those artists could have done if they had known about sobriety and had they been able to stop, and if they were sober." Imagine what the great artists who died of alcoholism and drug addiction could have created had they found sobriety and been able to stop. It's powerful, powerful stuff.

Janine: A lot of people think, "Oh I can only be a great actor with drugs and alcohol. That's the only way I can possibly be passionate." It's the opposite. The drugs and alcohol will block any sort of passion and creativity. If you're sober, you can find a much deeper well. Of course, for those who are listening who don't know, you and I are both sober!

Janine and Maureen: Woo!!!

Maureen: Amen! Where two or more are gathered.

Janine: I'm twenty-seven, and you have twenty-nine. Are you twenty-nine?

Maureen: And as we know, it's for people who want it, not people who need it. Else we wouldn't see so many tragedies. They have to want it, like the quote says. That's why that movie is so realistic.

Janine: No room for a threesome. So, Maureen, are you twenty-nine or are you thirty?

Maureen: I'm twenty-nine years sober. Oh my gosh, you're twenty-seven.

Janine: I have twenty-seven, yep, yep! And I met Maureen in Los Angeles.

Maureen: Woo!

Janine: And I saw her, and she was so funny and had such a bright, lovely, upbeat countenance, and energy. And I'm like, I want that, and I thought, I want her to teach me about sobriety.

Maureen: You know, God bless you, and you know that's exactly what keeps me coming back, is the laughter. It's not an ugly world sober. We understand how blessed we really are. We laugh because we have escaped great tragedy, we laugh because we are in the lifeboat, we laugh because we have cried, not because we are clowns. We know how blessed we really are. I'm speaking for us, of course.

Janine: And you and I became best buddies, and we went around town together, getting our cars towed and laughing.

Maureen: Yes, and we laughed and somehow we knew.

Janine: It's sobriety.

Maureen: And lo and behold! Here's the good news, is that it's possible, it works.

Janine: It works if you work it.

Maureen: You have to want it. To me, it's one word, it's God, and God is love.

Janine: To wrap this up, cause we promised everyone in these segments around ten minutes. The thing that I talk about that is so amazing to me is that as a Christian I go to church and all these things, but the thing that's really interesting to me is that these alcoholics are people who need God so much to stay sober that there is a whole other level of faith there. There is a different faith, just God, Higher Power. People say, "I get on my knees and I have to ask God to help me get through the day." So, there's this need, and love, and appreciation of God.

Maureen: It's a hunger.

Janine: It's a need like a lifeboat.

Maureen: Just like the Bible says, we thirst after God. He's our food, He feeds our soul, our very lives. We hunger and we thirst after God. Our very lives are dependent upon God. Think how cool, just as in *The Days of Wine and Roses*, our little girls are being raised in a sober environment. Our children know what it is to face a world without drugs or alcohol, with sober parents, in a sober environment. And this goes out from here to their friends and their parents.

Janine: And happy times, sad times, difficult times, joyous times. You can deal with it all in sobriety.

Maureen: We are in the "No Matter What Club"! No matter what, we trust God, we don't drink or use.

Janine: We teach our children, and I have to stop talking now. (Laughing)

Maureen: We could go on.

Janine: We teach our kids about sobriety, about the disease of alcoholism. That it's a hereditary disease. Teach them to never, never pick up.

Maureen: The other thing to teach them is that it is important for people to know where to go to get help. Some people are out there, and they say, "Wow, I didn't know where to go to get help, I didn't know about hope and faith and God. I didn't know that it was a disease." The American Medical Association declared alcoholism a disease.

Janine: A hereditary disease.

Maureen: We were sick, trying to get well. And when you approach it like that, like First Lady of the United States Betty Ford, then you can look at it and say, "She wasn't a *bad* lady, but sick." There's that "dis—ease". Alcoholics are sick trying to get well, rather than bad trying to get good.

Janine: There you go. Well, Maureen, we'll keep talking about this. God bless you. Thank you for listening out there, and I hope you have a blessed, wonderful day. Remember, Jesus is the reason for the season.

Maureen: Amen. One day at a time. Keep your humor!

Janine: Thank you for listening everyone. Have a great, blessed day!

The Janine Turner Show
December 2013

Holidays in Sobriety with Maureen Quinn

Even when the time feels dark as we were talking about, during the holidays. When it appears dark, because we are in a spiritual war, and we have the darkness and the light, we can shine God's light in honor of the spirit Christmas. We can convey that light and put that light forth into the world in the name of God and the name of love. If not us, then who?

—Maureen Quinn

Maureen: This is from the movie *The Bishop's Wife*—

Janine: I hope this one is more upbeat than yesterday.

Maureen: Remember the Turner Movie Classic?

Janine: No.

Maureen: I love some of these old school ones. To quote from the movie *The*

Bishop's Wife: "Tonight I want to tell you the story of an empty stocking. Once upon a midnight clear, there was a child's cry, a blazing star hung over a stable, and wise men came with birthday gifts. We haven't forgotten that night down the centuries. We celebrate it with stars on Christmas trees, with the sound of bells, and with gifts. But especially with gifts. You give me a book, I give you a tie. Aunt Martha has always wanted an orange squeezer and Uncle Henry can do with a new pipe. For we forget nobody, adult or child. All the stockings are filled, all that is, except one. And we have even forgotten to hang it up. The stocking for the child born in a manger. It's his birthday we're celebrating. Don't let us ever forget what we are celebrating. Let us ask ourselves what He would wish for most. And then, let each put in his share, loving kindness, warm hearts, and a stretched out hand of tolerance. All the shining gifts that make peace on earth."

Janine: Oh, that's so cool. Wouldn't that be an interesting idea, to have a stocking for Jesus? That's a great conversation. What would you put in Jesus's stocking?

Maureen: That's great. What would you put in it? Love, kindness, joy, forgiveness, humanity—

Janine: That's an interesting thought, Maureen, because there is nothing you can put in his stocking that is tangible, because what Jesus represented was spiritual. The things we do, our spirit, it's love and kindness, joy, forgiveness, mercy.

Maureen: That's right. Even when the time feels dark as we were talking about, during the holidays. When it appears dark, because we are in a spiritual war, and we have the darkness and the light, we can shine God's light in honor of the spirit of Christmas. We can convey that light and put that light forth into the world in the name of God and the name of love. If not us, then who?

Janine: Well, God works through us on this earth.

Maureen: In the midst of that spiritual war, if you will, is God's light. God's light is saying, "Go forth from here, carry this on, not just in the stocking, but into the world, and be the light." That's the gift to pay it forward.

Janine: Maybe you could take little pieces of paper and write "mercy," "compassion," "love," "empathy," "forgiveness," things of this nature, because that's the only thing you can put in Jesus's stocking. That might be a cool thing to do with the family. What if we put a small piece of paper with words of love into Jesus's stocking? What would Jesus want you to represent in the coming year? Fold it up, put it in the stocking, and everybody pull it out and read it. That'd be pretty cool!

Maureen: Even moving into the New Year one day at a time, make every day a new beginning.

Janine: And the gift of God, grace is a gift He gives us. In return we give God our will. Okay Maureen, love ya!

The Janine Turner Show
December 2013

Booze, Big Business, and Prohibition

Keeping Americans inebriated was big business for the German beer makers, wineries, and other distillers during the turn of the century. It was also big income for the federal government. The government received 70 percent of its federal income from the liquor tax. Keeping Americans drunk was big business for the federal government until the Sixteenth Amendment, the income tax, diluted it.

It is hard for us to picture what life was like during the saloon days, when brothels and barrooms lined the streets. Men laid strewn about the town or, having journeyed home, administered abuses on the wives and children. Insult upon injury occurred when the wives realized that their husbands' paycheck had been exhausted too.

Men were despondent. Women were helpless. Children were emotionally scarred for life. Starting at age fifteen, the average man consumed eighty-eight bottles of whiskey a year.

And it was more potent, having a much higher alcohol content than those drinks consumed by our Founding Fathers.

"Alcohol was a sign of masculinity that robbed a man of his masculinity," according to the PBS Special, *Prohibition*, by Ken Burns and Lynn Novick. America had become a "Nation of Drunkards."

I haven't had a drink in over two decades, and I have a familial familiarity with the cycle of sorrows alcohol reaps. As a Constitutionalist, I disagree with the Eighteenth Amendment. As one who knows the insidiousness of alcohol, I see the virtues of the Prohibition movement.

Something had to be done.

Enter American freedom and American freedom of speech. American true grit. American women. The journey of Prohibition is the journey of a social justice that clashed with the rights of the people. Should not a lesson be learned here? The government does not have the right to tell American citizens what they should or should not eat, drink, or buy.

The Eighteenth Amendment did not work. The movement did. After the Eighteenth Amendment was repealed by the Twenty-First Amendment, the lasting effects of social justice were felt. The saloons and brothels were diminished, and awareness curbed abuses, to an extent. Things were better.

Lessons were learned with the Eighteenth and Twenty-First Amendments. A social movement can have a positive impact. Invasive government, intruding into people's private lives and their rights, does not work. Should the government decide if you get to drink a beer or eat a Twinkie? Does the government get to decide if you get "approved" as a recipient of medicine, that you are a life worth saving?

Something had to be done to bring awareness to the crisis of alcoholism, and, frankly, the best work was done not by the amendment but by the women's movement. Like whirlwinds, they who could not even vote banded together to create a force with which to be reckoned. Women set out to save their men and their children, and as a result, their country.

They were spat upon, doused with liquor, and sent outside into the cold snow by men in the saloons. The women took it in stride—the abuses at home were probably no different. They marched, they lobbied, they prayed. Women like Francis Willard and Carry Nation, having watched loved ones succumb to booze, were stewards of their wounds.

The repeal of the Eighteenth Amendment did not diminish their arduous, emotionally charged mission. Enlightenment shone upon the evils of alcohol.

Yet, the battle against booze is a highly personal one. Alcoholism is a disease. An amendment can no more cure a disease than Obamacare can ensure proper and fair healthcare to every American.

The battle rages on in our American culture. We live in a culture that laughs at people in "blackouts"—thinking it's funny that they don't remember what they did the previous night. We accept a culture that permeates the television with images of laughter and "getting the sexy girl" when men have a drink in their hand.

They don't show the rape, the drunken driver, the vomiting over the toilet, or the tears of wives, husbands, and children. Why would they? It's a business, after all. Why show the truth if the truth doesn't sell?

The current crisis doesn't end with alcohol. The next wave of cultural demise is prescription drugs. The "it's okay because my doctor prescribed them to me" drugs. It's not just Hollywood stars who are succumbing. It is the American populace and the future generations.

In America, another wave of addiction is upon us. We need more whirlwinds to change the course of the downward spiral of addiction. It may not be as bad as it was at the turn of the twentieth century, but it is a dark abyss destroying our nation's future.

Janine Turner
October 3, 2011
janineturner.com

Dialogue with Bob Beckel—On Sobriety

You and I both know that the first start on the road to sobriety could be rough and bumpy. But in time[...]it is the most remarkable world that you are looking at—that you never saw before—because you were looking at it through alcoholic eyes.

–Bob Beckel

Bob Beckel is the first Democrat I ever interviewed, but it was fun and painless, especially when I brought up our mutual sobriety. What I like about this interview is it shows that even though we differ politically, we have common ground. We, as Americans, have forgotten that we have common ground with each other. We have stopped looking for it. As a result, we are polarized, and conversations where we can reason with one another and share ideas have become obsolete. George Washington warned about this in his Farewell Address. He warned that the party system would be the demise of America because we would care more about the party than America—we would care more about the party than about each other. We have forgotten about the humanism that connects us. This interview with Bob Beckel poignantly demonstrates how we can connect with our political opposites, and how we should connect. We, once again, need to have a national conversation with each other, person to person, American to American—not Democrat to Republican.

Janine: Okay. Can I ask you a sobriety question?

Mr. Beckel: A sobriety question?

Janine: Yeah, I am sober. I have twenty-five years of sobriety.

Mr. Beckel: Oh, God bless you. I didn't know that. Good for you.

Janine: So if you don't want to talk about it in the air, I will cut this out. But if you want to talk about—

Mr. Beckel: Oh, no, I have no problem talking about it at all. I am actually quite happy to talk about it.

Janine: I have been intrigued hearing you talk about it. So I thought you might want to chat about that for sixty seconds or so.

Mr. Beckel: Well, the reason that I talked about it, there is actually two reasons. One, there is a little selfish reason because I think people would doubt me if I didn't, maybe more conservatives. But more importantly, when I talk about it, there are people out there [who] inevitably get in touch with me who have got problems. And if I can help five people, who will never recover from this, but put this horrible disease in advance, then it's well worth talking about it. I mean I think people hide that they are alcoholic. Look, I was—and you can understand this, but I have been sober for twelve years; I had a chance to live a second life. And if it hadn't been for being sober, I would be dead. So I have been blessed and so I have a responsibility as somebody in the program to reach out to people who need help, and I am proud to do it, and I am not at all ashamed of it.

Janine: I am not either. I feel that it's—you think it's the worst thing that could ever happen to you, and it ends up being the best thing to ever happen to you. And it's such an amazing gift, and it's like peeling the layers of the onion and seeing life in vibrant colors, and it's a spiritual awakening. It's such an amazing process. And I admire that you talk about it. I didn't talk about it for a long time, and I am starting to talk about it more. I want to start another foundation once I get this one rolling called "Your Friend in Sobriety" to encourage college kids and high-school kids and anyone in general, to just stay away from the pressure in high school or college to pick up the drink.

Mr. Beckel: Twenty-five years is—there are not many people who have that many years, and I admire you for doing it. And you have a lot to give to people on that regard. You have got to talk about it. Don't be afraid about it at all. Look, I am proud of you.[...] And you and I both know that the first start on the road to sobriety could be rough and bumpy. But in time[...]it is the most remarkable world that you are looking at that you never saw before because you were looking at it through alcoholic [eyes], I mean it's a blessing. But somebody who is drinking, it's a very hard thing to imagine that they could stay sober for the rest of their lives. And they don't stay sober for the rest of their lives; they are sober today and maybe—

Janine: Yeah, one day at a time, one minute at a time.

Mr. Beckel: Yeah, one minute at a time. I've been there, I should tell you.

Janine: I know. Well, for the person listening out there, who thinks, "Oh my God, I have too much stress in my life, I can't possibly—I can't lose my best friend, this bottle of alcohol. I had to have it for the stress." What would you say?

Mr. Beckel: I would say everybody has stress. The problem with answering that hole—and generally, stress is about a hole, and I also think it's a spiritual hole mostly, is that when you fill it with alcohol or drugs, you are filling it with something that's going to kill you or somebody else because you are drunk, and you are driving, or something. And what it's doing is making your stress worse. There was nothing about alcohol and drugs, except it momentarily will make it feel like stress has gone away. But the next day, the stress is worse as a result of it. And so stress is a lousy excuse. Everybody has got it, but you don't have to drink it away. There [are] ways to deal with it. And I think—so that's my view.

Janine: Primarily, for me, it's the connection with God. I am powerless. Here is one thing I want to finish with. I promise that this will be my last. To me, the disease of alcoholism, what's so fascinating to me about it is that God is the only one [who] can heal it, and there is a lot of eastern medical philosophy, and as you know, it's not so much about taking a pill or it's not a medicine. And look at the miracle: it's God, it's the spiritual healing that heals the body of alcoholism. And I don't think there is really any other disease out there where that can be said.

Mr. Beckel: That's right. It drives me crazy when I hear about these miracle cures for alcoholism. There is only one cure, and that is you have to stop drinking one day at a time and you have to turn your life over to God. I mean if you are willing to do that and you can understand it, you could absorb it after a while. But Bill Wilson was brilliant when he put this together because he knew that talking about God might scare a lot of people who were drinkers. So he talked about a higher power, but we know what he was talking about. And eventually, when you get enough sobriety under your belt, you realize that your higher power is in fact the Lord. And when you come to that—look, I didn't believe before I got sober. Now, if nothing else, what a great blessing that was.

Janine: Oh, so true. The higher power. God is literally our power to get through the day to stay sober. Well, listen, I know you have other things to do. I love you on the Five. You did a great job on Hannity. And thanks for being the first liberal on my radio show.

Mr. Beckel: I am honored, and I will remember this day forever. Thank you, Janine.

Janine: [Laughing] Come back. Okay, thanks so much.

Mr. Beckel: Okay, God bless you. Okay.

Janine: God bless you. Bye-bye.

The Janine Turner Show
August 27, 2012

Chapter Eight

Dealing with Dad's Death

Spiritual resonance is what changes the world.

—Monsignor Don Fischer

Preface

As I was compiling this book, my father died. The loss of having my father in my life has been devastating and the effects surreal. There really is a valley in the shadow of death. It has only been two months since he died, so I know I will be experiencing more stages of grief in the days, months, and years ahead. Through the haze of sadness and, at times, a maze of madness, I have journeyed forth into the land of the living. As Shakespeare said, and C.S. Lewis etched on his tombstone, "Life is enduring the going hence."

In this chapter, the final chapter of this book, I have included a transcript from a radio interview I did with my dad, a tribute to him, and poetry. My father was one of those men who was larger than life. His spirit resides in heaven but his presence is etched in the air—here—everywhere, everywhere. I love you, Dad, but I know you know that.

Janine: *Okay Dad, listen, you have got to come back on the show again because we have so many more stories. But thanks for those stories. This is really great. Thanks, Dad, I love you.*

Mr. Gauntt: *Love you, baby.*

Interviewing my dad
The Janine Turner Show
2011

Dialogue with My Father, Turner Maurice Gauntt, Jr.

Well, it was pretty tough. The whole program was tough, and especially the first year, called plebe year—it was extremely unpleasant… Because they wanted to see if they could break you down and then build you back up.

–Turner Maurice Gauntt, Jr.

My father, though a man of few words, would occasionally share some of his stories about his days at the United States Military Academy at West Point and in the United States Air Force. I often wanted to write them down, record them, and videotape them. Now that he has passed, I realize the intricate value in doing so. I am immensely grateful that I have this radio interview with him where we had a chance to reminisce about his days at West Point and in the Air Force. My father was a treasure and this interview a gem.

Janine: So we are talking about lots of military things tonight, including George Washington's military genius and the West Point Military Academy. I was going to try to get my dad on the show last week, but we ran out of time. Tonight my father is here! My father Turner Gauntt is from Athens, Texas, and he was plucked out of high school early to prepare for West Point. He didn't get to graduate with his class in Athens, Texas; I didn't either, Dad, because I moved to Hollywood. So we thought it would be fun to speak to my father, who happened to be at West Point at the same time as General Palmer. General Palmer was in class of '56, and Dad, you were the class of '57. Welcome, Dad, to *The Janine Turner Show*.

Mr. Gauntt: Hi.

Janine: Hi. [Laughing] Okay, so, Dad, tell me about West Point. What's your favorite memory of West Point?

Mr. Gauntt: Graduating.

Janine: [Laughing] Oh, come on.

Mr. Gauntt: Well, I have a lot of fond memories, but I have always said throughout my lifetime it's a nice place to be from, not necessarily be at.

Janine: And why is that?

Mr. Gauntt: Well, it was pretty tough. The whole program was tough, and especially the first year, called plebe year—it was extremely unpleasant.

Janine: [Laughing]

Mr. Gauntt: Because they wanted to see if they could break you down and then build you back up.

Janine: And back then in the day when it was really hard, you couldn't go home for the first year, yeah? You couldn't visit your family.

Mr. Gauntt: No, we didn't. In fact, there was an old saying, we were known as plebes, and the sophomores were known as yearlings, and the juniors were known as cows, and there was an old saying up there, "until the cows come home," which meant that long before me, not only did I not get to go home my first year, but before that, I forget what period of history it was, they didn't get to go home for the first two years.

Janine: Wow. But your family could come visit you, you just couldn't go home, yes, or they couldn't even come visit you for the first little bit, right?

Mr. Gauntt: Well, they could come visit, but you know, my mother came up at Christmas while we were there.

Janine: And you were there on the football—you don't really, it's not really a football scholarship, is it, because I mean—well anyway football was one of the reasons, your brilliance of course, Dad, as well, but you played football for West Point.

Mr. Gauntt: Well, yes. I was there at the same time the general [General Palmer] was, and we had a guy [who] I played with named Hollander, who was very famous, he was an all-American. And during the Vietnam War, he was killed going out to rescue one of his men [who] had been wounded, and they named the gymnasium after him—Hollander Hall—which the general would have known.

Janine: Oh yes, I forgot to bring that up, didn't I, Dad? I think you told me that earlier, I forgot.

Mr. Gauntt: And then there was a little guy, of course, Earl Blaik was the head coach, a very famous head coach, and there was a little guy [who] was his assistant coach that year that I was there, named Vince Lombardi.

Janine: [Laughing] Few people out there know that name.

Mr. Gauntt: Yeah.

Janine: Pretty famous, okay. So, but you were quarterback, you had lot of different positions, yes?

Mr. Gauntt: Quarterback, halfback, and actually for one year I was on a track team with the general.

Janine: Oh, you are kidding.

Mr. Gauntt: No.

Janine: Wow, we should have gotten you all on the show together. Juliette loves track. Were you a sprinter or a long-distance runner, Dad?

Mr. Gauntt: Well, I was a sprinter, but we had a little guy in my class named Bob Kiveski who was very, very fast. In fact, he wiped out all the records that were set previous to him.

Janine: Oh my goodness. Well let's talk about the B-58 Hustler a little bit. Back then, it was the Air Force or Army at West Point, and you chose the Air Force, and I want to be a proud daughter here and say you were one of the first to fly twice the speed of sound, Mach 2, in the 1960s. You always had that little cool Mach 2 pin. We have got to figure out where that is, though I did rescue your West Point uniform, so we do have that. But, Dad, talk about the B-58 Hustler, because it was really unsafe. I remember I put this on Twitter, and I got like hundreds and hundreds of feedback [saying] what a dangerous aircraft the B-58 Hustler [was]. It was because the fuel went from one wing to the other, just kind of free-floated back and forth, right?

Mr. Gauntt: Well, the wing was a delta wing with a 60-degree sweep, and it was two big fuel cells with very little, if any, baffling in between. So when you were accelerating to Mach 2, the fuel would get heavy and stack in one wing. But they corrected that with a little black box that would put in some yaw that sloshed the fuel back in the center.

Janine: How did it feel to fly twice the speed of sound, Dad? What does it feel like? What is your favorite thing about flying when you are up there and going that fast; what does it feel like? What did it feel like?

Mr. Gauntt: Really, you are kind of busy.

Janine: [Laughing] No time to think about it, huh?

Mr. Gauntt: At that altitude, it's mainly just a sensation. You get a little bump going through the speed of sound and little bump coming back out, but other than that, it's just an indication on the airspeed indicator. You are going about 1,300 miles an hour.

Janine: Oh, that's so fast. So this aircraft, the B-58 Hustler, I mean just tell me [a] little bit [about] what it looked like. What did it look like when you were going 1,300 miles per hour in the B-58 Hustler, which could just stack that oil at anytime and send you flying off? I mean, would clouds just fly? I guess, I mean, was it beautiful?

Mr. Gauntt: Well, it depends. You might have been in the weather or at night-time, which we did a lot of and you really can't see that much. But the sensation was a thrill, of course. And there were 116 of them built, but thirty of them were experimental. So the Air Force only got about eighty-six of them operational. And at that time, we were on the gold standard and the airplane was worth more than its weight in gold.

Janine: Wow.

Mr. Gauntt: The program cost $3 billion, and they really got operational in about 1960, early '60s, and then it cost so much money to operate them that they discovered they could operate three B-52 wings for what it cost to operate one B-58 wing. And the surface-to-air missiles had really taken the original advantage of it away because it was designed for a Mach 2 dash end of the target. But when the missiles came along, they could shoot you out of the air, so they had to go back and go lower level.

Janine: So they B-58 Hustler was high, was high up going twice [the] speed of sound, but the missiles could get you from the ground, so now everyone had to fly lower? Did I get that right?

Mr. Gauntt: Yeah. We flew it 50,000 feet Mach 2 because we couldn't go higher, because we had no pressure suit in operation, but the test pilots actually took the airplane to 84,256 feet.

Janine: That's amazing. So there were missiles that could go that high?

Mr. Gauntt: Yeah, during the early '60s or middle '60s.

Janine: And so that kind of outdated the B-58 Hustler, because they needed planes that would be lower?

Mr. Gauntt: Well it didn't outdate it; it was still a wonderful airplane and the best bombing system that the Air Force had.

Janine: Yeah. And your mission was in Russia, yes, the Cold War?

Mr. Gauntt: I had five targets in Russia during the Cold War.

Janine: Wow.

Mr. Gauntt: And the airplane carried five nuclear weapons—all external—hung on the wing.

Janine: So you had five targets, so we hear over and over about alert, you had to be ready on alert, sitting by the airplane in case you got a call for the Cold War and had to go. And you talked about the fact if you had gone to Russia, you would have had to refuel, you might not come back, right, because there was—

Mr. Gauntt: Well, we weren't even planned to recover. We were going to recover in Turkey.

Janine: But it might not have made that, huh?

Mr. Gauntt: Yeah. And it took two refuelings just to get over there.

Janine: Oh yeah, talk about that. You had to refuel them in air, right?

Mr. Gauntt: Right.

Janine: So you were at 50,000 feet, twice the speed of sound, you didn't refuel twice the speed of sound, did you?

Mr. Gauntt: Oh no, no, no.

Janine: [Laughing] Oh gosh, but that's a bit interesting to refuel those aircrafts. Well, listen, I think we need to cut to commercial break. Dad, when we come back, can you talk about when your engine caught on fire, and then we will wrap up the interview?

Mr. Gauntt: Sure.

Janine: Okay. We are going to cut to commercial break, and when we come back, we are going to talk about when my father's engine caught on fire in the B-58 Hustler. Janine Turner on *The Janine Turner Show*. We are talking to my dad, Turner Gauntt. We will be right back.

Janine: Welcome back to *The Janine Turner Show*. We are talking to my father, who is a graduate of the United States Military Academy at West Point. He flew the B-58 Hustler. Dad, last question, are you there?

Mr. Gauntt: Yes, I am.

Janine: Okay. Tell us about [when] your engine caught on fire. Tell us about that.

Mr. Gauntt: Well, four of those eighty-six airplanes that I told you about were what we called TB-58s. They were trainers that had two pilot seats. Normally, there was only one pilot seat. And we were in tandem. And we were out on a training mission, I was giving them a check ride, and when we rotated and took off, we thought the number-two engine had failed because all the instruments went to zero, all the indications. So we went out and dumped fuel and then came back in to land, and what had actually happened was a burner can, outboard burner can, had failed and rotated, and at 425 knots it was just an acetylene torch. But when we came in, the B-58 had no flaps. It landed with about a 13- to 15-degree deck angle. And when you pick that up, it slowed up to about 200 knots, and it sucked that flame over the wings and started burning the wing, which was just honeycomb. We had no idea of this because you couldn't see out of that airplane.

But they had a mobile control on the panel that was monitoring everything, and they said "You are on fire, put in on the ground, and get out." So we did, and the only way you got out of that, you had these devices, escape ropes that were inertial, and you just jumped out and it lowered you onto the ground. The airplane was pretty far off the ground when the rear was down. And of course the flame, the burning was on the left-hand side, and my escape device was on the left-hand side. I am going down to the ground looking at all this blue flame on the ground from fuel on the ground, going up over the wing and over the honeycomb. So we ran like the devil. They put the fire out later. But then the engineers did some study, and they said if we had flown another ninety seconds, we would have blown up.

Janine: Oh, my gosh. Well, that's just an amazing story, Dad. I think about that Johnny Cash song, "Down, down, down, the burning ring of fire," something like that, right? That's what happened to you. Okay, Dad, listen, you have got to come back on the show again because we have so many more stories. But thanks for those stories, this is really great. Thanks, Dad, I love you.

Mr. Gauntt: Love you, baby.

Janine: Okay. All right, talk to you soon, Dad. Thank you so much. Those are great stories.

Mr. Gauntt: Bye-bye.

Janine: Thanks for sharing.

The Janine Turner Show
June 2, 2011

You Went to Heaven and I Went to Hell

You went to heaven and I went to hell
The day you went away
Gone in an instant
Like a switch that went—"click"

And I didn't get to say good-bye

You went to heaven and I to hell
It swelled inside me—
Darkness, hate, sadness and pain
Like Helen Keller, I grappled with reality

You shed your self
Leaving me here to dream
Of stopped hearts and bleeding fingers
Climbing on hands and knees
Fainting with arrhythmia

Leaving me with funeral music
That sucked the soul from my carcass
As I peered into your cold, cruel coffin
Filled with your still, nil—
Nothingness

I saw they broke your nose, flattened your hands
And tainted your skin bright orange
Rage ran riot inside me
I screamed at strangers
And wailed at walls that refused to move

Your hands were graceful
Your nose Roman like a god
What have they done to you!
I turned inside out
With wild, uncontainable woe

When you went to heaven and I to hell

Leaving me to grope through days
With furrowed brow and trembling hands
Your empty chair
You're not there—
Hallowness all around me

You live in photos,
Or inside your clothes
In the hair of your comb
Or the yellowed cologne

You live in never-mores and yesterdays

Because you are in heaven and I in hell

You fly and I cry
You run and I stumble
You radiate and I darken
You know and I know not
You love as I debate—
Not satisfied with empty answers and vacant pride—

You float as I drown
Down into the dark abyss
Of losing you

Because you went to heaven and I to hell

And the days get no better
Stronger not I rise
I carry forth days
With empty bitter
For you are not here to cleanse them

Besieged I wait in murky feelings
Fiery hot and never yielding
Your old demons haunt and taunt
Me
Eager for a host

They fly around
Not backing down
Watching, waiting,
Hoping, hopping
Knowing

That you went to heaven and I to hell

—Janine Turner; April 7, 2014;
Two months after Dad died

You Know

The shadows where you used to be
Hang like a heavy haze,
In a daze
I can't believe you're gone

I sit in a pit of darkness
Vacillating in the valley of death

And you know

So you clear the chaos
Clear the fear
And reside here—
Inside me

Because I seek you and refuse to let you go.

Like a locked gear
I seer into your infinity
Steadfast, true, dire—
I reach out to touch your hand

Sometimes in bursts
Sometimes subtle
Sometimes in streams of steady, ready certainty
I feel you—

Until I wreck it with thunderstorms of thought and passion

And you know

When it clears, I see,
I am born of your eternity
Your you, in my me
Living in dual consistency

Because I seek you and refuse to let you go

So you take my shattered pieces
And forge past my weak forsaken
To teach that willingness, if taken,
Will lift my misery

And I know you know

I know you know

All the answers to the questions now

And you will guide me

Be beside me

Be all around me

Be—

Because I seek you and refuse to let you go

And you know

—Janine Turner
April 16, 2014
Two months after Dad died

A Death Discussed—Dear Dad

Men must endure their going hence

—Shakespeare, *King Lear*

Dear Dad,

I really can't believe you are gone.

Though it is painfully obvious in every corner of the room that you are not here, I still feel your presence. You fill up all the spaces in my mind and in my ears. Your loud voice echoes. I see you sitting there, masterful and handsome, as you sing select pearls of wisdom and exude fatherly love.

As I walk in the house I hear you, "Put your keys on the hook when you walk in, Janine, that way you won't lose them." You and I both know I was always losing my keys. So, I walk in the door, hang my keys on the hook, talking to you as I do. "There you go, Dad. I hung them on the hook." Your "Hi, girls!" greets me as I enter the den. "How are you?" "Fine, Dad. How are you?" "Still here," you say.

But you are not here.

You always had command of the room, though mom fought you for it. Almost every day you'd point to the photo of you and mom on your wedding day. It beams joy from the mantel. You'd point and say with a twinkle in your eye, "See that photo. Your mother is so beautiful and she works so hard." You loved mom, dearly. That's why you married her three times. The third time, you cried. You always had such a tender heart behind your tough West Point veneer and famously broad shoulders. I connected to your tenderness. You were my gentle ledge of tender.

I can't believe you're gone.

How I wish I could have said good-bye, but as you told me, saying good-bye wouldn't have made it any easier. Every time I walked out the door, I knew that it might be the last time I would see you. I had hope though, because you always had this miraculous, remarkable ability to rebound—to endure. Still, I knew that one day you would not. Every time I said good-bye, even if I was just going to the store, I'd walk back in and say "I love you" again. I'd kiss you once and kiss you twice. One time you said to me, "We've been through this…" Then one day you did die, January 24, 2014. I wasn't there when you died, and even though I had all those good-byes, I really had none. I had no final good-bye. It was a surprise that was expected.

I miss you so very much.

I sat on the edge of the bed, scared and saddened the other day. I heard you, clear as day, reciting one of your favorite poems by Rudyard Kipling. Mom used to tell me how you would stand up at dinner parties and recite poems from memory. You recited Kipling often, even as recently as a couple of weeks before you died. You sat in your chair, bright and commanding, "Then it's Tommy this, an' Tommy that, an' 'Tommy, 'ow's yer soul?' But it's 'Thin red line of 'eroes' when the drums begin to roll." Breathlessly, I realize I never discussed with you what you believed it meant, or did we? I hear your thunderous recitation again and again in my head, and I cry. Clear as day, loud as thunder, I hear your voice.

You are still so present.

It hasn't been three months yet. I've kept all your things, even though others are eager to give them away. Not me. Not me, Dad. I want to hold things of yours near to my heart—wear them, smell them, put some of your hair in a locket. I have photos of you everywhere. I stare at them. They speak, synopsizing your life's journey. I realize, even more so now, how much you endured in your life. Shakespeare says it best, "Men must endure their going hence."

I have to endure life without you now.

How I want to see you again. As a child I was always desperately afraid something would happen to you. I would watch through the windows until you came home. I am blessed that you lived to the age of seventy-nine. One would think it would be easier, but it is not. Nevertheless, as I appraise your life, my mind racing to a thousand places and back again, I appreciate now, in a more meaningful way, how much you endured. You lost your father two months after you graduated from the United States Military Academy at West Point. You loved your dad. You didn't get to say good-bye to him either. You often talked about the night you were told your dad died. It's a moment one never forgets. You remained haunted by it always. You were in Air Force training, and your superiors came to your bedside and awakened you. You looked up at them and said, "My dad died." I didn't get a premonition when you died, Dad. Why is that, I wonder? Throughout your life, you cried every time you mentioned your father. I always understood.

Now, I understand on a deeper level.

The day, the hour, the minute I was told you died, a moment I too will never forget, I began to run through the house, clutching my heart. I felt like something had been ripped out of my soul and yet at the same time I felt the immensity of your soul in me—carrying me through the moments. I kept repeating, "Oh no, oh no, oh no, oh no . . . he wasn't ready to die!" Or were you? I also kept saying, "He's with his father now. He's with his father now." You are reunited with your father, Dad, finally, after fifty-seven years. That was a long time to endure, Dad. You always said, "No one loved me like my father." I remember standing there, even up to the last month you were alive, thinking, I do. I love you that much. Somehow you couldn't see it.

You see it now. This I know. You know how much I loved—and love—you.

I, too, know more. So many things carry a different understanding. Now I know that no one can love you like your father and no one can replace that love. Maybe that's what you meant. One week after your father died, you returned to active duty in the Air Force. You had to continue your training. As you hurdled the physical rigors of the test, I know you were heaving your heavy heart along with you.

Did anyone ever teach you how to cope?

The Air Force gave you a "compassionate transfer" to be near your mother in south Texas. I marvel, as I struggle to endure your loss, that you sought, and found, your brilliant, beauty-queen bride six weeks after your father's death—and married her four months later. That is a remarkable rebound. I do not feel that resilient, though it gives me hope. Of course, I am at a different point in my life now than you were then. What I am realizing, as I put together the pieces of your life, is the divine plan of God. If your dad had not died, you would not have had your "compassionate transfer." If you had not had your "compassionate transfer," you would not have met mom in San Antonio. If you had not met mom, I would not be here. Ironically, because of your father's death, I am here. I would not have wanted any other dad but you, Dad.

God sees eternity in perspective. I was meant to be your daughter.

You married mom, became a father, and flew twice the speed of sound, Mach 2, in the 1960s, one of the first. You flew twice the speed of sound in the very dangerous B-58 Hustler. It was the plane that killed many pilots. You were in this aircraft when you heard the voice of God. This moment in your life must have had a big impact on you, and affirmed your faith, because you recalled it often. You were in great danger when the fuel from the Delta wing stacked over onto one side, into one wing. You were fighting for control at 1,300 miles per hour. During this desperate moment, you heard a voice say, "Hold on, Tex." You mastered the aircraft and completed your mission instead of aborting it. This, I might add, is a testament to your bravery and determination. Afterwards, you inquired about who said, "Hold on, Tex." No one involved in the mission said it. No one. When I asked you, "Dad, who said, 'Hold on, Tex?'" You answered, "God." God was telling you to "Hold on,"—and you did, Dad. You held on for so many years, through all kinds of challenges. You endured. I know this is what you are telling me to do now, Dad, hold on. I am. I am. Through hurricane-force emotions, I am "holding on."

I am holding on for you, for sweet Juliette, for mom, and for the purpose God's destined in me.

It was your time to finally let go, Dad, on January 24, 2014. It makes me so very sad. How I wish I had been with you the last week of your life. I know you were desperate, and I know you were scared, and it breaks my heart. When I asked you how you were, you said, "Same old stuff." Brave again. You had rallied so many times. We didn't know. You didn't know. But on some level, you let go, and that's okay, Dad. You endured. You thrived. You excelled. You loved. You laughed. You succeeded. It was your time. But it's hard as hell to be left here.

You went to heaven and I went to hell.

I am looking at your photo in your flight suit right now. It's on my desk. I am struck by how genuinely happy you look. You didn't always look happy. You had more of a Marlon Brando smoldering look most of the time. When you were "acting" during your "extra role," on *Northern Exposure*, you brooded, just like Marlon Brando. I will never forget how intense you were sitting there, at Holling's Bar. You looked up and gave someone a dirty look. Yep, "Marlon Brando," I said. I laughed. But in this photo, in your flight suit, you look so very happy. The happiest photo I've seen. You loved to fly. You were one of the "elite pilots" chosen to fly the B-58 Hustler and to be a part of the Strategic Air Command. Then, during a routine mission flying the B-58 Hustler, your engine caught on fire. You didn't even know it. Over the radio they told you to evacuate the airplane. You rappelled out of the plane, through the fire, and ran for your life. You endured, but afterwards your heart was in atrial flutter. I say, "Hell yes, of course it was skipping some beats. You had the adrenaline rush of a lifetime." After your post-flight exam, they told you were in atrial flutter and left you sitting there for hours. You didn't even know what atrial flutter was, though you were about to discover how it could alter your life.

It's these life-altering situations that challenge our fortitude and character, right, Dad?

It was a condition that could easily be corrected, and it was, but the Air Force grounded you. They said you could never fly again. I was just a little girl, maybe three years old, but I remember that this was something tragic for you and our family. They don't ground pilots for atrial flutter anymore, and even though three out of four doctors said you were fine to fly once the rhythm was corrected, the head doctor vetoed it. You were grounded. All of your dreams, all of your aspirations, the sacrifices, your dedication and willingness to die for your country (your mission was in Russia during the Cold War), the grueling years at West Point where they ripped you apart to put you back together again—the entire slate was wiped clean after one adrenaline rush. From the day when you were company commander at West Point, to the day you were one of the elite pilots chosen for the B-58 Hustler, everyone thought you would be a general. Now, it was "over and out."

One thing we've learned in our lives, Dad, is that only God can truly call, "over and out."

You endured. You held on. You moved on. You served your time in the Air Force and then moved to Euless, Texas, to launch many entrepreneurial projects. You started an insurance company, becoming one of the top companies in the country. You became a real-estate broker, creating Texas' first real-estate franchise, which succeeded brilliantly. You embarked on your favorite job, the impetus for moving to Euless, Texas: you were hired by Braniff International Airlines. Your flying career resumed, barely missing a beat, Dad! You flew for Braniff for the next two decades of your life.

You were back into the wild blue yonder. No, "over and out," for you, Dad. You had such guts and gusto.

At mid-life, a time when life is supposed to be on "auto-pilot," you, once again, were grounded, so to speak, when Braniff International dismantled as a company. Deeply disappointed but not discouraged, you re-invented yourself—again. Determined to stay in the wild blue yonder, you worked as a private pilot and then flew

737s for Conoco Phillips in Alaska, flying to the North Slope and beyond! One month before you died, as I was going to be meet one of the doctors who made the decision to ground you in the Air Force, you said, "You tell him that I continued to fly until I was sixty-nine years old!" Oh, how you endured, Dad. You picked yourself up by your bootstraps, brushed yourself off, and began again—and again.

Your tenacity is the wind beneath my wings.

You were one of the best pilots, ever. Your landings were smooth as silk. Mom used to say, "Pay attention now, his landings are the best!" You commented on all the sights and entertained the passengers. You landed planes in all kinds of conditions, a few times on ice. I asked you what you did in these conditions, and you said you had to throw the plane into reverse throttle. You always got your passengers home safely. As I was going through your things, I found a letter in which the author applauds you for the wonderful flying experience he had with you at the helm. I am going to frame it. You touched many people's lives. People often stop me on the street and tell me how much they loved and respected you. Many of these people were men you instructed in the 737. You taught at the simulator until you were seventy-six years old. You endured, Dad, as does your legacy.

I am so proud of you, Dad. You knew I was proud of you, didn't you, Dad?

Every time I see an airplane, I think of you. When you were alive, I only thought about them at random. Now I seek them out and see you in them. I think about how you would always bring me presents from your trips. I was always delighted, even if it was just a bar of soap from the lavatory, which often it was. It wasn't the soaps at all, was it, Dad? It was the fact you were home. I loved you. Once, when I was about six years old, you returned home from a trip and I ran to the staircase in my pajamas to greet you. You were at the bottom of the stairs in your uniform, and you said, "Hi, D'anine." I ran to you and you lifted me up into your arms. That's it. That's the moment. That's the love in you that I miss, Dad.

I wish I could hug you one more time.

You would bring me gifts from your exotic trips. You flew the first Braniff plane to Hawaii in 1968. You brought back a little doll in a hula skirt—I still have it, Dad. When you were in Mexico you brought back a big black piggybank with hot-pink flowers. I still have it, too. I remember when Tim slid into my bedside table and the piggybank started to fly off the table. Tim reached out and caught it as if it were the winning catch in a football game. He was immensely relieved that it was not broken. He knew how important it was to me. You brought back a stuffed toy llama from South America—I was fascinated by it. I still have it, too. As I got older

I would ask you, "How was your trip, Dad?" You would answer with one word, "Uneventful," which meant it was a good trip. You always were a man of few words. You taught me, "A fish that opens its mouth gets caught."

I am growing to appreciate days that are "uneventful."

When I was a teenager, I remember that I would ask you over and over, "Dad, are you happy?" Do you remember that, Dad? You would respond, "Happiness is relative." I guess it is, Dad. I actually never knew what you meant by that, and still don't. It's too late to ask you now. I suppose I understand it, and you, more and more since you have passed away, though. *The degree of happiness is relative to the pain you carry with it.* Is that what you meant, Dad? What is true happiness?

Whatever it is, I know you are experiencing it now and that makes me happy—relatively.

So you endured the loss of your dad by creating your own family. You endured the loss of your esteemed flying career in the military by creating a new career, flying for a major airline. You often said that if you had not been grounded in the Air Force, we would have never moved to Euless, Texas, near Dallas, and my career as a model, which led to my acting career, never would have happened. You did have a philosopher's heart after all, Dad.

You saw God in the thread of life, even if you couldn't understand Him.

You often told me about your startling God-experience in Athens, Texas. You were a young boy walking down the street thinking about God, which led you to your next thought, "Who made God?" You said that you got so scared you ran home, went straight to your room, and closed the door.

That's the problem with thinking too much, especially alone.

You managed to chip away cerebral constraints long enough to teach me to see God in the sunset. Many times, you and I watched the sunset over Eagle Mountain Lake. We saw God together, even if He was never mentioned. He was there in the midst of us. God endured in you as you endured, Dad. We know God by just knowing, not thinking. You *really know* God now, Dad. You have all the answers.

How I wish you could tell me.

You had to endure another devastating loss, the early loss of your sister when you were thirty-two years old. Your dad died, then ten years later, your sister died. Actually, I don't know how you endured that loss. You loved your sister dearly. You held that loss close to your heart. I was in first grade. I remembered how you cried. I was sitting in the backseat of the car. I was very still. Your sobs were so deep, so vulnerable, as if your heart were shattering. You seemed so young and vulnerable.

Did anyone ever teach you how to cope?

You persevered though. You endured. I wonder what kept you going. You never said it, but it must have been your family. You were a family man in your own unique way. I appreciate now how you were always there for me. Even if you were there in various ways, you were there. Now you are gone. You said to me once regarding someone's death, "Here today, gone tomorrow. I know it well." You are gone now, Dad. Gone. Your vacancy has left a hole in my soul.

The only thing that saves me is the feeling of your presence. It is etched in the air here.

As your life continued, you endured three divorces and four marriages. Three of those four marriages were to mom. Now *there* is an endurance story. You ran an endurance race of enduring love for mom. You often told stories about how you always rushed home to be by her side. One such time was in the Air Force after you returned from a long trip to Spain. You landed in Nebraska and immediately got in your car, driving non-stop from Nebraska to San Antonio, Texas. You stopped on the side of the road, only briefly, napping until it was too cold to bear. Mom talks about the connection the two of you had. Often, when you were returning from these trips in the middle of the night, mom, having heard no sound, would open the door just as you approached the threshold, knowing you were there. Your depth of soul was deep, Dad. You loved and you loved profoundly.

Maybe this is why your presence is so vibrant now. Love is eternal, and your capacity for love was endless.

Coping was hard for you. Your endurance matched your physical strength, but not quite your emotional strength. You were a rare combination of genius, beauty, determination, and bravery, with a body of steel. Most people have one or two of those attributes, but rarely five of them. You were special, Dad. You still are. You were always so strong. When I was a little girl, you would put me on your back and do push-ups. "Come on. Come on!" you'd say and throw me on your back. You were quite the football player, I am told. You won every award possible in high school, and at West Point you played the positions of quarterback and half-back.

I don't think I ever saw you throw a football.

I remember when we were at West Point for your ten-year reunion. I was five years old. Your mom looked out onto the field and said, "You father could throw the football from one end of the stadium to the next." I sat there and tried to picture it, looking left then right. Athletics was a big part of your life. This aspect of your life, I took for granted. It is super sharp to me now. You jogged all the time. I remember when you went jogging in Central Park around the reservoir in a blinding snow storm. I was fifteen years old, modeling in New York City. When you returned home, your knit facial mask was covered in ice. You said the reservoir was a white blanket of snow and that not one soul was in the park. I joked with you, telling you that they were the smart ones.

I remember loving New York City because you loved New York City.

It had been a big part of your life. It reminded me of you, New York State, at least—West Point. I remember when you and I saw *A Chorus Line* for the third time on Broadway. We saw *A Chorus Line* for the first time in London when I was twelve years old. I recommended it and then worried the entire time. "Is dad enjoying it?" You were. We got so lost afterwards. Do you remember? You insisted that we walk back to the hotel. It was pitch black on the streets of London. We wandered forever, sort of like Moses in the desert. What could we do? You were in charge. You loved classical music, too. Tchaikovsky's *1812 Overture* was your favorite. I remember vividly, as a very young girl, sitting in your lap as you conducted my arms to the music and those booming canons. Your *1812 Overture* version used West Point canons for the crescendo. I was enthralled.

I played 1812 Overture *at your funeral, Dad. I hope you liked it.*

In my teenage years you discovered golf. Shall we talk about golf? You were, shall we say, an avid golfer. Mom was never very happy when you played golf on holidays, especially Mother's Day. One year, she put me into the car and drove up to the putting green. I remember how you sauntered over to her and said, "Janice, how many times do have to tell you. You are not my mother." Vintage you, Dad. Vintage you. You stopped playing golf when you rediscovered ranching. You rediscovered ranching after I purchased mine. "What are you going to do with one hundred acres?" you bellowed. Shortly thereafter, you were captivated and purchased your own ranch. My love for ranching was borne of your love for ranching. Your love for ranching began as a young boy in Athens when you bought five cows with money you had saved from working at the bottle factory.

Hey, Dad, did you realize when you played your last game of golf, it would be your last game of golf?

Dad, I look at my ranch now and my longhorn cattle and realize it's all you. Mom certainly isn't a rancher. You and I share an affinity for the great outdoors, cattle, and ranching. You and I are so much alike. After you died, I sat outside with the longhorns and breathed in your vision. One of my longhorn steers, Prairie Don Juan, did something that no other longhorn has ever done. He walked up to me, standing with about one foot distance between us, and stared deeply into my eyes for quite a while. Animals have a sixth sense.

What was he trying to tell me, Dad?

I hear your voice, clear as a bell, "When are you going to get some real cows, Janine?" I always reminded you that longhorns epitomize Texas—the Chisholm Trail, cattle drives. I know what you wanted, Dad. You wanted me to get real beef cows. Well, I did, Dad. After you died, I purchased my first Black Angus bull. He's a teenager. We named him Henry Lee after Patrick Henry and Richard Henry Lee.

I will have to close my eyes, not name the cows, and be a real rancher now—to honor you, Dad.

Do you remember when my only home at the ranch was my camper, which perched forlornly on three hundred acres? I was by myself when, in the middle of the night, I heard a noise, as if someone was stealthily walking around the camper. I was scared out of my wits. I picked up my gun and it misfired. The bullet wildly ricocheted around the camper and lodged in the door. I couldn't hear a thing. I called you at your ranch and screamed, "Dad, I heard someone outside and I accidently misfired my gun. Come help me!" Do you remember what you said, Dad? You said, "Well, whoever it was is gone now." That was not exactly what I wanted you to say. You came anyway, didn't you, Dad? You always did protect me, even if begrudgingly. When you arrived at the gate you called me and said, "I'm here. Don't shoot." Then, when you were at the door of the camper you said, "I'm here. Don't shoot." No one was there. It was probably an armadillo. A few years later, you had to sell your ranch. I know how much you relished being a rancher. That little boy who saved his money from the bottle factory had been living his dream. You swallowed that sorrow and endured yet again.

I had a vision of you the other day, Dad. You were in heaven. It was very bright. You were standing there in your jeans, boots, and cowboy hat, with your arm thrown over my beloved mare's, Maggie, neck. You were both beaming with clarity and happiness. You and she were so vibrant and so filled will joy.

That's what heaven is like, right, Dad? Living your dream with the Lord.

Your health started to take a turn for the worse in your seventies. But that didn't stop you. You were a warrior. Patton-tough, and oh, how you admired Patton. Juliette, mom, and I watched the movie with you many times. There is no better example of your determination then when you were playing cards at Winstar in Oklahoma. Your heart went into ventricle tachycardia. You fainted into the stranger's lap beside you. Your defibrillator in your chest shocked you and then you promptly sat back up—and continued playing cards! The medics rushed to the table and tried to get you to go to the hospital. You declined and continued your game. Patton has nothing on you. What a general you would have been. Well, Dad, you were the general in our house.

You were the general of my life.

When you were seventy-two years old, we attended your fiftieth reunion at West Point so that Juliette could see you there, in your element. You had a hard time walking the field. As you huddled over, gasping for breath, you said, "If I'd known I was going to live this long, I would have taken better care of myself." You always did have a sense of humor, Dad, and there was a bit of Wild West in your living.

I guess that's where I get my pioneer spirit.

You endured years of ill health: heart disease, heart arrhythmia, a stent for clogged arteries, a stroke, lung disease, kidney disease, liver disease. You lived much, much longer than your doctors predicted. You had a survivor's instinct and endurance. You were constantly able to rebound and keep on, keeping on. You endured until God called you home. You lived until your purpose was complete, God's purpose. It doesn't feel complete to me. I feel very incomplete.

Now it is I who must endure my "going hence."

But you endured a long time, Dad, and I am so very thankful that you did. God knows your life was far from perfect, but you were always there. As I struggle to endure your loss, I have been drawn to Exodus 14:14. It says, "The Lord will fight for you: you need only to be still." This is important to me. I have always put God first in my life, but you, Dad, you always fought for me. You fought for me because—you were my dad. You were always on "alert" for me. Since you have been gone, I call on God over and over and over again, reciting, "The Lord will fight for me. The Lord will fight for me."

Please God, please God, fight for me, help me to endure.

Dad, not only did you endure your hardships, you left your enduring mark on my heart and in my life. Many of your qualities endure, Dad, as a guiding light for my "going hence." You taught me about honor with your character, your honesty, and your integrity. You taught me about love—with your unswerving love for me, for mom, for our family. You taught me the value of the family name with your ardent passion for the Gauntt lineage, familial respect, and the lessons wrought from their history. You taught me to seek knowledge with your keen intellect, your quest for wisdom, and your innate common sense. You taught me about love of country with your heroic service, your dedication to our Republic's principles, and by heeding your call to duty at an early age at West Point. You taught me to seek adventure with your insatiable travels, your exploration of new frontiers, and your experiments with new challenges. You taught me to be brave with your daring dalliances in the sky, your tenacious reinvention of yourself over and over again, and with your very stoic strength during your ailing years. You taught me to seek God with a questioning mind that resolves on belief.

All of your endurances culminated in your most powerful, singular attribute—hope. Hope endureth all things.

You resilience has taught me to take all of your accomplishments, and all of your challenges, and champion them into higher resolve. This is what you did with your life, Dad. You took the Gauntt name, ratcheted it up a notch, and made the legacy proud. That's the goal of every rising generation, and you achieved this dad, with flying colors. You have instilled all of these values into the fiber of my being. I learned from your greatness, Dad. I also learned from your weaknesses. I learned from your highs and I learned from your lows. I watched you vacate the valleys and climb the hills. When you got down and dirty, you got back up and got in the saddle again. Just like when I fell off my pony. You were there beside me. You picked me up and put me right back in the saddle. That's what I have to do now, isn't it, Dad?

I have to pick myself back up from the canyon of your death and seek the distant horizon. You are there in that horizon. You always have been.

I have to endure as you did—with dignity, grace, and purpose, and though I am engulfed in the valley of the shadow of death, I know you are my advocate in heaven. I know because the other day I was praying in earnest for mom. I was very concerned about her. It was probably one of my most fervent prayers. Sometimes the only thing one can do is pray, right, Dad? Later that day, she returned home and said that a strange women sitting in Starbucks approached her and said, "The Lord has told me to lay hands on you today." As you know, Dad, mom is not really "evangelical," but she took the woman's hand. A peace was over her for the rest of the day. But you know this, don't you, Dad? You were up there advocating for her, for me, for God. I know God heard my prayer, and I know that you did, too.

My Lord will fight for me and I know you still fight for me. I felt it. I feel it. I know it.

Something else I have felt during these past two-and-a-half months is an innate and better understanding of what heaven is. I have this feeling that you are free, Dad. You no longer have to endure, even though you did it so valiantly. You are free. You are free from the demons that bound you here on earth and released from earthly limits and challenges.

You are no longer trapped in your humanness.

This is what heaven is, isn't it, Dad? A glorious place with God where there are no demons. They are not allowed. This is why there is no sadness or sickness, no fear or shame. It is simple, unadulterated love. It is a love—an energy—that is boundless. You are now the truest form of your spirit: your essence. You are the you God made you to be. You are the wonderful, mesmerizing, grand, and glorious you. You are purely Turner Maurice Gauntt, Jr.

You are the good you, the loving you, the protective you, the eternal you. You.

I rejoice that you are sublime now. You gave it a heroic turn here. The memories of you symphony all around me—seasons, sounds, and senses. Your voice is still so clear, your image still so vibrant, your impact still so earnest, your love still so prevalent. You endure, Dad. You endured and you endure.

You endured here in body. You endure here in spirit.

Now, it is I who must endure without you. "Men must endure their going hence." I thank you, Dad, for teaching me how to endure. You came, you saw, you conquered. Go rest with God now. May your happiness have no more "relatives." May your happiness be complete. I love you, Dad.

I love you—enduringly.

–Janine Turner
April 15, 2014
Two-and-a-half months after Dad died

West Point Association of Graduates Memorial

Turner M. Gauntt, Jr. '57
No. 21472 • Dec. 18, 1934–Jan. 24, 2014 • Died Dallas, Texas
Interred in Dallas Fort Worth National Cemetery, Texas

Turner Maurice "Tex" Gauntt, Jr. was born in Dallas, TX, the son of Turner Maurice Gauntt, Sr. and Marguerite McKinzie Gauntt. He graduated from Athens High School where he excelled academically and athletically. His accomplishments included National Honor Society, President of the Key Club, Captain of All-District Football and Basketball teams, Captain of the Athletic Association, Babe Ruth Sportsmanship Award, President of the Senior Class, and Most Handsome. He was considered one of Texas' best high school quarterbacks. His outstanding record led to an appointment to West Point by Congressman John Dowdy of the 7th District of Texas.

During cow year at West Point, Tex roomed with Bruce Turnbull and "Andy" Andrews. Having attended college for two years and the USMA Preparatory School before joining our class, Andy excelled at academics. He was famous for retiring early and then maxing the next day's classes! After lights out, Tex and Bruce studied by flashlights under their Red Boys. Bruce recalls that at the reveille cannon blast, Andy would shoot out of bed, switch on the sink light, and sing as he shaved. Meanwhile Tex and Bruce yearned for peace and quiet. A trip to Hoffman's Hardware in Highland Falls resulted in the purchase of a camera flash bulb which was screwed into the sink light fixture. The next morning when Andy hit the light switch, the flash bulb exploded in a blinding flash. Andy reeled backwards crashing over chairs and desks. So ended Andy's early morning antics.

Firstie-year Tex was selected as Company Commander of I-1. This came as no surprise to those who knew him. He was greatly respected and admired. His leadership qualities were evident from his first days at West Point. Under his leadership the company was awarded the Trill Prize for Best Company and two drill streamers.

Tex roomed with Jack Apperson, the Company Executive Officer, and Dana Mead, the Battalion Commander. Jack recalls Tex doing vertical pushups by standing on his hands, feet straight up, back against the wall, pushing up from the floor.

Before Graduation Parade, rumors circulated about our class running, instead of marching, to join the reviewing party. In 1957 the reviewing party included

General Maxwell D. Taylor '22, then Chief of Staff, United States Army, in addition to the Superintendent and the Commandant of Cadets. At the command for the graduating class to march forward, a rebel yell erupted from H-1's Rabble Rousing Carl Burgdorf. He pulled out a hidden Confederate Flag and took of running like a jack rabbit. Despite I-1's proximity to running companies on both flanks. I-1's firsties marched on, not missing a drum bet, mainly because their leader, Tex, was having none of the rabble running. Instead he led the company with back straight, chin set, and eyes forward. Both Jack Apperson and Tom Adcock recall Tex turning his head slightly to his right and commanding. "Don't run, don't run!" Of the 24 cadet companies all but four ran. The runners soon learned that they would spend major parts of their final cadet days confined to their rooms.

Tex was commissioned in the Air Force. His first training was at Hondo Air Base. While there he met Janice Agee who was attending Trinity University in San Antonio. They were married on Dec. 22, 1957.

Tex was assigned to the Strategic Air Command and was selected to pilot the revolutionary, delta-winged B-58 Hustler. This bomber was capable of flying at Mach II (twice the speed of sound). B-58 crews were elite, hand-picked from other SAC bomber squadrons. Tex became SAC's youngest B-58 squadron commander.

In 1965 an in-flight emergency occurred on Tex's B-58 as an engine caught fire during a training flight over Arkansas. He ordered his two crewmen to bail out and received permission to land his aircraft. He was able to land his B-58 safely despite the engine fire. Unfortunately a heart arrhythmia was found during a post-incident physical exam. He was told he could never return to Air Force flight status, which was a huge disappointment. Tex telephoned close friend and classmate Stan Cass to transfer to Army Aviation.

But before the transfer began, Braniff Airlines made Tex an offer too good to refuse. The couple returned to Texas where Tex joined Braniff and in time moved into the captain's seat. His career with Braniff was a grand one until Braniff went out of business in 1992.

In keeping with his love of flying, Tex became an instructor with High Power Aviation in Grand Prairie until 2012. In 2006 he received the Wright Brothers "Master Pilot" Award from the Federal Aviation Administration. He also flew for Conoco Phillips, flying to and from the north shore of Alaska. In 2012 he was presented an award for Leadership, Professionalism, and Exemplary Contribution.

Tex also became a Real Estate Broker and opened his first office with wife

Janice in 1968. He created Texas' first real-estate franchise. This award-winning company later became Century 21 Lake Country at Eagle Mountain Lake. It and a second office in Colleyville are now owned by son Tim.

Tex's love for flying was exceeded only by his love for his family. He was proud of them and almost any conversation quickly turned to his wife, children, and grandchildren, and their many successes.

He is survived by wife Janice, his son Tim and Tim's wife Roslyn Gauntt, his daughter, actress Janine Gauntt Turner, and grandchildren Tiffany Gauntt, Turner M. Gauntt IV, Bobby Gauntt, and Juliette Turner. His family loved and adored him and wishes him blue skies and tailwinds forever.

–Janice Gauntt and classmates Tom Adcock, Jack Apperson, and Bruce Turnbull
The Association of Graduates of West Point Magazine, TAPS

Notes

Chapter Two

What Would Our Founding Fathers Think of America Today?

Benjamin Franklin, Way to Wealth (Bedford MA: Applewood Books, 1986)

A Republic, If You Can Keep It

"Perspectives on the Constitution: A Republic, if You Can Keep It," Dr. Richard Beeman, accessed June 25, 2014, http://constitutioncenter.org/learn/educational-resources/historical-documents/perspectives-on-the-constitution-a-republic-if-you-can-keep-it

Farewell To All My Greatness

Benjamin Franklin, Way to Wealth (Bedford MA: Applewood Books, 1986)

No Nobility

"Just 53% Say Capitalism Is Better Than Socialism," Rassmussen Reports, April 09, 2009, http://www.rasmussenreports.com/public_content/politics/general_politics/april_2009/just_53_say_capitalism_better_than_socialism

Duty Would Bind the Constitution

"Definition of Duty," The Free Dictionary, accessed June 25, 2014, http://www.thefreedictionary.com/duty

John D. Rockefeller's Speech on July 8, 1941: http://www.rockarch.org/inownwords/pdf/ibelievetext.pdf

William J. Bennett, *America: The Last Best Hope* (Nashville: Nelson Current, 2006)

Ibid

"Nathan Hale Quotes," Brainy Quotes, accessed June 25, 2014, http://www.brainyquote.com/quotes/quotes/n/nathanhale161330.html

What In The Name of Common Sense

Alexis de Tocqueville, *Democracy in America*

Exclusive Right to Their Writings and Discoveries
> Karl Marx, *Communist Manifesto*

> Emily Dickenson, *1176* (Canada: Little, Brown & Company)

Chapter Three

Title Page
> Patrick Henry, *Give Me Liberty or Give Me Death*, March 23, 1775

> Thomas Jefferson, 1801: http://www.heritageresearchinstitute.org/founders.html

Satellites, *Northern Exposure*, and America's Future
> "Kahlil Gibran Quotes", Good Reads, http://www.goodreads.com/quotes/10271-your-joy-is-your-sorrow-unmasked-and-the-selfsame-well

> Jackie Gingrich Cushman, *The Essential American* (Regnery Publishing, 2010)

> Claire Berlinski, *There Is No Alternative: Why Margaret Thatcher Matters* (Basic Books, 2011)

> Patrick Henry, *Give Me Liberty or Give Me Death*, March 23, 1775

A Call to Arms
> William J. Bennet, *The American Patriot's Almanac* (Nashville: Thomas Nelson, 2008) pg8

> Alexander Fraser Tytler

> John & Abigail Adams, *The Letters of John and Abigail Adams* (New York: Penguin Books, 2004)

Czars: The Enemy In The Field
> "A Judicial Watch Special Report: President Obama's Czars," September 15, 2011, http://www.judicialwatch.org/wp-content/uploads/2014/02/Special-Report-President-Obamas-Czars.pdf

> H.R. 3226, July 15, 2009, http://www.gpo.gov/fdsys/pkg/BILLS-111hr3226ih/pdf/BILLS-111hr3226ih.pdf

Why Are We Selling American Liberty to China?
> Brett M. Decker, William C. Triplett III, *Bowing to Beijing* (Washington DC: Regnery Publishing, 2011)

> Aleksandr Isaevich Solzhenitsyn, *Détente, Democracy, and Dictatorship* (New Jersey: Transaction Publishers, 2009)

House Leaders Should Enforce Constitutionality Rule
> "Constitutional Authority Statements: In Defense of House Rule XII," Horace Cooper and Nathaniel Stewart, accessed June 25, 2014, http://www.constitutingamerica.org/docs/WhitePaper.pdf

The Real "Game Change"

"Sarah Palin's Former Aide Accuses HBO of Reneging on Promise to Let Him Fact-Check 'Game Change'," The Hollywood Reporter, February 22, 2012, http://www.hollywoodreporter.com/news/sarah-palin-game-change-hbo-fact-check-aide-293941

"Palin associates angrily denounce HBO's 'Game Change'" LA Times, Robin Abcarian, February 22, 2012, http://www.latimes.com/nation/politics/politicsnow/la-pn-palin-game-change-preview-20120222-story.html

"Q&A with Palin Advisor-Turned-Novelist Nicolle Wallace," TIME, Claire Suddath, October 5, 2011, http://entertainment.time.com/2011/10/05/qa-with-palin-advisor-turned-novelist-nicolle-wallace/

America's Hope That Obama Is Determined to Change

"What North Dakota Could Teach California," Wall Street Journal, Stephen Moore, March 11, 2012, http://online.wsj.com/news/articles/SB10001424052970203370604577265773038268282

"Why Prosperity Is Hip, And Raises Living Standards," Forbes, Stephen Ferra, March 15, 2012, http://www.forbes.com/sites/peterferrara/2012/03/15/why-prosperity-is-hip-and-raises-living-standards/

Does America's President Understand America?

"An Update on the HHS Mandate," Preserve Religious Freedom, accessed June 26, 2014, http://www.preservereligiousfreedom.org/video/

"For Imposing Taxes on Us Without Our Consent"—The Declaration's Words

Benjamin Franklin, *Way to Wealth* (Bedford MA: Applewood Books, 1986)

The Gate Called Beautiful—How Common Sense Compassion Heals

"May Job Numbers: Why Are 15% Of Americans On Food Stamps in An Improving Economy?" Policy Mic, Ben Fogel, June 7, 2013, http://mic.com/articles/47001/may-job-numbers-why-are-15-of-americans-on-food-stamps-in-an-improving-economy/900895

The TRUTH Act

"H.R. 1417," Thomas.gov, accessed June 26, 2014, http://www.gpo.gov/fdsys/pkg/BILLS-113hr1417rh/pdf/BILLS-113hr1417rh.pdf

Chapter Four

Title Page

Janine Turner, *Holding Her Head High* (Nashville: Thomas Nelson, 2008)

Barack Obama: President of Replicants

"The Life of Julia," Organizing for Action, May 3, 2012, http://l.barackobama.com/truth-team/entry/the-life-of-julia/

Chapter Five

Title Page
> "Oriana Fallaci Quotes," Brainy Quotes, accessed June 26, 2014,
> http://www.brainyquote.com/quotes/quotes/o/orianafall336428.html

Success—A Social Crime
> "Super People," New York Times, James Atlas, October 1, 2011,
> http://www.nytimes.com/2011/10/02/opinion/sunday/meet-the-new-super-
> people.html?pagewanted=all&_r=0

We Should Reject the Race Card as King Did
> Martin Luther King, Jr, *Letter from a Birmingham Jail*, April 16, 1963

Virtue and the Pursuit of Happiness
> Hillsdale College, *The U.S. Constitution: A Reader*, (Hillsdale College Press, 2012)
>
> Ronald Reagan's Farewell Address, January 11, 1989

Town of Greece, New York vs. Galloway: With Victory Comes Responsibility and Respect
> "Supreme Court Decision of the United States, Town of Greece, New York v. Galloway et al," Justice Kennedy, accessed June 26, 2014, http://www.law.cornell.edu/supct/pdf/12-696.pdf

John Quincy Adams Says It Best
> John Quincy Adams, *Letters of John Quincy Adams, to His Son, on the Bible and Its Teachings*, (Forgotten Books, 2012)

Chapter Seven

Title Page
> F Scott Fitzgerald, *The Great Gatsby*, (Scribner, 2004)

Booze, Big Business, and Prohibition
> Ken Burns and Lynn Novick, *Prohibition*, PBS

Acknowledgments

In the play *As You Like It*, Shakespeare says it best: "All the world's a stage, And all the men and women merely players; They have their exits and their entrances, And one man in his time plays many parts."

My life thus far has had many stages, and I feel I have played many parts. I believe, as well, that I am merely a player for God's higher purpose. As I compiled the pages of this book, I saw with clarity of mind the vital role other players, both protagonists and antagonists, have had in my life, and how they have shaped my exits and entrances from my many stages. Isn't life amazing? My role? My role was, and continues to be, to show up, stay sober, and keep reaching for God's hand, or as we say here in Texas, to simply "cowboy up."

The making of this book has stages as well, seven to be exact. I thank not only the people who helped bring this book to fruition, but also those whom I have encountered during my many stages of life.

For stage one, I thank my ancestral lineage of mothers and fathers whose delicate tapestries weaved the fabric of my character. I thank God for breathing life into my earthly body through my wondrous mother Janice and beloved late father Turner, and I thank my parents for their humanness and dedication to love and principles. I also thank my brother Tim, who always seeks enlightenment, and my sister-in-law Roslyn for her love and compassion. I am also grateful for those I have loved along the theatre of life who challenged my resiliency. I also thank Monsignor Don Fischer for his spiritual guidance and for his saving grace after the death of my father.

For stage two, I thank the greatest gift of my life, my sixteen-year-old daughter Juliette, who is my inspiration and my joy. Having written two books of her own, I am grateful for her sharp eye regarding content. She lovingly, and with patience beyond her years, sat beside me as a co-editor. I thank Cathy Gillespie, the dearest, most special friend anyone could dream of having, for entering the stage of

Constituting America with me and for delving into the drama of convincing people that the Constitution and The Federalist truly are relevant and non-partisan.

For stage three, I thank Peter Roff and Horace Cooper for shaping my raw love of country and Founding Fathers into that of a professional opinion editorial writer, radio talk-show host, and political pundit. I thank Lynne Jordal Martin at foxopinion.com, Mark Tapscott at *The Washington Examiner*, the late Andrew Breitbart and his team at breitbart.com, and Bryan Preston at PJ Media for giving me such prestigious outlets for my opinion editorials.

For stage four, I thank Jim Gracie and Richard Frish, who, after hearing my homespun podcasts, gave me a microphone at KLIF in Dallas, Texas, on Saturday nights. I thank John Hogan, Carl Anderson, and Darryl Parks at Clear Channel for cultivating my radio personality and performances both on KPRC and iHeart. I thank Senator Ted Cruz and Senator Rand Paul for their dedication to preserving our republic, upon which our freedom rests, and for visiting with me on the radio.

For stage five, I thank my dear friend, sobriety sister, and creative partner, Maureen Quinn, for her constancy of support in sobriety and healing humor. And I thank Marsha Haufrecht, my acting coach and dear friend. I thank Grandpa J.B., my great-great-grandfather, for his courageous willingness to write about his withdrawals from alcohol at the turn of the twentieth century. I thank Bob Beckel for his profound, personal radio conversation with me about the seriousness of alcoholism.

For stage six, I thank my gentle ledge of tender, my father, whose depth of soul spoke, and continues to speak, to my inner essence of being.

For stage seven, last but certainly not least, I thank David Dunham, a true champion and a man of character, for calling me out of the blue, just at the right time, and encouraging me to do this book. I also thank his exceptional partners at Dunham Books, Joel Dunham and Crystal Flores, plus his gifted design team, Amy Dennis, Josh Hailey, and Darlene Swanson, and editors Emily Prather and Rachael Price for their kindness, care, and keen eye. I thank Rick Hersh, my literary and commercial agent, whom I respect immensely both professionally and personally, for his generosity of time and talent. I thank the oh-so-patient and talented Brandon Vanderford, Amanda Hughes, and Tanya Toll who helped me with the tremendous undertaking of compiling the many different pages and genres of this book. And I thank Cindi Berry who generously took on the task of reading the original four hundred and fifty pages—the first to do so!

Thus, all the world's a book, with many pages and players—I thank them all for their many parts.

About the Author

Janine Turner is an Emmy and three-time Golden Globe nominee actress most known for her beloved performance as Maggie O'Connell in *Northern Exposure*. Other memorable credits include *Cliffhanger, Leave it to Beaver, Dr. T & the Women, Steel Magnolias, Friday Night Lights,* and *Solace* with Anthony Hopkins. As a single mother, Turner, inspired by her father, a graduate of the United States Military Academy at West Point and Air Force hero, has championed the cause of preserving American principles with her foundation, Constituting America, her radio show, *The Janine Turner Show,* and as a columnist and political pundit. She travels the country speaking on a wide array of subjects from her faith, her sobriety, to women's issues, as well as her call to action—non-partisan dialogue regarding American principles. She also enthralls audiences with her stories of tenacious triumph over the canyons of her life, often reciting passages from her poetry. Janine continues to be a steward of her wounds with her first published best-selling book, *Holding Her Head High,* and now with a new glimpse into her private life in *A Little Bit Vulnerable.* She lives on her cattle ranch in Texas with her beloved, sixteen-year-old daughter Juliette.